*Into the Perfect Likeness*

Jonathan Fletcher

# *Into the Perfect Likeness*

## Scratching the Surface of Christian Transformation

ST MAXIMUS
SCRIPTORIUM

*Into the Perfect Likeness*. Copyright © 2020 by Jonathan S. Fletcher. All Rights Reserved

Printed in the United States of America. No part of this book may be used or reproduced in any manner whatsoever without written permission except in the case of brief quotations embodied in critical articles and reviews.

Published in the United States
by
St. Maximus Scriptorium
Hopkins, SC
www.stmaxscriptorium.com

ISBN-13: 978-0-9838399-1-0
Printed in the United States of America

All quotations in the text are used under fair use guidelines except where permissions are noted in the footnotes.

Cover Art: *Sermon on the Mount* by Carl Heinrich Bloch (1834–1890)

*To*

**Kathryn Larisey, Sam and Janet Roberts, Joan Savage, and Kathryn McCormick**
without whose shared journey toward Christ this effort would never have taken place.

*In Memory of*

**My Mother – Gertrude Park Fletcher**
who gave me a priceless experience of unconditional love.

**and**

**My Father – Robert Sturtevant Fletcher**
who showed me an equally priceless example of personal integrity.

Both of which are essential elements to understanding the idea of being transformed

*Into the Perfect Likeness*
*of*
*Jesus Christ*

# Contents

| | |
|---|---|
| Contents | vii |
| Preface | 1 |
|    Logistical Issues and Approach | 2 |
| Acknowledgements | 4 |
| Introduction and Background | 6 |
| *1* A Starting Point: Christian Orthodoxy | 19 |
|    In Search of Roman Catholic Orthodoxy | 21 |
|    In Search of Eastern Orthodox "Orthodoxy" | 24 |
|    In Search of Anglican Orthodoxy | 26 |
|    In Search of Protestant Orthodoxy | 28 |
|    So, What Are We Going to Do? | 30 |
| *2* Christian Transformation | 32 |
|    Translation vs. Transformation | 32 |
|    Christian Translation | 36 |
|    Christian Transformation | 37 |
|    Blow the Trumpet | 39 |
| *3* Who is the God of whom Jesus is the Son? | 42 |
|    The Connection to Israel – God of the Story | 44 |
|    The Narrative Priority | 45 |
|    The Mystery of God | 46 |
|    The Character of God | 47 |
|       God as Wholly Other Creator | 47 |
|       God as Eternal | 50 |
|       God as Perfectly Free | 50 |
|       God as Perfect Love | 50 |
|       God as All-powerful | 51 |
|       God as All-knowing | 51 |
|       God as Ever-present | 52 |
|       God as All-demanding | 52 |
|       God as Awe-inspiring | 53 |
|       God as All-holy | 53 |
|       God as the One Who Chooses Me | 54 |
|    A Promise Unfulfilled | 55 |
| *4* Jesus as the Messiah of Israel | 56 |
|    Prince | 60 |
|    King | 60 |
|       The Fallen Booth of David | 61 |
|       A Shoot from the Stump of Jesse | 62 |

|  |  |
|---|---|
| Warrior | 63 |
| Teacher | 64 |
| Shepherd | 65 |
| Priest | 66 |
| Prophet | 68 |
| Suffering Servant | 68 |
| Bearer of Good Tidings | 71 |
| Son of God | 72 |
| Jesus as a Lens | 73 |
| 5  Who is Man? Who is Woman? | 75 |
| The Image of God | 76 |
| Image vs. Likeness | 78 |
| Doctrinal Development | 80 |
| The Grace of God | 80 |
| More on the Image | 83 |
| The Transformation of Women and Men | 85 |
| 6  Transformed from What? | 89 |
| The Fall | 89 |
| Many Levels of Meaning | 91 |
| What is Sin? | 92 |
| Descriptive v. Prescriptive | 93 |
| Characteristics of a Sinner | 94 |
| Attachment | 95 |
| Satan | 96 |
| The Accuser | 96 |
| The Battle between Satan and Michael | 97 |
| The Power and Traps Associated with the Image | 98 |
| Geraldine | 98 |
| Screwtape | 99 |
| Possession, Therapy, and Exorcism | 101 |
| A Call to the Journey Back | 102 |
| 7  Transformed into What? | 104 |
| The Sermon on the Mount | 104 |
| The Model is Jesus | 108 |
| Freedom from Sin | 109 |
| Indistinguishable | 110 |
| A Caveat | 111 |
| Trying on Jesus | 112 |
| The Incarnation as the Model | 115 |

| | |
|---|---|
| *8* Who Was Jesus? Divine vs. Human | 117 |
|    The Incarnation | 117 |
|    Human Characteristics | 119 |
|    Divine Characteristics | 120 |
|    The Endpoints | 121 |
|    The Early Heresies | 122 |
|    Some Basics of Orthodoxy | 123 |
|    The Nicene Creed | 124 |
|    The Chalcedonian Formula | 126 |
|    Kenosis – the Blind Trust | 130 |
|    Prayer | 133 |
|    Free Will, Temptation and Sin | 136 |
|    Ignorantists | 138 |
|    The Holy Spirit | 139 |
|    Traps | 142 |
| *9* How Was Jesus God? | 144 |
|    What Jesus Said About Himself | 145 |
|    A Speculation | 149 |
|    What Was Said About Him | 151 |
|    The Human Face of God | 153 |
|    The Deep Structure of God | 157 |
|    The Meaning | 160 |
| *10* Who Was Jesus? Particular vs. Universal | 165 |
|    Jesus – a Particular Man | 165 |
|       A Meditation | 167 |
|       The Last Temptation of Christ | 169 |
|       Just as We Struggle | 174 |
|       Trying and Choosing | 174 |
|    Jesus – the Universal Man | 177 |
|       Transparent and Self-giving | 178 |
|       Truthful and Loving | 180 |
|       Tough Love | 182 |
| *11* How Does Jesus Open the Door for Transformation? | 185 |
|    Formulas of Salvation | 185 |
|    Three Meditations | 190 |
|    A Hebrew Context | 205 |
|    Irenaeus | 205 |
|    Anselm | 207 |
|    Baptism | 209 |

| | |
|---|---:|
| *12* How Does It Look to Be Christ-like? | 212 |
|     Christ's Characteristics | 212 |
|     Dealing with the List | 214 |
|     Dealing with the Will of God | 215 |
|         The Imitation of Christ | 215 |
|         Just Like Jesus | 218 |
|     From the Perspective of God and the World | 221 |
|     The Characteristics of Jesus | 222 |
|     The View from Different Vantage Points | 224 |
|     A View from Scripture | 226 |
| *13* What is the Price of Transformation? | 228 |
|     Sacrifice | 228 |
|     The Challenge of Truth | 232 |
|         Thought vs. Practice | 235 |
|         Suffering | 236 |
|         Obedience and Willingness | 237 |
|     God's Perspective on Suffering | 237 |
|     Two Aspects of Suffering | 238 |
| *14* What is the NET Price of Transformation? | 240 |
|     Tallying Up the Debits and Credits | 240 |
|     Going to Heaven? | 242 |
|     The Peace of God | 244 |
|         The City of God | 245 |
|         Hebrew Scripture | 246 |
|     Integrity | 247 |
|     As It Is in Heaven | 247 |
| *15* How Much Transformation Has Been Offered to Us? | 250 |
|     Pickin' and Choosin' | 250 |
|     Be Perfect | 254 |
|     A Radical Transformation | 256 |
|     Maximus the Confessor | 257 |
|     A Transformation of Being | 261 |
|     Becoming the Father | 262 |
|     The Only Point | 266 |
|     Something about Mary | 267 |
|     Miracles | 271 |
|     Trying on the Words of Jesus | 272 |
|     A Journey into God | 277 |
| *16* What is the Process of Transformation? | 278 |
|     The Divine Desire | 278 |

| | |
|---|---|
| The Posture of Jesus | 279 |
| The Ladder of Divine Graces | 280 |
|    It's a Ladder | 283 |
|    Perfection as a Process | 284 |
|    A Collaborative Effort | 285 |
|    Humility and Openness | 285 |
|    More on Detachment | 286 |
|    Compassion | 290 |
| A Relationship with Jesus | 291 |
| **17 The Community of Faith** | **294** |
| Knowledge | 295 |
| Opportunity | 298 |
| Compatibility | 301 |
| Dialogue | 303 |
| Safety | 304 |
| Responsibility and Accountability | 305 |
| **18 Transformation in Action** | **309** |
| Prayer and the Life of the Spirit | 310 |
|    The Rosary | 312 |
|    Speaking in Tongues | 313 |
| Spiritual Exercises | 315 |
| How is Driving Transformed? | 316 |
| How is our use of Technology Transformed? | 318 |
| How is Dieting Transformed? | 320 |
| How is Fear Transformed? | 321 |
| How is Pride Transformed? | 322 |
| How is Sex Transformed? | 323 |
| How is Ambition Transformed? | 327 |
| How is Competition Transformed? | 329 |
| How are Politics Transformed" | 332 |
| How are Violence and Anger Transformed | 334 |
| How is Humor Transformed? | 336 |
| How are Church Ministries Transformed? | 339 |
| How is Happiness Transformed? | 342 |
| **19 Some Final Thoughts** | **344** |

# Preface

This book arose out of a class I taught over a span of several years in a parish Sunday school setting. The class was called *Scratching the Surface of Christian Transformation*, or *How Would Jesus Play Basketball*. The class addressed what appears to be a general confusion among most Christians about what actually happened over 2000 years ago. Who was this man Jesus? Was he a superman? Was he just an average Joe who happened to be a powerful speaker? Or was he something much different—much more challenging and enticing and even compelling? And who am I? Just exactly what has been offered to me? What am I challenged to *be* because this man Jesus lived?

Who was he, and who am I? The answers to these questions define what it means to be Christians. As followers of Jesus Christ, we must at some point come to terms with just how radical the call is for us to be changed into someone new. The questions, therefore, form the foundation of any Christian spiritual journey. They also point clearly to the differences between the many Christian denominations, since they cut to the core of any Christian belief system. They also form the basis of comparing Christianity with other religions and may just inform us about what it means to be humanity at its best. Because these defining questions and their answers are so important to serious religious dialogue, both with those inside and those outside our religious institutions, there seemed to be a need for a consideration of them in some accessible form. This task, therefore, forms the foundation of this book.

Let me say a word about the tone of the book. This is not intended to be a scholarly work. I am not a biblical or theological scholar. That will be abundantly clear as you read. I am just trying to find some answers to some very simple questions. We might call this the "view from the pew." Consequently, I will try not to take myself too seriously. We are talking essentially about God here. One premise that may be important to get out on the table now is that God, in God's very essence, is unknowable to us. Paul's words will be an important guide, "For now we see through a glass darkly, but then face to face" (1 Corinthians 13:2, King James Version). None of us has a lock on the mind of God. There are many ways to access the mind of God and in some way, we may be called to emulate the mind of God, but in this life our understanding of that mind is always imperfect. So, for me to write anything at all would be the height of audacity without a large dose of humility up front.

If, during the course of this exposition, it looks like I am speaking disparagingly about any religious tradition, I hope I am evenhanded in my attempt to point out the traps that we all tend to fall into—myself especially. No denomination is without flaws and no individual I know is either. Let me poke at myself first, lest you think that I place myself above those whom I may be discussing. I am self-centered, but I taste enough of the other-centeredness of Jesus to know that that is where I want to be. I can be small and petty, but I have seen the compassion of Jesus and know that that is where I want to be. I am easily angered in a way that is certainly not righteous, but I have seen the righteous anger of Jesus, and I know that that is where I want to be. If I may be so bold, let me assert the following statement of personal faith: I am flawed, yet I have a savior who is Christ Jesus, and in him are my hope and my salvation. And it just may be that you are as flawed as I am. So, we have a lot in common, you and I.

## Logistical Issues and Approach

Let me make quick mention of a few logistical issues before we begin. Regarding my use of capital letters, I have decided not to capitalize pronouns, such as "he" or "him," when referring to God or Jesus. Some authors do this out of reverence, and I do not disagree with the practice. Because of the possible breadth of the

## Preface

reading audience, I will leave it up to the reader to allow the Spirit to move him or her in that direction.

I have chosen to capitalize the word Scripture as a pointer to its fundamental importance for all we say and do as Christians. As far as the word "Church" is concerned, my tendency is to capitalize it when referring to the Church as a whole and use a lower case when referring to one or more local parishes. My capitalization of the word expresses my hope that someday the implied unity will be realized. I would also like to lighten the cumbersome load of the "him/her" pronoun problem. I will state right now that I believe, as a whole, the Church is moving in a more inclusive direction. I will, therefore, try to be balanced in my use of each different gender pronoun in those situations in which inclusive language is appropriate.

Throughout the text and quotations, you will notice that I have italicized key words. Sometimes the italicized words are those of the original author and sometimes they are my additions for emphasis. In any case, one of us meant for there to be emphasis. I have avoided the cumbersome practice of constantly placing in square brackets the designation [my emphasis] or [author's emphasis]. If it is critical that one should know the source of the italics, I would encourage the reader to consult the original text. At this level of scholarship, I hope that will not be an issue. Most of them are mine.

I might also note that most of my biblical quotations are from the Revised Standard Version. While there are some important aspects of the translation that are helpful, it does not use more inclusive language that is found in the New Revised Standard Version. For example, the use of the word "man" should usually be taken to mean mankind.

# Acknowledgements

I would like to acknowledge some of those who have been integral to my own journey, and consequently have been formative in the development of this book. To all those who have participated in "Scratching" I owe much thanks for the opportunity to discuss and share the deepest parts of our spiritual journey toward Christ. For at least thirteen years I met with a few seekers from my church. We called ourselves the Tuesday Morning Breakfast Club That Meets on Monday Mornings. From the beginning Sam and Janet Roberts, Kathryn McCormick, Joan Savage, and I grappled with all the questions addressed here. That dialogue has been essential in my own process of formulating and clarifying these ideas.

I simply cannot say enough about their importance in my own spiritual journey. Jim Cutsinger, a Professor of Religion at the University of South Carolina, was a priceless sounding board for me as I struggled to make sense out of the variety of ideas and questions that came my way. He rarely agreed completely with me but was always gentle with his comments. His recent passing represents a great loss to many.

Blaney Pridgen, when he was Rector of St. Mary's Episcopal Church in Columbia, South Carolina, gave me important encouragement and an opportunity to share many of these ideas with parishioners and those studying for the permanent diaconate in the Episcopal Diocese of Upper South Carolina. And of course, Fletcher Montgomery, at that time pastor of St. John's Episcopal Church in Columbia, allowed us to take the first steps in teaching "Scratching" at St. John's. This whole effort would simply not exist without his support and encouragement.

I would also like to say a word about a very special soul friend who was a powerful force in my own spiritual development. Kathryn Larisey was a spiritual force to be reckoned with. With

## Acknowledgements

tremendous courage, a nuclear will, and a colossal desire for God, Katherine changed all who encountered her spirit. I am deeply indebted to her for the gift of grace that God bestowed on me through her. I have been privileged to know her. You will encounter some of her spirit in Chapter 11.

I would like to thank Fr. Gregory Caruthers, S.J. of St. Augustine's Roman Catholic Seminary for his willingness to engage me on a number of issues raised in the development of these thoughts. He has been an invaluable guide and spiritual friend as this manuscript was refined.

Several folks were kind enough to read and comment on earlier versions of the manuscript. They include Jeffrey Morehouse, Nicholas Beasley, Bruce Marshall, and Emerson Smith. Many thanks to them for their time, energy, and insights.

Finally, I need to offer very special thanks to Michael DeVries for the inestimable care he took in editing an early draft of this manuscript. My own shallow thinking did not escape his rapier intellect and insightful suggestions for clarifying points, improving the flow, and correcting blunders. There were many times I felt unworthy of his efforts to keep this project on some sort of even keel.

If there is value here, it is a product of all the folks who have been on the journey with me. It there are errors or any weaknesses in the arguments and conclusions presented here, they are alone my responsibility.

Jonathan Fletcher<br>
May 24, 2020<br>
Hopkins, SC

# Introduction and Background

> And we all, with unveiled face, beholding the glory of the Lord, are being *transformed into his likeness* from one degree of glory to another.
>
> *2 Corinthians 3:18*[1]

> For those whom he foreknew he also predestined to be *conformed to the image of his Son*, in order that he might be the first-born among many brethren.
>
> *Romans 8:29*

What we are trying to do in this book is to start at the beginning and uncover orthodox doctrine concerning Jesus, how it developed, why is it important, and how it might become the foundation of our own personal transformation *into the perfect likeness of Jesus Christ*.

If you as a child loved baseball, and you wanted more than anything else to be a great baseball player, your father might say, "Sure, go out and *be* Babe Ruth," assuming that both of you knew that he did not mean to become all the particular qualities of that particular man at the particular time in which he lived. But there is no doubt in the power of the image. It is not the same as being "like" the Babe. The power of the image is somehow diminished. To *be* the Babe is to imagine yourself standing at the plate blasting home runs, and the crowd cheering wildly as you trot that inimitable trot around the bases. Somehow for a moment you are transformed into a new being with new and wondrous possibilities. You step up to the plate with a new demeanor, a new bravado, a bit of a swagger. And of course, when you strike out, you immediately take great solace in the fact that the Babe

---

[1] The word "transformed" is translated simply as "changed" in the RSV.

## Introduction and Background

struck out a lot, too. It may be only after several times at bat, with no home runs and no hits and no walks, that you start to realize that "being" the Babe would take a lot of hard work. *A lot!* At which point you may simply join your friends for ice cream.

The title of this effort as I originally conceived it was "On Being Jesus." As you can see, the title eventually morphed into its present form. To contemplate "being" Jesus is essentially the same thing as to contemplate being transformed into the "perfect likeness" of Jesus Christ. The word "perfect" is used for precisely the same reasons that the word "being" was originally used. The objective is to remove doubt and wiggle room. We are talking about a radical transformation such that when someone sees us, they "see" or have an intimate encounter with Jesus Christ. The book is an attempt to explain what this kind of transformation is all about.

What we are talking about here is the power of the image. The power of the Incarnation of God is not in the theology, or Christology, or ethics—or any other conceptual perspective for that matter. It is in the power of the image. Once there was a real man. Someone you can picture. Someone you can not only emulate in some fuzzy and safe way, but someone you can picture so clearly that you can start on the path to being that person in some profound way. Of course, what we mean by that is what this book is all about. Let me emphasize this. The fact of the matter is that it is a heck of a lot easier to *be* Jesus than it is to *be* Babe Ruth. You don't need any inherent athletic talent to be Jesus. You just need *you—all of you*. What we are talking about here is a distinction between the physical attributes of someone like the Babe that we may or may not possess and the completely accessible universal mental and spiritual attributes of Jesus of Nazareth. There is no question that we do not have the same physical attributes of Jesus. When Paul admonishes us to take on the mind of Christ (1 Corinthians 2:16), he is talking about a new state of *being*, one that is patterned on Jesus. A state of being that is available to all of us.

The power of the image that is captured in the painting by Carl Heinrich Bloch (1834–1890) may be worth noting. In his painting *The Transfiguration*, Bloch depicts the biblical story (Matthew 17:1–9) of Peter, James, and John going with Jesus up

the mountain, at which point Jesus is transformed, or more appropriately transfigured, into a radiant image who then enters into conversation with Moses and Elijah. Clearly it is meant as a definitive sign of Jesus' divine son-ship. But for us, there is more to the story. While the Apostles in the foreground are apparently blinded by the light emanating from Jesus, and Moses and Elijah

# Introduction and Background

are engulfed by the light, we know from "the rest of the story" that, not only is the light blinding, but it is also *inviting*. It is inviting us to participate in that divine light. So now we see ourselves at Jesus' feet with the Apostles being possibly blinded at first but then invited by the light to participate in the perfect likeness of Jesus Christ. In other words, we are not only called to be *transformed* but ultimately *transfigured* in such a way that the light of Christ shines forth from us as it did from him. In other words, we are to take seriously Jesus words to us:

"I am the light of the world."    *John 8:12*

"You are the light of the world."    *Matthew 5:14*

My spiritual journey has taken me from cradle Episcopalian into, at various times, Methodist, Baptist, Wesleyan, Roman Catholic—and back. I hope this perspective will inform rather than confuse the effort. When I wrote the bulk of this manuscript, however, I was an Episcopalian. Thus, there is some good news and some not-so-good news. Because of their history, Anglicans and their Episcopal offspring in the United States have been in a unique position to view, assess, and appropriate with considerable freedom the theological traditions of both the Protestants and the Catholics, both Roman and Eastern Orthodox. This balance can be a huge value in assessing the facts independent of some predetermined vested interest in any one tradition. The not-so-good news is that by not having been exposed to a very tightly integrated tradition, Episcopalians may be less apt to settle on—let alone agree to—a coherent expression of their own theology. There may be an inclination to "inclusivity" to the detriment of the need for some important critical thinking. So having said that, I hope to approach this whole subject of being transformed into the likeness of Christ with an open mind, look at a wide range of sources, seek whatever is true, and come to some conclusions that may have value for members of a wide range of both Christian and non-Christian traditions.

Because I believe in the universality of the theme of transformation, I have chosen to refer to the Christian Old Testament as the Hebrew Scripture, emphasizing its broader reach than simply the Christian community of faith. While we assert that Jesus Christ is the fulfillment of that Scripture, we also acknowledge and stand by Jesus' statement:

> "Think not that I have come to abolish the law and the prophets; I have come not to abolish them but to fulfil them. For truly, I say to you, till heaven and earth pass away, not an iota, not a dot, will pass from the law until all is accomplished. Whoever then relaxes one of the least of these commandments and teaches men so, shall be called least in the kingdom of heaven; but he who does them and teaches them shall be called great in the kingdom of heaven.
> *Matthew 5:17–19*

Because the answers to the defining questions differ among Christian denominations, and because we tend to hold our religious beliefs to be, if I may say it, *sacred*, dealing with these questions often places one in a contentious position. If you choose to go down this path—clarifying and exposing wishy-washy thinking—you will undoubtedly find yourself in some form of conflict, threatening those who hold a different opinion. This will be your first taste of what it is like to *be* Jesus. This is the life he led—constantly challenging fuzzy thinking. The question we must all address is whether any given answer is true and whether the truth is of any value to others and ourselves. If you are willing to come with me on a wondrous journey of discovery

## Introduction and Background

and possible enlightenment, then take a deep breath, say a prayer for fortitude, and start to entertain the idea that in some very special and mystical way Christianity is about only one thing—being transformed *into the perfect likeness* of Jesus Christ.

Let me say something about the pathway I have chosen. Everything in Scripture points in some way to the kind of life that is offered to us in God, and I am asserting here that this life is intimately related to the transformation that has been offered to us in Jesus Christ. There are virtually an infinite number of pathways one could take to get to the same destination. It is as if there were a forest of dots between the starting point and the goal, and we need to find just one pathway that connects the two. Some may be better than others, some straighter, some more tortuous, but the first and foremost challenge is to find at least one. So, the way to think of this whole effort is a process of connecting enough dots that get us from point A to point Z in a way that is as clear as possible. There are undoubtably other pathways and even better pathways. I just hope this one gets the job done.

From the very beginning of Jesus' ministry and his gathering of a small group of followers around him, those followers and the rest of the world have been asking this question: Who was this man, Jesus? The Apostles were in a constant quandary. It was only after the resurrection that their understanding took a quantum leap forward. How did this understanding evolve? From their first-hand experience of Jesus, we get a body of oral traditions[2] that were passed from Christian community to Christian community as well as a set of writings—the Gospels, the Acts of the Apostles, and certain letters—that give us insight into

---

[2] Clearly Paul was drawing on some form of shared understanding among the other apostles concerning what had taken place. Since his letters are considered to be the earliest written documents that now make up the New Testament, we must assume some form of oral transmission that predates his writings and therefore predates the Gospels.

that understanding. This body of information, which was eventually codified in what we now know as the Bible, is known as the *apostolic tradition* and forms the foundation for the early Church's understanding of who Jesus was. Since there were many ways in which the apostle's understanding of the Christ event was passed along through the Christian communities, not the least of which were the written documents, this "tradition" is considered to be all-encompassing as well as a bit vague. Suffice it to say that the result of an organic process of transmission was a shared understanding that eventually needed to be defended from dilution, degradation, and corruption. This understanding of Jesus Christ and the nature of the Christ event that has been passed along to us today is what is known as the Church's Christology.

Paul was digesting and formulating the oral part of this tradition as it was passed along to him (long before the Gospels were written) into his own set of letters that enunciate and clarify its meaning for the new Gentile churches he founded. In other words, Paul offered his own clarification and amplification of the Christ event, just as Peter, James, John, Matthew, Mark, and Luke offered their own interpretation that was consistent with the historical facts of Jesus' life, death, and resurrection as they experienced them. Thus, the process of clarification and amplification began with the first encounter of the Apostles with Jesus and continues today. This process is what we call *doctrinal development*, with Paul's writings being a clear and early example. His formulations have become an integral part of that apostolic tradition.

Before and following the gathering together of these early writings into what we call the New Testament canon (officially sanctioned by the Church in the fourth century A.D.), the early Church had to deal with a number of controversies that threat-

## Introduction and Background

ened to shake the apostolic foundation. Heresies arose that challenged certain teachings of the early Church. Early Church leaders wrote extensively on these issues to clarify the apostolic teaching, giving the Church additional doctrinal development. We now call these writers the *Church Fathers*. They were constantly trying to refine our understanding of this man, Jesus. In so doing, they all participated in the process of developing what they would have called correct or *orthodox* doctrine. The result was a body of thought that has detailed answers to the question, who was Jesus Christ?

One cannot answer the question about who Jesus was, however, without addressing his relationship to others. We might assert that the Christ event was principally one of how we are to live in a world of people to whom we must relate. If we are created in the image of God, and God is love, then somehow we are called to reflect this love in the world through our relationships. My very being is therefore a reflection of a profoundly mysterious relationship between God and man that calls us to a special kind of relationship among humanity. We therefore must focus our interest on the nature of human beings. In other words, we must ask the question: Who am I? And just exactly what has been offered to me by this Jesus of Nazareth?

To address this question, we must go way back. One of the most powerful admonitions in the early Church that has continued to this day is to "follow Jesus." In fact, the earliest description of Christianity was the moniker "The Way." In other words, being Christian was less about an intellectual assent to a set of beliefs as it was a way of living.

Many folks in the recent past were wearing small wristbands that said "WWJD" which stood for "What would Jesus do?" The ideas of following Jesus' teachings and emulating his behavior have been centerpieces of Church preaching and teaching. Is that the basis of the answer to the question? Is it that I am the one who is capable of emulating Jesus behavior? Am I the one he has offered simply the example of a set of behaviors? Is that all there is, or is it simply a very good starting place? Could we go beyond mere emulation—to something much deeper?

The Apostle Paul uses even stronger language when he suggests that we take on the mind of Christ (1 Corinthians 2:16). Episcopalians, for example, are called to live into the "full stature of Christ."[3] What is that full stature? In both their writings and in their behavior, the Apostles pointed toward a more radical interpretation of what it means to *follow*. The premise of this book, and it is an ancient one, is that orthodox apostolic teaching intended not for us to *follow* in the usual sense of the word, but to *be*. In other words, the transformation offered to us is not simply one of action or behavior, but also one of *being*. As the philosophers would say, we are talking about an *ontological* (having to do with *being*) transformation.

So here we are with a host of tough questions regarding Jesus and us. Was Jesus truly God, and if so, did he exhibit all the qualities traditionally ascribed to God: omniscience (all knowing), omnipotence (all powerful), and omnipresence (present everywhere at one time)?[4] If Jesus was human, what do we mean when we say that he was the Son of God? Does Jesus offer all of who he was to us or only a part? In other words, does he hold something of himself back from us? If Jesus was God, am I called to *be* God? It brings up a host of questions that also seem trivial yet cut to the core of the Church's Christology. If Jesus

---

[3] *Book of Common Prayer* (New York: Seabury Press, 1979), 302 that is based on Ephesians 4:13.

[4] These qualities are those that have been articulated over the centuries as a result of doctrinal development within the setting of the Church—however you might want to define the term doctrinal development. Scripture alone cannot unequivocally prove any of the manifold qualities of God that we today use as the basis of our theological understanding.

## Introduction and Background

was God and he played golf, could he have made a hole-in-one on every hole? Am I supposed to be able to walk on water or raise the dead? If Jesus was God, did he ever get sick? Or was Jesus really God? There are, in fact, clear answers to these questions, if we are willing to do some work and if we are willing to define our words carefully. Here we will be asserting that the answers to these and many more questions are the *good news* and indeed are worth the effort.

To talk about becoming anything new involves a radical *transformation*. This transformation is one of the most powerful admonitions of Christ—to be "born anew" (John 3:3). To understand the nature of this transformation, we must again understand who Jesus was. Notice that I deliberately use the word *was*. When Jesus was in his earthly ministry, he manifested certain characteristics that resulted from what we call the *Incarnation*. This is the "enfleshment" of God or God made man. While he was in the temporal (in time) world, as opposed to the eternal world (not in time or not temporal) he was limited in some very important ways. When we understand this, we can understand more readily what or who he calls us to be. When he says, "You, therefore, must be perfect, as your heavenly Father is perfect" (Matthew 5:48), we need to know what he meant. This process of transformation is the subject of this book.

My hope is to explore the ideas of the Church that have been developed over the last 2000 years, but mostly were crystallized within the first 500 years. The answers we are seeking are the answers of the Apostles. The questions we're asking about the nature of Jesus while he walked the earth are addressed under the general topic called *Christology*, the study of Christ. As such, Christology forms a subset of the field of *theology*, the study of God. Among the many possible answers, there are some that the Church has determined to be correct or "orthodox," and have been incorporated into a body of beliefs called Church *doctrine* or Church *dogma*. So this book is an attempt to expose the basics of *orthodox Christological doctrine*. I know this is a mouthful, but I think you will get used to the terms as we go along. The compact meaning found in such terms can be very helpful in developing these ideas about Jesus. Let me say a few words about three concepts that will play an important role in what we are about: apologetics, the distinction between doctrine and dogma, and finally, the idea of doctrinal development.

Christian apologetics is the process not of apologizing for something we have done wrong, but of arguing for the validity of an idea. While we will be trying to uncover orthodox Christology, we will certainly put forth arguments for the validity and importance of those ideas. But this book is not essentially apologetics. It is expository. It is intended simply to expose what the Church says about Jesus, not necessarily to defend it. I hope that once we see this exposition, we will be captured and challenged by its stunning implications.

All reflection about God results in ideas about how the pieces fit together. Creation, incarnation, atonement, and the Trinity—all are fundamental ideas that require some understanding of how some of the pieces, such as God, the world, humanity, Jesus, and the Holy Spirit, fit together. Anyone who puts forth a description of how any of this works, is articulating doctrine. All theologians state doctrine. Calvin had his doctrine of predestination. Luther had his doctrine of justification by faith. Paul had his doctrine of the role of women in the Church, and so forth. Some of these doctrines have been accepted by the Church or by a denomination, thus becoming *Church doctrine*. A smaller set of doctrines is determined to be essential to the faith and is called *dogma*. In the Roman Catholic tradition, the distinction between Church doctrine and dogma is not large because they would say that all of it is important. The Anglican tradition would allow for more wiggle room and designate a

## Introduction and Background

much more limited set of doctrinal statements as dogma. In the non-creedal traditions, the distinction is not so important, since they would simply point to their "dogma" as Scripture, with no emphasis on any form of other doctrine that would inform Scripture. Here we will use the term *orthodox Church doctrine* to be essential and therefore synonymous with the word *dogma*.

Finally, before we start, I need to say something about *doctrinal development*. This process has been poorly understood, and this misunderstanding has been the major cause of many of the splits in the Church over the last 2000 years. As a touchstone for these thoughts, I will draw on an imposing "essay" written in the 1800s by a former Anglican priest who eventually converted to Roman Catholicism and became a cardinal in the Catholic Church, John Henry Newman. The book, entitled *An Essay on the Development of Christian Doctrine*,[5] discusses the necessity for a formal process for doctrinal development. In fact, the apparent lack of such a process was one of the reasons Newman left the Church of England. He felt the Church did not have in place an effective means for doing doctrinal development. Here is the point. Recall that the Protestant source of authority is *sola Scriptura* (only Scripture). What the Church found in the early years was that there were many issues that were simply not straightforward from Scripture. We would not have had the controversies that we had, if everything had been perfectly clear. The biggest problem surrounded the understanding of Jesus' humanity versus his divinity. Some groups stressed one at the expense of the other. What was the proper balance? How was the Church to state its understanding in such a way as to preserve the power of the Christ event? Where were we to put our emphasis, on his life or on his death and resurrection? Did he come to

---

[5] J. H. Newman, *An Essay on the Development of Christian Doctrine* (Notre Dame, IN: University of Notre Dame Press, 1989).

make a place for us in heaven, or did he come to show us how to live on earth—or both—or neither? All the answers to these questions needed to be codified through doctrinal development into what we call orthodox doctrine.

# 1
# A Starting Point: Christian Orthodoxy

To begin our journey toward being transformed into the perfect likeness of Jesus, we first want to know who Jesus was. This may seem like a pretty simple question since many of us have grown up with a notion of Jesus. We Christians are all conditioned by Christmas pageants, Easter celebrations, Sunday school activities, and ubiquitous pictures of Jesus with children and lambs, and finally images of Jesus hanging on the cross. If we don't think about it too hard, it somehow makes sense, probably because we all have been told from our youth that it makes sense.

But what if we start seriously to *think* about it? What if we start to ask the basic questions about what it all means? Most of us know the story of Jesus' birth and ministry and death, but when someone starts to use common language to talk about an itinerant Jewish preacher who was the son of a carpenter, we start to feel uncomfortable. It all seems a little bit too earthly. We grew up with a beautiful story, one that was more like a fairy tale than a documentary. We love and are somehow comforted by the happily-ever-after stories of Cinderella, Snow White and the Seven Dwarfs, Jack and the Beanstalk, Winnie the Pooh, Mickey Mouse, and Superman. Deep inside, do we somehow envision Jesus in the same comforting way? Sadly, many of us do. So how do we move beyond this sweet story to something more meaningful?

Years ago, I visited Sea World in Orlando, Florida. One of the exhibits was something called "Shark Encounter." The idea was to take people beyond their own misconceptions to a much more meaningful understanding of what sharks are. To do this, they sat us in a dark theater and showed us a movie about sharks. While interesting, it was hardly life changing. Then they dramatically raised the screen to reveal a huge aquarium behind glass, and for the first time we witnessed sharks in their own, although somewhat artificial, realm. This certainly was a kind of encounter, but again it was still at a safe distance. Finally, they led us all out a door at the bottom left side of the glass wall and into a large Plexiglas tube through which we walked. At this point the sharks were swimming all around us. It was intimate. It was stunning. This was indeed a *shark encounter*. None of us probably thought of sharks the same way we used to ever again.

The question is whether it is possible to have an intimate and transformative encounter with Jesus Christ, one that is so real and resonates so much with us that we are never the same. What would such an encounter look like? To start along a path toward this *Christ encounter*, we need to know where to start. This chapter is about the starting point. It is called Christian orthodoxy, and it must be clearly defined and understood.

The word "orthodox" means to be right or correct—literally *right belief*. From the beginning of the Church's struggle to understand the meaning of Jesus, there have been areas of confusion and dissention. Within the first 100 years after Christ's death, factions arose with conflicting explanations of just exactly what happened during the life and death of Jesus. While this book cannot deal exhaustively with the way the Church handled these problems, some basics are important. To do this we need to refine our understanding of the word "orthodox."

When we look around at the vast array of different Christian denominations just in our own communities, it is clear that there are considerable differences in our definitions of what is orthodox. The idea of orthodoxy is a relative one, as is the word "heresy." If orthodox teaching is "right" or in agreement with the teachings of a particular denomination, then heresy is that which is "wrong" or contrary to the teachings of that denomination. What is orthodox for the Presbyterians may be heresy to the Catholics and *vice versa*. Therefore, what we need to do is to be clear whose orthodoxy we are talking about. What we need to do then is to say a few words about the Roman Catholic, Eastern Orthodox, Protestant, and Anglican sources of authority, other than Scripture, that form the basis of their respective understandings of their own "orthodox doctrine."

Unfortunately, this treatment is scratching the surface of an historical process that began at the great break between the eastern and western branches of the Catholic Church in around A.D. 1000, ramped up during the Reformation around A.D. 1500 and continues today. It is worthy of a much more insightful treatment than I am able to do here. This is a complicated history to which I will not do justice. Please forgive me for that, but we need some foothold on these ideas as a foundation.

## In Search of Roman Catholic Orthodoxy

In its most simple terms, sources of authority for Roman Catholic orthodoxy are Scripture and Tradition—the Bible and the interpretation of the Bible through a complex historical process that involved dialogue, struggle, and accommodation. Because during the first 1000 years of the Church, there was relative unity, the Roman Catholic sources of authority prior to the first major split are common to the Roman Catholics and the Eastern Orthodox. Prior to the split between the spheres of influence of Rome and Constantinople, the Church spoke as one concerning conflicting ideas on theology and Christology. To address any problems, the Church called together all the important leaders from all the major centers of the faith. These gatherings were called Ecumenical Councils. They could be called ecumenical because everyone was invited, since at that time there were no major divisions in the Church as there are today. The following is a list of the first seven Ecumenical Councils.

> **Nicaea (A.D. 325)**
> **Constantinople (A.D. 381)**
> **Ephesus (A.D. 431)**
> **Chalcedon (A.D. 451)**
> Constantinople II (A.D. 553)
> Constantinople III (A.D. 680)
> Nicaea II (A.D. 787)

The first four councils are highlighted in bold letters. The Anglicans hold these councils to be authoritative sources of their Christology. The Eastern Orthodox hold the first seven to be authoritative, and the Roman Catholics have had councils all the way up to the modern day, including the Second Vatican Council in 1962. There were two important results of the first four councils. The first of the two was the Nicene Creed, which was formulated at the Council of Nicaea in A.D. 325. and revised into its present form at the Council of Constantinople a little more than 50 years later. (It is actually correctly called the Nicene-Constantinopolitan Creed, but because nobody can say that, the Church has settled on the simpler designation.) It is amazing that it took more than 300 years to clarify some of the most basic tenets of the Christian faith. The second important result of the first four councils was the source for our understanding of the person of Jesus Christ. It came out of the Council of Chalcedon. This formulation of the nature of Jesus forms the basis of Roman Catholic, as well as Eastern Orthodox and Anglican Christologies.

As an integral part of the disputes that were addressed in the councils, the writings of certain influential Church leaders

## A Starting Point – Christian Orthodoxy

formed the basis for the eventual formulations of the councils. These early writers were usually bishops or other Church leaders and are often classed for convenience as to whether they were influential before (ante-) or after (post-) the Council of Nicaea. We call these writers, because at that time they all happened to be men, the Church Fathers. The following is a list of many of the important Church Fathers.

**Church Fathers**
- Ante-Nicene Fathers
    - Irenaeus (125-202)
    - Clement of Alexandria (150-215)
    - Origen (185-254)
- Nicene Fathers
    - Athanasius (296-373)
- Post-Nicene Fathers
    - Gregory of Nazianzus (329-390)
    - Gregory of Nyssa (330-395)
    - Basil of Caesarea (330-379)
    - St. Augustine of Hippo (354-430)

Although the writings of these apologists (and remember, that is exactly what they were doing, making arguments for the validity of a doctrinal position) are not considered to be without error, many of their ideas form the basis for current Roman Catholic doctrine concerning Jesus. One of the most important of these was Athanasius. He was instrumental in formulating many subtleties surrounding Catholic Christological doctrine and will be discussed again in a later chapter.

Because of the hierarchical structure of the Roman church, it was able to administer doctrinal development more effectively than those churches that tended to shy away from a strong hierarchy. Consequently, the best and most accessible source of current orthodox Roman Catholic doctrine is the *Catechism of the Catholic Church* that was recently revised in 1999.

## In Search of Eastern Orthodox "Orthodoxy"

The sources of authority for the Eastern Orthodox would be the same as those for the Roman Catholics: Scripture and Tradition. The Eastern Orthodox Church as a separate entity arose from a gradual breaking away process that culminated in the mid-11th century, ostensibly as a result of two issues: (1) the primacy of the Bishop of Rome, called the Roman Pontiff or Pope, and (2) some wording in the Creed called the *Filioque*.[6] The first related to authority, while the second related to doctrine.

In the early Church, the patriarchate of Rome was the largest and most influential of the geographical divisions. It took its position of preeminence from the assumption that the Roman Church was established by the Apostle Peter and that Christ had designate Peter as the head of the early Church. As the Church grew and expanded geographically, the Bishop of Rome was assumed by many, especially those in Rome, to be the most influential Bishop among the major divisions, including Alexandria (Egypt), Antioch (Syria), and Constantinople (modern Turkey). As this preeminence continued to assert itself during the conciliar period, the Eastern Church, centered in Constantinople, felt slighted and eventually refused to recognize this difference in authority. They insisted on a more equal collegiality of leadership without the need for a single head.

The doctrinal issue was more subtle. In the Roman version of the Nicene Creed, there is the statement that the Holy Spirit

---

[6] For a good overview of the historical relationship between the Orthodox and the Roman Catholic Churches, see Thomas Bokenkotter, *A Concise History of the Catholic Church* (New York: Random House, 2007).

## A Starting Point – Christian Orthodoxy

"proceeds from the Father and the Son." The Eastern Church argued that the creed that was agreed to in council stated that the Holy Spirit proceeded only from the Father. In other words, there is a hierarchy among the Father, Son and Holy Spirit that the Western (Roman) Church denied. The Eastern Church asserted that, if you want to change the creed, it must be done in another ecumenical council. Because the two never could come to an accommodation, a permanent break (called the Great Schism) occurred in A.D. 1054. This situation is a good example of very large divisions that often turn on apparently very small differences of opinion and wording. The point is that many perceived that these differences had a huge effect on the overall resulting doctrine and the ultimate long-term viability of the Christian community of faith.

One important distinction between East and West is their spiritual and legal emphasis. The Eastern, or predominately Greek Church, was much more interested in the spirit or *pneumos* of the Church while the Roman or Latin Church, because of the tradition of Roman law, became more interested in rules and order. Many of the great mystics in the Church came from the east, while many of the great systematic theologians came from the west. We will be drawing from both traditions.

What we find as far as orthodoxy is concerned is that the Eastern Church froze its doctrinal development as of the seventh ecumenical council in A.D. 787. The writings they use as their source of authority are the Greek and Latin Church Fathers up to that date. Since Christological doctrine was pretty well established by the seventh council, we would expect that the Eastern Church would hold to the same doctrines and call them orthodox as those in the Roman Church. In practice, the picture is not so straightforward.

## In Search of Anglican Orthodoxy

The sources of authority for the Anglicans is an expansion of the Catholic sources and adds Reason to Scripture and Tradition. This system yields what has been called the Three-legged Stool. While the Catholics would say that they exercised reason in the context of the conciliar process, Anglicans prefer to expand the use of reason to include that exercised by individuals. The best way to describe the Anglicans is the way they have described themselves from the very beginning—the *via media*, or middle way. When Henry VIII broke away from Rome in 1534, the Church *in* England was essentially Roman Catholic. Because this occurred right in the middle of the Protestant Reformation, there were powerful forces operating that wanted to reform the English Church into a Calvinist institution. Consequently, the entire early history of the Church of England was one of tension between its Roman roots and its Calvinist leanings. The influence of Rome or Geneva (the center of Calvinism) depended on who was in secular power. Therefore, a little political history may be in order.

The Protestant Reformation is usually dated from the point at which Martin Luther posted his Ninety-five Theses on Indulgences in 1517. The Church in England at this time was Roman Catholic. By the early 1530s, Henry VIII wanted to divorce Catherine of Aragon for not producing a male heir, and he appealed to the Pope for a way out. Because the Pope refused to annul the marriage for various political reasons, Henry convinced Parliament to pass the Supremacy Act of 1534, which made the king the head of the Catholic Church in England. At this point we still should talk about the Church *in* England not *of* England. Henry was a committed Catholic, so the foundation of the English Church had the same theology as before the split.

Just for information sake, Catherine bore a daughter named Mary. Since Henry's last name was Tudor, she is known as

## A Starting Point – Christian Orthodoxy

Mary Tudor. The one thing we need to take with us is that Henry and his Archbishop of Canterbury, Thomas Cranmer, established the Ten Articles, which set forth the fundamentals of the Church in England. In addition, they accepted as authoritative the first four Ecumenical Councils. Thus, the formulation of the fourth council at Chalcedon in A.D. 451 forms the basis of Anglican Christology and is found at the back of the modern *Book of Common Prayer*.[7]

Upon the do-it-yourself annulment of his marriage to Catherine, Henry married Ann Boleyn, who bore him a daughter, Elizabeth—Elizabeth Tudor. Ann also failed to give Henry a male heir, so he trumped up charges against her and had her executed. Eventually Henry married Jane Seymour, who gave him a long-sought-after son, Edward Tudor. When Henry died in 1545, Edward VI took the throne. Since he was an avowed Protestant (as "avowed" as one could be at the age of nine) and had Protestant advisors, the Church in England took its first shift away from its Catholic roots. Under Edward and Archbishop Thomas Cranmer, we got the first and second editions of the *Book of Common Prayer*, the Forty-two Articles of Religion, which were pointedly anti-Catholic, and the first Uniformity Act, which started to hold English clergy's feet to the fire. A derivative of the Forty-two Articles is found in the modern *Book of Common Prayer* as the Thirty-nine Articles.[8]

When Edward died in 1553, Mary Tudor took the throne. She repudiated the Supremacy Act and took the English Church back to its Catholic base and back to its original relationship to Rome. When she died in 1558, Elizabeth Tudor took the throne. She repudiated the repudiation with a true effort to unify the Church with what is called the Elizabethan Settlement. At this

---

[7] *Book of Common Prayer*, 864.
[8] *Book of Common Prayer*, 867–76.

point we have a true reflection of the *via media*. One consequence of this effort was the retention of some Catholic dimensions such as an episcopal (having bishops) hierarchy. These characteristics were codified in the Uniformity Act of 1559 that reintroduced the Book of Common Prayer from Edward's reign. In 1571 the *Thirty-Nine Articles* were promulgated as a doctrinal statement of the Church.[9]

At this point, we have a truly consolidated Church *of* England. Today, the *Book of Common Prayer* is the central source of Anglican orthodoxy. Since it points to its Catholic roots in the Chalcedonian formula and its Protestant roots in the Thirty-nine Articles there is a bit of confusion as to a clearly defined Christological orthodoxy. What we can say is that there has been no clear repudiation of Catholic Christology throughout the history of the Church of England.

## In Search of Protestant Orthodoxy

Protestant orthodoxy is a little more complicated. During and after the Reformation, there was a terrific reaction to the hierarchy of the Roman Church that had promulgated a number of abuses that became intolerable to many in the Church. This reaction resulted in two shifts that are important to our search for Protestant Christological orthodoxy.[10] First, by abandoning the hierarchic structure, the tight control on doctrinal development pretty much came to a halt. By reducing their sources of authority to *sola Scriptura* (only Scripture), they again gave up any control over how the scriptural gaps were filled in. Therefore, doctrinally

---

[9] See the Wikipedia article at https://en.wikipedia.org/wiki/Elizabethan_Religious_Settlement.

[10] For a classic treatment of the Protestant Reformation and its roots and consequences in Christian doctrine, see Williston Walker, et. al., *A History of the Christian Church* (New York: Scribner, 1985, Fourth Edition).

## A Starting Point – Christian Orthodoxy

they had to rely on their founders as their primary source of doctrinal formulations. Luther, Calvin, the Wesleys, Arminius, etc. were not only writing theological *opinion* that was placed into the crucible of the broader community of faith to be refined, but they were also creating what amounted to *Church doctrine* for specific denominations without the historical winnowing processes that characterized the first 1000 years of Christianity.

Lutheran, Calvinist, Baptist, and Methodist doctrine has, in fact, been shaped over the years, but is a bit harder to nail down an understanding of the process. For example, while the Presbyterians look to Calvin for a doctrinal foundation, subsequent events have influenced that doctrine considerably. Predestination, an idea that was not one of Calvin's central themes, became much more important to one of his followers, Theodore Beza. A Church of England gathering called the Westminster Assembly (1643-1652) was convened to formulate a set of doctrinal statements. Although both "episcopal"[11] and Calvinist supporters were invited, the episcopal delegates didn't come, so the resulting document, the *Westminster Confession*, was essentially a Calvinist document and became a cornerstone of Presbyterian/Calvinist doctrine.

While there are a number of statements that imply a Christology, it is difficult to find specific answers to some basic questions about Jesus. The same thing might be said of the other Protestant confessional statements. Thus, we have a bit of a problem in finding current Christological doctrine that is widely accepted among the Protestant churches. With that limitation in mind, however, we can at least point toward key documents for the different mainline Protestant confessions. If we were to look

---

[11] Here "episcopal" refers to bishops who supported the hierarchy of the Church of England.

for Lutheran doctrine, we would first look at the *Augsburg Confession* written in 1530 and the small and large catechisms written by Luther. For the Presbyterians, we would look at Calvin's *Institutes of Religion* written in 1599, and the *Westminster Confession* (1646). For the Baptists, we might look at the *London Baptist Confession of Faith* (1689). And for the Methodists, we would look at the *Book of Discipline* that has been revised continually through modern times.

A final note regarding the Methodists: while I have grouped them with other mainline Protestant churches, they arose out of the Church of England and have their roots in the Anglican tradition. Consequently, they see their sources of authority as the same as the Anglicans with the addition of a fourth leg of the stool, Experience. The fact that they have a foot in both the more Catholic pool as well as in the more Protestant pool creates the same kinds of christological confusion as we found among the Anglicans. This has resulted in considerable political struggle within the denomination that is not unlike that found among the Anglicans.

## So, What Are We Going to Do?

The history of each of the Christian denominations mentioned above is all very complex and the brief discussion could be viewed with some justification as wholly inadequate. The fragmentation that has occurred among these denominations is a testament to the difficulty the whole Church has had in defining and agreeing on a coherent set of statements concerning Jesus Christ that is not so trivial as to be utterly useless. Unfortunately, we have to make a decision and pick a direction.

Somewhere around 1995, I had lunch with my Episcopal pastor, at which I presented him with a set of questions concerning the nature of Jesus Christ. That set of questions prompted a

## A Starting Point – Christian Orthodoxy

quest for the orthodox Jesus.[12] After questioning a number of clergy and seminary professors, it became clear to me that the Catholics were the only ones who were consistent. This is not necessarily to assert that they were right, but their answers were, so to speak, doctrinaire, as one might expect. Church doctrine is a much stronger influence for the Catholics than for any other denomination. In addition, the answers they gave were not trivial and appeared to point us in the direction of profound transformation. You might say that my choice of direction is a bit self-serving, but I really wanted to explore where such a radical transformational doctrine would take us. So for lack of anything clearer, I will "go Catholic" and see where it takes us. We actually have a pretty good precedent for this. C. S. Lewis, one of the most highly respected and most widely quoted Christian apologists, is said to have interpreted Catholic doctrine for Anglicans. Hold on to your hats—and let's have at it.

---

[12] The book that evolved out of those questions is entitled *The Quiz: On the Nature of the Incarnation of Jesus Christ* (Denver: St. Maximus Scriptorium, 2012).

# 2
# Christian Transformation

Now that we have addressed the sources of our understanding of who Jesus was, it is important to talk generally about the nature of transformation. What does it mean to be transformed? We certainly talk a lot about it, and most pastors and priests would endorse the concept as one of the most important aspects of our Christian journey. But could it be that, if we really grasped what was at stake, we might not be so interested? Could it be that, if we dwelled on some of the radical words of Jesus regarding transformation, we might actually run the other direction? If the idea of transformation has this ability either to attract, bore, or repel us, we might say that our Christian journey somehow hinges on our understanding of the kind of transformation Jesus calls us into. This is why defining or at least setting some boundaries around the word "transformation" is one of the pillars that will support the entire structure of our understanding of the call to be transformed *into the perfect likeness* of Jesus Christ.

## Translation vs. Transformation

Let me start by introducing a book entitled *One Taste* by Ken Wilber, a non-Christian eastern mystic. This book was written as a collection of diary entries for specific days in his life. The one of particular interest is for Tuesday, February 11, 1997, entitled *A Spirituality That Transforms.* He opens by quoting Hal Blacker, the editor of *What is Enlightenment?*

> All too often, in the translation of the mystical traditions from the East (and elsewhere) [here we will take

## Christian Transformation

this to include us Christians] into the American idiom, their profound depth is flattened out, their radical demand is diluted, and their potential for revolutionary transformation is squelched.[13]

The whole entry is extremely rich in perspective, and I am sure I will not do it justice here. But let me acknowledge a few major points Wilber makes. First, he makes a distinction between lateral or horizontal *translation* and vertical *transformation*. For Wilber, translation is the work the Church does to comfort us, to make it possible for us to cope with the exigencies of life. Particularly, it is Scripture, liturgy, community, and pastoral work that allow us to know that we are safe and cared for. Transformation, on the other hand, is the work the Church does (or does not do, as is often the case) to prod us and poke us to change so radically that we become instruments of comfort for others. This doesn't seem so strange so far, since most churches encourage us to reach out and minister to others. But Wilber goes much further.

In discussing the issue of translation, Wilber talks about the *self*. We will call it the ego. While the Church is wearing its translational hat, it helps to protect the ego, shield the ego, and even give the ego a sense of meaning in the context of a community of faith. "The self is given a new belief—perhaps holistic instead of atomistic, perhaps forgiveness instead of blame, perhaps relational instead of analytic—to diminish the terror inherent in the heart of the separate self."[14] This idea of bolstering and protecting the separate self or ego is central to his idea of translation. I just have to let him speak for himself here.

---

[13] Ken Wilber, *One Taste: Daily Reflections on Integral Spirituality*, (Boston: Shambhala, 2000), 26.
[14] Ibid., 27.

But with transformation, the very process of translation itself is challenged, witnessed, undermined, and eventually dismantled. With typical translation, the self (or subject) is given a new way to think about the world (or objects); but with radical transformation, the self itself is inquired into, looked into, grabbed by its throat, and literally throttled to death.

For authentic transformation is not a matter of belief but of the death of the believer; not a matter of translating the world but of transforming the world; not a matter of finding solace but of finding infinity[15] on the other side of death. The self is not made content; *the self is made toast.*[16]

For those of us who have gained great and wonderful solace from the Church, these are harsh words, and Wilber admits it. Although he is clearly disparaging translation as the central goal of religion and holding up transformation as the ultimate ideal, he then goes on to tell a couple of stories that make the case that translation is indeed an essential function of religion. The question he poses is whether we should stop there.

To establish this point, he makes a distinction between legitimate religion and authentic religion. We might translate this into accepted religion and true religion. The world accepts what it finds comforting, but the question is, what is really true? We must look to a higher authority than worldly consensus to find the answer. But what Wilber would say is that true or authentic religion is inherently transformative. While translational religion

---

[15] This is a bit of "theology" that we don't need to struggle with. His theology is not the point here.
[16] Ibid., 28.

creates the foundation for transformational spirituality, it must not stop there. The bottom line is that "transformative authentic spirituality is one of the most precious jewels in the entire human tradition. . . ."[17]

> [E]ven though you and I might deeply believe that the most important function we can perform is to offer authentic transformative spirituality, the fact is, much of what we have to do, in our capacity to bring decent spirituality into the world, is actually to offer more *benign and helpful modes of translation.*[18]

Having offered a masterful if confrontational explanation of the importance and nature of transformation, Wilber goes on to one of the most encouraging and insightful sections of the piece. The question he addresses concerns what one does if one finds translational spirituality insufficient, which he clearly hopes we all do at some time in our spiritual journeys.

> Thus, the authentic spiritual camps have the heart and soul of the great transformative traditions, and yet they will always do two things at once: appreciate and engage the lesser and translative practices (upon which their won successes usually depend), but also issue a thundering shout from the heart that translation alone is not enough.
> And therefore, all of those for whom authentic transformation has deeply unseated their souls must, I believe, wrestle with the profound moral obligation to shout from the heart—perhaps quietly and gently,

---

[17] Ibid., 31.
[18] Ibid.

with tears of reluctance; perhaps with fierce fire and angry wisdom; perhaps with slow and careful analysis; perhaps by unshakable public example—*authenticity* always and absolutely carries a *demand* and *duty*. You must speak out, to the best of your ability, and shake the spiritual tree, to shine your headlights into the eyes of the complacent. You must let that radical realization rumble through your being and rattle those around you.[19]

## Christian Translation

Ok, so that is Ken Wilber. While to the Christian there are many foreign and contrary thoughts in the details, his overall ideas are powerful and insightful. The question we must ask is whether his major premise is "orthodox" or not. Let's look at some important pieces of Scripture that may shed some light on whether Jesus would have agreed with Wilber. Here are a number of scriptural passages that might be considered translational:

> The LORD[20] bless you and keep you: the LORD make His face to shine upon you, and be gracious to you: the LORD lift up his countenance upon you, and give you peace.[21]     *Numbers 6:24–26*

> The LORD is my shepherd, I shall not want;

---

[19] Ibid., 35.

[20] Whenever the Hebrew Scripture refers to the unspeakable name of God, YHWH, the reader would substitute the word Adonai or Lord. In English Bibles, to represent the Hebrew word Adonai, the word LORD, in capital letters, is substituted.

[21] Note the word for peace, *shalom*, was considered by the Hebrew people to be deeply transformational, implying the kind of peace that comes from oneness with God.

> he makes me lie down in green pastures.
> He leads me beside still waters;
> > he restores my soul
> He leads me in the right paths
> > for his name's sake.
> Even though I walk through the valley of the shadow
> > of death,
> > I fear no evil;
> for thou art with me.
> > thy rod and thy staff,
> > they comfort me. *Psalm 23:1–4*

> Come to me, all who labor and are heavy laden, and
> I will give you rest. *Matthew 11:28*

These are all very comforting words, and we all would agree they form the foundation of all the bold, courageous, or confrontational parts of our ministries. So, Wilber seems to be right on the mark by integrating his translational aspects of our spiritual journey into the fabric of a more transformational movement. The question we as Christians must ask is whether he is also correct in his indictment that we, along with other religions, usually stop with translation.

## Christian Transformation

Let's now look at some passages that have a different twist.

> He who finds his life will lose it, and he who loses
> his life for my sake will find it. *Matthew 10:39*

If we equate "their life" with our current self-centered materialistic life, then to lose this life is to die to that self-centeredness.

## Into the Perfect Likeness

Jesus here is using radical language to point to a kind of transformation that goes far beyond a comforting translation. This transformation redefines the very definition of "life."

> "Truly, truly, I say to you, unless one is born anew, he cannot see the kingdom of God." *John 3:3*

Again, the language of death and rebirth is consistent with a call to a radical transformation that totally reshapes our motives, interests, and willingness.

> We were buried therefore with him by baptism into death, so that as Christ was raised from the dead by the glory of the Father, we too might walk in newness of life. *Romans 6:4*

Here Paul is relating our own spiritual death and rebirth to the physical death and resurrection of Jesus. This is important for us, because we will be asking what this transformation is supposed to look like. Here, Paul is making something explicit—look to Jesus for your model of transformation.

> [P]resent your bodies as a living sacrifice, holy and acceptable to God, which is your spiritual worship. Do not be conformed to this world but be transformed by the renewal of your mind, that you may prove what is the will of God, what is good and acceptable and perfect. *Romans 12:1–2*

Here Paul makes explicit the distinction between the life of "this world" and the life that is offered by God. He now is pointing specifically to a transformation that resides in the "renewal of your mind" and not just our actions—and he ends with the word "perfect." We will be spending considerable time on the idea of perfection and the question of whether some sort of perfection has been offered to us here in our temporal earthly lives.

> For I through the law died to the law, that I might live to God. I have been crucified with Christ; it is no longer I who live, but Christ who lives in me; and the life I now live in the flesh I live by faith in the Son of God, who loved me and gave himself for me.
> *Galatians 2:19–20*

This last passage is a perfect blend of translational and transformational language. It not only has the strong language of death and rebirth, but also the comforting words of love and sacrifice for our sake. What we can say at this point is that Scripture and the Christian tradition taken as a whole is a wondrous balance of translation and transformation. But there is no question that Jesus expects us ultimately to be transformed.

## Blow the Trumpet

Finally, I would like to consider Wilber's last point about our own personal responsibility to "shout." Look at the following passage from Ezekiel.

> The word of the LORD came to me: "Son of man, speak to your people and say to them, If I bring the sword upon a land, and the people of the land take a man from among them, and make him their watchman; and if he sees the sword coming upon the land and blows the trumpet and warns the people; then if any one who hears the sound of the trumpet does not take warning, and the sword comes and takes him away, his blood shall be upon his own head. He

heard the sound of the trumpet and did not take warning; his blood shall be upon himself. But if he had taken warning, he would have saved his life. But if the watchman sees the sword coming and does not blow the trumpet, so that the people are not warned, and the sword comes, and takes any one of them; that man is taken away in his iniquity, but his blood I will require at the watchman's hand.   *Ezekiel 33:1–6*

It is clear that our Christian tradition that flows from the Hebrew Bible is full of strong pointers to the responsibility of those who know the truth, or even think they know the truth, to speak it clearly to those who may not. Even in the story of Cain and Abel, where Cain has killed his brother, God asks Cain where his brother is. Cain's response is, "Am I my brother's keeper?" (Genesis 4:9) The implication is that if Cain, the murderer, renounces his responsibility for his brother, he probably has some.

Once we are sensitized to the issues that Wilber raises, we can probably say with some conviction that Christian transformation is not preached boldly enough today in our churches. Perhaps this is because we are too busy trying to do all the translational work that needs to be done in such a broken world. When the preacher keeps emphasizing, "God loves you," we now should see those statements as only one part of the equation. When the preacher comforts us by saying that we are going to heaven after we die, we should see that as only one part of the equation.

What Wilber, Ezekiel, and especially Jesus say unequivocally is that transformation must be preached in some form. We must at least point in the direction of transformation and try to place our translational movement in the broader context of transformation. Clearly Jesus' ultimate objective was not to make us feel better —but to utterly change us into new beings. From now on, our task is to discover just exactly what those new beings should look like. How much transformation is enough? How much transformation are we called into in order to have "life and have it abundantly" (John 10:10).

# 3
# Who is the God of whom Jesus is the Son?

My heart is always warmed when someone tells me how much like my father I am. My dad was a wonderful, generous soul who offered me a model of integrity and love. He sacrificed many of his own personal desires so that his family would have a roof over our heads, food on the table, and a family life that was nurturing. He taught me how to be a baseball catcher, and he stepped in to be my scoutmaster when the previous one resigned. I simply cannot imagine having a better father as model and friend. I assume he is listening when I express my heartfelt thanks for the life he gave me. I was truly blessed.

This intimate relationship between father and son, or Father and Son, is central to our understanding of Jesus. There are two statements that form the foundation of Christian orthodoxy regarding who Jesus was. The first is that he was the Son of God. This he and others state very clearly. The second is that Jesus was, in fact, *God*. Jesus' and others' statements about this second assertion are somewhat less clear and have, over the last two millennia, required considerable clarification. Nonetheless, we are left with the first pressing question about Jesus. "What presuppositions were inherent in the Jewish understanding of this God? Who is this God of whom Jesus is the son? In the name of which God did Jesus claim to speak? Who raised Jesus from the dead?"[22]

---

[22] David Yeago, *The Faith of the Christian Church* (pre-publication manuscript) Chapter 3, 51.

## Who is the God of whom Jesus is the Son?

Thus far, we have tried to establish the definition of what we will call the "truth." Our first question was: What are the *orthodox* answers to the questions concerning the nature of Jesus and his call to us? Second, we have spent some effort to get a clear picture of just what we mean by the concept of *transformation*. As a continuation of this foundation-building effort, we now turn to our first purely theological question. If we are to understand the meaning of Jesus' call for a radical transformation, we need to know who Jesus was. If we start from the premise that Jesus was the Son of God, we are first compelled to look carefully at the question of who is this "God" of whom Jesus is the Son? What is interesting here is the fact that our understanding of Jesus depends on our understanding of God and our understanding of God depends on our understanding of Jesus. This circularity seems to present a dilemma.

The dilemma arises out of the Christian belief that in Jesus Christ we see an *incarnation* or enfleshment of God. As the Son of God, Jesus is ultimately seen in the Christian understanding, not simply as a representative of God but as "one being"[23] with God. Therefore, we first need to understand who the God of Abraham, Isaac, and Jacob is as depicted in Hebrew Scripture.

In other words, the interconnectedness of Hebrew Scripture and the Christian New Testament is essential to appreciate. This remarkable tradition of Israel, the nature of their God, and the New Testament understanding of a messiah, who is "sent" by that God, sets the stage for the radical transformation that Jesus offers. This transformation would have made no sense without this context. What is important to stress at this point is that we

---

[23] The Catholic term in the Nicene Creed is "consubstantial" or "of one substance." A full discussion of the complexity of this Trinitarian doctrine is far beyond the scope of this work.

are going to point toward some subtleties that make all the difference. With this rather daunting challenge on the table, let us start with some basics concerning the God of Israel.

Let me also acknowledge that much of this chapter is based on an insightful manuscript entitled *The Faith of the Christian Church* by David Yeago, written when he was a theology professor at the Lutheran Theological Southern Seminary in Columbia, South Carolina. Consequently, we are taking a decidedly Christian view of Hebrew Scripture.

## The Connection to Israel – God of the Story

What is the most interesting thing about the search for the nature of Israel's God is that we learn what we know not from some dogmatic dissertation, but from a series of stories.

> Then Moses said to God, "If I come to the Israelites and say to them, 'The God of your ancestors has sent me to you,' and they ask me, 'What is his name?' what shall I say to them?" God said to Moses, "I AM WHO I AM." And he said, "Say this to the people of Israel, 'I AM has sent me to you.'" God also said to Moses, "Say this to the people of Israel, 'The LORD, the God of your ancestors, the God of Abraham, the God of Isaac, and the God of Jacob, has sent me to you': this is my name forever, and thus I am to be remembered throughout all generations."
> *Exodus 3:13–15*

This riddle clearly places this God in a different realm than the Greek and Roman gods. There is a sense that we must watch

Who is the God of whom Jesus is the Son?

what this God does in order to learn who he is.[24] This is further reinforced by such often-repeated statements like:

> "I am the LORD your God, who brought you out of the land of Egypt, out of the house of bondage."
> *Exodus 20:2*

So, to understand who this God is, we are tied to the stories of the Hebrew Scripture. As much as many Christian churches might like to call themselves "New Testament" churches, orthodox Christianity finds its foundation in and on the Hebrew Scripture.

## The Narrative Priority

One of the powerful things that Yeago does for us here is switch around how we use language—words—to describe God. He puts forward the idea of *narrative priority*. He is saying that the meaning of the metaphors, the images used to describe God such as *king* or *rock*, must be interpreted in a new way. We must be willing for God to give us the new meaning. God is not simply the most powerful king or the most solid rock, but God himself must interpret the idea of *kingship* and "rock-hood," when talking about God. God not only has reinterpreted this meaning within the context of the historical Hebrew Scripture but reinterprets them afresh for us within the context of our respective spiritual journeys.

The same thing is true concerning the descriptors such as *loving*, *compassionate*, *steadfast*, etc. These words do not define the character of God as much as God defines the character of

---

[24] In fact, the term YHWH is based on the Hebrew verb "to be." In other words, the essence of God is *being*. The action of God flows out of his very being.

these words. Now you might say that this puts us in an intractable dilemma, and there is no doubt that it forms a kind of paradox. But it also preserves the mystery of God. And this mystery is absolutely crucial to what will follow.

## The Mystery of God

If we say that God is not just the biggest, strongest, meanest kahuna on the block, then who or what is God? This is where it is so helpful to turn to the Church Fathers. They help us immensely to clarify that God is "creator of heaven and earth, and of all that is, seen and unseen."[25]

God is not of this world, but is totally "other" than this world. God is not a *being* in the sense that we are beings. Many of us, when asked who God is, would say that God is a *supreme being*. We could be a bit more correct by saying, as Paul Tillich did, that God is not a being at all but the "ground of all being."[26] But this doesn't even capture the total "otherness" of God, because "ground" implies some kind of continuity with our being. It would be like saying that the carpenter is the "ground" of the table he has made. Not exactly. He is the *creator*, totally other than the table. "God is not in a class [with other entities]. God is God, and no one else is like him."[27]

In other words, God is total mystery. But from this position of total otherness, God chooses to enter our world, to make himself known, and to influence our lives. God chooses not only to act, but also to act locally, to be manifest in a burning bush, to wrestle with Jacob, and to speak with Moses. This free choice of a wholly other God is the pattern for our own free choice. What is even more important, many of God's characteristics that we

---

[25] Nicene Creed.
[26] Charles W. Kegley, ed. *The Theology of Paul Tillich* (New York: Pilgrim Press, 1982), 194.
[27] David Yeago, 54.

see in the stories that reveal his nature are the same characteristics we see in Jesus. This relationship between the characteristics of God and those of Jesus will be the most essential part of the case we are making here for our own transformation. So let's spend some time here considering several of these characteristics.

## The Character of God

Before we dive into this, we need to begin with the realization of what we are dealing with here—*mystery*. Let us take off our shoes when we tread here, as the Hebrews did when they entered a holy place. Let us leave behind our western, scientific, analytical mentality that seeks to control through *comprehension* and allow our hearts to descend somewhat to a deeper level of *apprehension* of the mystery that we call God. I will try to do this by using a different style here. This will be more like a meditation than an exposition in order to stress the question rather than the answer.

### God as Wholly Other Creator

I don't know. I cannot know, yet I need to know who you are. I desire to know, I yearn to know, I need to know more than anything else in my life. As I am on my knees, Lord, speak to me through your word. Let your light shine upon me. Let your countenance fall upon me and be gracious to me, Lord, my beginning and end, my life and my light.

> Thus says the LORD:
> "The wealth of Egypt and the merchandise of Ethiopia,
> and the Sabe'ans, men of stature,
> shall come over to you and be yours,
> they shall follow you;

> they shall come over in chains and bow down to
> > you.
> They will make supplication to you, saying:
> > 'God is with you only, and there is no other,
> > no god besides him.'"
> Truly, thou art a God who hidest thyself,
> > O God of Israel, the Savior.
> All of them are put to shame and confounded,
> > the makers of idols go in confusion together.
> But Israel is saved by the LORD
> > with everlasting salvation;
> > you shall not be put to shame or confounded
> > to all eternity.
>
> For thus says the LORD,
> > who created the heavens
> > (he is God!),
> > who formed the earth and made it
> > (he established it;
> > he did not create it a chaos,
> > he formed it to be inhabited!):
> "I am the LORD, and there is no other.
> I did not speak in secret,
> > in a land of darkness;
> I did not say to the offspring of Jacob,
> > 'Seek me in chaos.'
> I the Lord speak the truth,
> > I declare what is right.
>
> "Assemble yourselves and come,
> > draw near together,
> > you survivors of the nations!
> They have no knowledge

Who is the God of whom Jesus is the Son?

> who carry about their wooden idols,
>   and keep on praying to a god
>   that cannot save.
> Declare and present your case;
>   let them take counsel together!
> Who told this long ago?
> Who declared it of old?
> Was it not I, the LORD?
> And there is no other god besides me,
>   a righteous God and a Savior;
>   there is none besides me.
>
> "Turn to me and be saved,
>   all the ends of the earth!
> For I am God, and there is no other.
> By myself I have sworn,
>   from my mouth has gone forth in righteousness
>   a word that shall not return:
> 'To me every knee shall bow,
>   every tongue shall swear.'
>
> "Only in the LORD, it shall be said of me,
>   are righteousness and strength;
>   to him shall come and be ashamed,
>   all who were incensed against him.
> In the LORD all the offspring of Israel
>   shall triumph and glory."   *Isaiah 45:14–25*

Though you are the God who conceals himself, you are also the God who chooses to be experienced and heard. Though you are the creator of this world, you are not of this world. You are wholly other, total mystery, incomprehensible, invisible. You have created even the things that I cannot see, the things I cannot

## Into the Perfect Likeness

comprehend. You are the wholly other God. You are not of this world, but you are the creator of this world.

### God as Eternal
You are not of our own time and space. You are beyond time and space. You do not last "forever." Your lasting has nothing whatsoever to do with "lasting" in time. You are not constrained by time. You are not temporal. Neither are you constrained by space. Dimensionality simply does not apply to you.

### God as Perfectly Free
While you are wholly other, total mystery, and not in any way constrained by that which you have created, you, in your complete freedom, chose to make yourself accessible to our history in time and space. You reveal yourself to us in the stories you share with us. But why? Wouldn't it have been simpler and easier to leave us alone? We are a stubborn bunch, hardheaded, and hard hearted. You are also perfectly free not to. So why?

And you made us free like you. Why? Wouldn't it have been easier on all of us, if we had been created to be good —without the possibility of being bad? Wouldn't it have been easier for you to make us just—without the possibility of being unjust? Why did you curse us with this horrible freedom, this same freedom you have? Why did you bless us with this wondrous freedom, this same freedom you have? Is it that you desire that we be in some way like you?

### God as Perfect Love
Did you, in your perfect love, choose to participate in our lives that we might be saved? But saved from what? From ourselves? From our own freedom? Is it about love? I don't understand this love. I have felt love from Mom and Dad. That deep, abiding,

Who is the God of whom Jesus is the Son?

steadfast, unconditional love that only parents have for their children. I have felt this. Is that it?

Or is it even deeper than that? Is it something more fundamental; something you build into the very fabric of our lives—something that is in the very fabric of *your* life? The only thing I can think of is the love I have for my hand or my foot. I don't think about it. I don't stroke my hand or my foot as if I needed to express this love I have for a part of me. It just is. It is intrinsic to who I am. It *is* the "I." Is that sort of it? You love me as if I were a part of you, and extension of you. But I cannot be. You are the wholly other God, the total mystery. How can I be an extension of you? Or is that your deepest desire—for me to be an extension of your love in the world?

**God as All-powerful**
Your omnipotence is not anything that I can imagine. It is not just bigger and stronger than the biggest and strongest thing I can imagine. My thoughts about your omnipotence must somehow take me out of myself, must draw me beyond this world. When I feel a lack of power in my own life, I turn to your strength. What I must know is that any understanding I have of your power must place me in an open and receptive posture, one that opens me up to possibilities that are far greater than I would be able to contemplate based on my own strength or even an extension of my own strength. If I wilt in the presence of your power, I wilt into your "arms." I submit to your rule. I surrender to overwhelming odds. Is that the point? Is that your steadfast desire that I be completely supple in the face of your unimaginable power?

**God as All-knowing**
You have given us free will that emulates your own free will, and we believe you are omniscient, or all-knowing throughout

all time. How can this be?[28] How can you have perfect knowledge of what I will do, and I have free will to change my mind, to turn toward your will or turn away from it? Is my future *predestined* or could it be that what you really want is for me to fall again into your arms in faith. How can you have perfect foreknowledge and I have perfect free will? Is this one of the great paradoxes of the faith? How can this be? Is it possible that the only proper response to this dilemma is for me to say, "I don't know" and get back on my knees?

**God as Ever-present**
If you are omnipresent, everywhere at the same time, or if there is no place where you are not, then I cannot hide from you nor can I be separated from your instantaneous availability to me. But I often would like to hide. I wish you didn't see me at my worst and yet, to know that you are closer to me than myself, is possibly the deepest of comforts. Should I be willing to trade the discomfort of my nakedness for the profound comfort of your loving presence? Help me to feel that deep comfort of your presence.

**God as All-demanding**
You are the God who told Abraham to sacrifice his own precious son, Isaac. Are you hard-hearted? Is it just my own self-centeredness to insist that "my God" would not do something that cruel? Are you just a big meany or is there something much deeper going on here? Are you saying to me that you want all of me and that you will settle for no less? Is that the only way for

---

[28] The omniscience of God is a bit of a struggle for some. Biblical references are not unequivocal on the subject. Some see this as very much a Greek concept that did not arise out of Hebrew Scripture as a necessity. For many modern theologians, however, this characteristic of God is taken as a given.

## Who is the God of whom Jesus is the Son?

me to participate fully in your life—to have the best that "life" offers me? Is your greatest desire for me to be perfectly one with your will, and that your will for me is precisely what you created me to be? Is it that I can only find true joy when I surrender completely to who I really am?

**God as Awe-inspiring**
How awesome are you? I recall standing at the foot of one of the World Trade Center towers and looking up, sighting along the side of the building as it soared upwards. It was dizzying. My small mind could not put that immensity into any kind of rational perspective. It was awesome. Is that it? Is it like a parent's feeling at the first sight of their first child? When my heart soared the first time I saw Lake Ontario from the Scarborough Bluffs, is it like that? When my breath was taken from me briefly upon my first glimpse of the Dolomites in Northern Italy, is it like that? When, from time to time, I am overwhelmed by something wondrous that I have difficulty putting into perspective, is that a small hint of your awesome nature. Are you like that, only much more? How can I apprehend[29] your awesome nature?

**God as All-holy**
You have given us the amazing ability to experience things that take us outside of our normal operating mode—transcendent things that lift us up, let us soar. These experiences are impossible for me to describe in words. Is holiness like that? Is that a little hint of your own holiness?

What is this holiness that takes me to a different and wondrous experiential place? What is this capacity you have given me to apprehend this "je ne sais quoi?"[30] Whatever it is, you are

---
[29] Recall, the word means to appropriate without comprehending with our intellect.
[30] French for "I don't know what."

the source of it all. Only the mystics are thought to have sensed your all-holiness.

I remember a wonderful story about the last lecture of a very special Old Testament Professor at Union Theological Seminary in New York City named Dr. James Muhlenberg. It is said that he was so highly revered by both Union and Jewish Theological Seminary students that, at his last lecture upon his retirement, they left their shoes out in the hall, as was the Jewish custom when walking on holy ground.

But can I start on that path by thinking about those most special times when I have experienced something so profoundly precious that I was brought to tears, when I was touched in a way that stilled my heart and quieted my spirit? Does this happen when the apparently disparate pieces of some puzzle all of a sudden come together to make an integrated whole that reflects profound truth. Is it when wholeness and beauty and love and truth come together to dazzle the spirit? Are you like that? Do you desire for me to exhibit that same kind of wholeness that has the capacity to dazzle the spirit?

**God as the One Who Chooses Me**
Is it possible that you choose me to participate fully in your life? Yes? What! Are you calling me? Is that your sweet tender voice I hear—beckoning me to come into your embrace? Is that your firm compelling voice sending me out to love as you love, to care as you care, to share in your compassion. How can this be? How can you, the great mystery of life, be calling me? How can you, the omnipotent one, the omniscient one, the omnipresent one be choosing me to be part of your plan? Where do I look for answers? Have you pointed toward the answers to be found in your Son?

Who is the God of whom Jesus is the Son?

## A Promise Unfulfilled

God's answer to these questions may be just one more way of understanding what it means to be transformed ***into the perfect likeness of Jesus Christ***. We need to look at Jesus not only from the perspective of the God of Israel of whom he is the Son, but also from the perspective of the one Israel is yearning for, the messiah. Within the stories of Israel's God, there is another important theme. The stories are not yet complete. They speak of things yet to be completed that will bring all these stories to some kind of fulfillment.

> "and in you all the families of the earth *shall be* blessed." *Genesis 12:3*

> "… for the earth *will be* full of the knowledge of the LORD as the waters cover the sea." *Isaiah 11:9*

As Yeago says so beautifully, "And so the Old Testament gestures toward a future whose outline it cannot fill out from its own resources. This is precisely the New Testament concept of the Messiah. The Messiah is the 'one who was to come,' the one who would fulfill the empty space which the Old Testament postulates, gestures towards, but cannot itself fill out."[31]

---

[31] David Yeago, 49.

# 4
# Jesus as the Messiah of Israel

It is impossible to understand the nature of the God of Israel without some understanding of his call to his people to righteousness. Jewish orthodoxy is based on the centrality of the Torah that included the Ten Commandments and other commandments (613 commandments of which made up what is called the Mitzvot) that comprise the entirety of the Law of Moses.[32] This call to right relationship or at-one-ment with the commandments of God drove Israel's understanding of its goal—its reason for existence.

When Israel had strayed from this path of righteousness, the consequences were dire (and with Jews, all consequences were seen to be the will of their God). As a result, they needed to see a way back. It was this drive to return to a state of righteousness that created pointers toward one who would lead such a return. This most generalized picture is the backdrop for our understanding of the Jewish context out of which Jesus' own role arose.

In other words, we cannot understand the Incarnation of Jesus Christ apart from its Jewish context—into which he was born and by which he was taught—and we cannot understand this context apart from to general drive toward righteousness in the law that was the cornerstone of the Jewish faith.

We Christians tend to take for granted the whole idea that Jesus was the Messiah—the one who was to come and save in the

---

[32] As usual, it is a bit more complex than this, but you get the idea.

name of God—the *anointed one*—anointed by God to be the savior of the world. He was *christos* in Greek—*mashiach* in Hebrew, uniquely sent by God the Father as his one and only begotten Son; the one who was pointed toward throughout the Hebrew Bible who fulfills the deepest yearning of the Jewish people.

Well, not so fast. It turns out that the concept of messiah in Hebrew Scriptures and in extra-scriptural writings, such as early rabbinic literature and the Dead Sea Scrolls, is highly complex, many layered, and not without considerable controversy. An important starting place is the idea of one who is *anointed*. In the Hebrew tradition both the king and the priest were literally anointed for their duties. So, being *mashiach* simply meant that one was anointed for a special role of public service to the Jewish community.

In addition, those who were proclaimed to be prophets were often considered to have been anointed by God. Consequently, the anointing had nothing really to do with some sort of anticipated activity in the future. The *maschiach* was not one who was anticipated, expected, or hoped for but one who was already there and fulfilling a role. It is only when we get to the period of the Babylonian Exile when there was neither king nor temple that the concept of messiah starts to take on future connotations.

The challenge is to understand that the messianic tradition from a Hebrew perspective is not monolithic. The diversity of Judaic sects and their equally diverse messianic concepts that arose in the various periods of Hebrew history are well captured in the book by Jacob Neusner, et. al., *Judaisms and Their Messiahs at the Turn of the Christian Era*[33] and the book by John J. Collins, *The Scepter and the Star: Messianism in Light of the*

---

[33] Cambridge: Cambridge University Press, 1987.

*Dead Sea Scrolls*[34]. The question we need to be asking is this: How does Hebrew Scripture inform our understanding of the Jewish carpenter, Jesus of Nazareth, whom Christians believe is the one unique and final messiah? This is a daunting task, but I will at least try to capture the variety of issues that arise. Most of what follows is taken from the work by John Collins. In fact, much of the richness of this tapestry comes from an intense study of the Dead Sea Scrolls and how thy have informed our understanding of early Judaic messianism.[35]

The challenge is to determine if there was to be one messiah with many roles or several messiahs each with one or more roles. The answer to this question is not at all clear from Hebrew Scripture. What we seem to have at minimum is a series of roles, ideals, and hopes for the future, all of which point toward a messianic fulfillment without drawing all the strains together into a consistent vision.

The Incarnation of Jesus Christ as the messiah of the Jewish people is profoundly informed by the various pictures of messianism that are found in Hebrew Scripture reflected in the Christian Old Testament. At the same time, these pictures themselves are clarified, focused, and fulfilled in the Incarnation of Jesus Christ as depicted in the New Testament. In other words, we are confronted with another kind of circularity. Jewish background, as represented in the Hebrew tradition informs our understanding of messiah as reflected in the Incarnation of Jesus Christ and the New Testament understanding of the Incarnation of Jesus Christ informs our understanding of what it means to be messiah. To set the stage, let's start with the Hebrew Scripture.

---

[34] Grand Rapids: Eerdmans, 2010, Second Edition.
[35] While the Dead Sea Scrolls are of considerable importance in this debate, we will be dealing here only with those writings that are found in the Christian Old Testament.

# Jesus as the Messiah of Israel

One of the most compelling pieces of Hebrew Scripture concerns the prophecy of Isaiah:

> The people who walked in darkness
> > have seen a great light;
> those who dwelt in a land of deep darkness,
> > on them has light shined.
> Thou hast multiplied the nation,
> > thou hast increased its joy;
> they rejoice before thee
> > as with joy at the harvest,
> as men rejoice when they divide the spoil.
> For the yoke of his burden,
> > and the staff for his shoulder,
> > the rod of his oppressor,
> > thou hast broken as on the day of Mid'ian.
> For every boot of the tramping warrior in battle tumult
> > and every garment rolled in blood
> > will be burned as fuel for the fire.
> For to us a child is born,
> > to us a son is given;
> and the government will be upon his shoulder,
> > and his name will be called
> "Wonderful Counselor, Mighty God,
> > Everlasting Father, Prince of Peace."
> Of the increase of his government and of peace
> > there will be no end,
> upon the throne of David, and over his kingdom,
> > to establish it, and to uphold it
> with justice and with righteousness
> > from this time forth and for evermore.

The zeal of the Lord of hosts will do this.
*Isaiah 9:2–7*

Hear we see a yearning for deliverance from darkness. This yearning is met by one who is seen to be "Wonderful Counselor, Mighty God, Everlasting Father, Prince of Peace." Let us have a look at these roles and how they are expressed in the Hebrew tradition.

## Prince

A prince is one who is royally born to fulfil a role—one who is in line to be King. A prince is endowed with power that emanates solely from his lineage and, consequently, represents the very essence of the royal line.

> Know therefore and understand that from the going forth of the word to restore and build Jerusalem to the coming of an *anointed one*, a *prince* . . . *Daniel 9:25*

A prince is a refinement of a set of royal characteristics, one who is set aside by birth for certain responsibilities and prerogatives. The juxtaposition of "anointed one" and "prince" implies that the prince is anointed by God for his role. Rulers of Israel assumed this intimate relationship with their God. To see Jesus as prince is to see him as one who reflects the responsibility and authority of one of the royal line of King David. Thus, it was seen by many that the one who was sent by God to save the people was, in some way, a prince.

## King

One of the most evident roles of the messiah in Hebrew tradition was that of ideal king. It was believed that the Davidic line had been instituted by God. As such, those kings of that line were seen to be anointed for their purpose. Two themes point clearly to the importance of the restoration of this line.

## The Fallen Booth of David

The Prophet Amos speaks clearly about the centrality of the Davidic line and the importance of its restoration. His writings are positioned long after the reign of King David but before the Babylonian Exile that was such a cultural and religious disaster for the Jewish People. His major concern was the movement of the people of God away from a state of obedience to the law.

> "In that day I will raise up
> > the booth of David that is fallen
> and repair its breaches,
> > and raise up its ruins,
> > and rebuild it as in the days of old;
> that they may possess the remnant of Edom
> > and all the nations who are called by my name,"
> > says the LORD who does this.
>
> I will restore the fortunes of my people Israel,
> > and they shall rebuild the ruined cities and inhabit them;
> they shall plant vineyards and drink their wine,
> > and they shall make gardens and eat their fruit.
> I will plant them upon their land,
> > and they shall never again be plucked up
> > out of the land which I have given them,"
> > says the LORD your God.
> > *Amos 9:11–12, 14–15*

## Into the Perfect Likeness

Here we see Amos admonishing the people of Israel to return to right relationship with God through the return to the Davidic royal line.

### A Shoot from the Stump of Jesse

The prophet Isaiah wrote a bit later than Amos but was dealing with the same issues: the movement of the people of God away from obedience to the law. Consider the following:

> There shall come forth a shoot from the stump of
>     Jesse,
>     and a branch shall grow out of his roots.
> And the Spirit of the LORD shall rest upon him,
>         the spirit of wisdom and understanding,
>         the spirit of counsel and might,
>         the spirit of knowledge and the fear of the
>         LORD.
> And his delight shall be in the fear of the LORD.
>
> He shall not judge by what his eyes see,
>         or decide by what his ears hear;
> but with righteousness he shall judge the poor,
>         and decide with equity for the meek of the
>         earth;
> and he shall smite the earth with the rod of his
>         mouth,
>         and with the breath of his lips he shall slay
>         the wicked.
> Righteousness shall be the girdle of his waist,
>         and faithfulness the girdle of his loins.

> The wolf shall dwell with the lamb,
>> and the leopard shall lie down with the kid,
> and the calf and the lion and the fatling together,
>> and a little child shall lead them.
> The cow and the bear shall feed;
>> their young shall lie down together;
> and the lion shall eat straw like the ox.
> The sucking child shall play over the hole of the
>> asp,
>> and the weaned child shall put his hand on
>> the adder's den.
> They shall not hurt or destroy
>> in all my holy mountain;
> for the earth shall be full of the knowledge of the
>> LORD
>> as the waters cover the sea.   *Isaiah 11:1–9*

Here Isaiah is calling the people back to right relationship to God by reinstituting a kingship that is from the "stump" of Jesse, who was the father of King David. Getting back to the source of right relationship through the royal line is one important messianic theme in the Hebrew Scripture.

## Warrior

One of the most compelling and yet confusing themes in the Hebrew Scripture is centered on the desire of the people of Israel to be delivered from their oppressors. Three episodes that loom large in the history of the Jewish people were the Exodus from

Egypt,[36] The Babylonian Exile, and the Roman rule that was extant during the life of Christ. In each case, there was a yearning for deliverance from the oppressive rule of those outside the Jewish faith.[37] This yearning often expressed itself as the desire for a person who would lead the people in military battle. Consequently, many Jews saw the messiah as some sort of warrior king. Bar Kochba in the Jewish revolt against the Romans in A.D. 132 is often cited as a failed example of such a warrior messiah whose goal was to free the Jews from bondage in the same way that Moses freed the Israelites from Egyptian bondage.

## Teacher

Throughout the history of the Jewish people, certain members of the community arose who had the ability to understand the will of God and to communicate that to God's people. Moses certainly was one of those. Once the tribe of Levi was established as the priestly caste, they took on the role, not only of mediator between the Jewish people and God but also of teacher.

> For they observed thy word,
>     and kept thy covenant.
> They shall teach Jacob thy ordinances,
>     and Israel thy law... *Deuteronomy 33:9–10*

The implication is that the elucidation of that Scripture, once codified, needed to be accomplished by those who had some

---

[36] The debate concerning the historicity of this event is complex. It is clear, however, that Jewish tradition assumes this event took place somewhere between the sixteenth and thirteenth centuries BC.

[37] In fact, it is even more complicated than this, since there were kings within the Jewish faith who were seen as problematic. The solution always seemed to be a return to the line of David.

level of knowledge above that of the average Jew. While the word *rabbi* refers to a master or teacher of the Torah, it is not found in the Hebrew Scripture. Clearly, the use of the word concerning Jesus indicated that, by the first century, the importance of a teacher of the law was established. The idea that a new kind of teacher would be needed to guide Israel's return to God is more obscure.

> Yea, O people in Zion who dwell at Jerusalem; you shall weep no more. He will surely be gracious to you at the sound of your cry; when he hears it, he will answer you. And though the Lord give you the bread of adversity and the water of affliction, yet your Teacher will not hide himself any more, but your eyes shall see your Teacher. And your ears shall hear a word behind you, saying, "This is the way, walk in it," when you turn to the right or when you turn to the left. [38]  *Isaiah 30:20*

Here we see a glimmer of an important aspect of one who was to restore Israel to its former state of obedience: he must be a teacher of the law. In more stark terms we see the elevation of the concept of teacher to that of one who has the power to restore.

## Shepherd

Since the time of King David, the image of a shepherd leading the people of Israel has been a powerful one. The shepherd was the one who tended, guarded, and guided the flock. Their entire

---

[38] The capitalization of the word "Teacher" is an aspect of the translation and not a reflection of the original Hebrew text. It seems to point toward the special role of the teacher as a source of hope. See https://www.christianforums.com/threads/isaiah-verse.7857134/.

wellbeing was dependent on the shepherd, so much so that if the shepherd were harmed or destroyed, the flock was in grave danger.

> The LORD is my *shepherd*, I shall not want; He makes me lie down in green pastures.
> He leads me beside still waters; he restores my soul.
> He leads me in paths of righteousness for his names's sake. *Psalm 23:1*

> O save thy people, and bless thy heritage;
> be thou their *shepherd*, and carry them for ever.
> *Psalm 28:9*

> He will feed his flock like a *shepherd*,
> he will gather the lambs in his arms,
> he will carry them in his bosom,
> and gently lead those that are with young.
> *Isaiah 40:11*

While these passages are calling on God, they also form the foundation for the understanding of one who would come as God's representative to accomplish these things within the Jewish community. The one who would lead the people to return to righteousness resulting in the favor of God would be seen as their shepherd.

## Priest

Hebrew Scripture developed the concept of a joint responsibility for ruling the Jewish nation: that of King and Priest. After the people of Israel demanded of God that he allow them to have a king like other nations, that kingship, particularly of David, always was seen in juxtaposition to the priesthood that was established in Mosaic times in the tribe of Levi within the line of Aaron.

> "Then bring near to you Aaron your brother, and his sons with him, from among the people of Israel, to serve me as priests—Aaron and Aaron's sons, Nadab and Abi'hu, Elea'zar and Ith'amar. And you shall make holy garments for Aaron your brother, for glory and for beauty. And you shall speak to all who have ability, whom I have endowed with an able mind, that they make Aaron's garments to consecrate him for my priesthood. *Exodus 28:1–3*

Here we see the establishment of the priesthood early in the life of the Jewish people. The priest was the one tasked with being a mediator between the people and God. The priest was the only one who could handle the Arc of the Covenant, enter the Holy of Holies in the Temple in Jerusalem, and offer sacrifices for the atonement of the Hebrew people. This special role in the life of the people of God placed the priest in the forefront of those who had the kind of relationship to God that could help the people return to a state of right relationship. As such, the priest could be seen as one model for the messiah.

> And Melchiz'edek *king* of Salem brought out bread and wine; he was *priest of God Most High*. And he blessed him and said,
> "Blessed be Abram by God Most High,
>   maker of heaven and earth;
> and blessed be God Most High,
>   who has delivered your enemies into your hand!"
> *Genesis 14:18–20*

Here we see the juxtaposition of both king and priest. This model is a powerful driver for the understanding of some of the Jewish people of the one who would deliver the people from sin and oppression.

## Prophet

While we often think of a prophet as a fortune teller, a more useful understanding is one of truth teller. Hebrew Scripture is multi-layered with translations and editing taking place at different times and under different circumstances. Sometimes writings that appear to foretell something might have been written after the fact. That makes understanding the meaning of the passage difficult. What we can assert, however, is that the role of the prophet was to be an unbiased (or at least biased in favor of God) witness to the truth.

Nathan in interacting with King David over his sinful behavior regarding Bathsheba is a perfect example of a prophet of God simply speaking the truth of God. In this sense, the prophets of Israel were the first to recognize when she had strayed from the path of righteousness and the first ones to declare the consequences. Once the Jewish community realized that it needed to return to a right relationship with God, it is not too much of a stretch to yearn for a prophet who could guide that return. References to such a messianic prophet can be found in some extra-scriptural sources.[39]

## Suffering Servant

Although this was not a common theme among Jews who looked to the future for a messiah, the quotation below from Isaiah

---

[39] M. Zetterholm, ed., *The Messiah in Early Judaism and Christianity* (Minneapolis: Fortress Press), p. 12.

## Jesus as the Messiah of Israel

clearly conditioned at some level the nature of any who claimed
to bring the Jews out of bondage.

> Who has believed what we have heard?
> > And to whom has the arm of the Lord been
> > revealed?
> For he grew up before him like a young plant,
> > and like a root out of dry ground;
> he had no form or comeliness that we should look at
> > him,
> > and no beauty that we should desire him.
> He was despised and rejected by men;
> > a man of sorrows, and acquainted with grief;
> and as one from whom men hide their faces
> > he was despised, and we esteemed him not.
>
> Surely he has borne our griefs
> > and carried our sorrows;
> yet we esteemed him stricken,
> > smitten by God, and afflicted.
> But he was wounded for our transgressions,
> > he was bruised for our iniquities;
> upon him was the chastisement that made us whole,
> > and with his stripes we are healed.
> All we like sheep have gone astray;
> > we have turned every one to his own way;
> and the Lord has laid on him
> > the iniquity of us all.
>
> He was oppressed, and he was afflicted,
> > yet he opened not his mouth;
> like a lamb that is led to the slaughter,
> > and like a sheep that before its shearers is

## Into the Perfect Likeness

    dumb,
  so he opened not his mouth.
By oppression and judgment he was taken away;
  and as for his generation, who considered
that he was cut off out of the land of the living,
  stricken for the transgression of my people?
And they made his grave with the wicked
  and with a rich man in his death,
although he had done no violence,
  and there was no deceit in his mouth.

Yet it was the will of the LORD to bruise him;
  he has put him to grief;
when he makes himself an offering for sin,
  he shall see his offspring, he shall prolong
  his days;
the will of the LORD shall prosper in his hand;
  he shall see the fruit of the travail of his soul
  and be satisfied;
by his knowledge shall the righteous one, my
  servant,
  make many to be accounted righteous;
  and he shall bear their iniquities.
Therefore I will divide him a portion with the great,
  and he shall divide the spoil with the strong;
because he poured out his soul to death,
  and was numbered with the transgressors;

yet he bore the sin of many,
  and made intercession for the transgressors.
          *Isaiah 53*

## Jesus as the Messiah of Israel

What is so amazing about these words is the fact that they turn the whole idea of messiah on its head. If we take the servant of God to be the one who could restore the people of God to right relationship and, if we take Isaiah's description seriously, then the one who restores is not simply a king or a high priest but one quite different. It is precisely these words that so clearly influenced the early Christian Church's understanding of the Christ event.

## Bearer of Good Tidings

For a people who struggled with sin and oppression throughout their history, it is no surprise that they saw the one who could return them to a state of right relationship with their God as a bearer of good tidings—a bringer of Good News.

> How beautiful upon the mountains
>   are the feet of him who brings good tidings,
> who publishes peace, who brings good tidings of
>   good,
>   who publishes salvation,
>   who says to Zion, "Your God reigns."
> Hark, your watchmen lift up their voice,
>   together they sing for joy;
> for eye to eye they see
>   the return of the LORD to Zion.
> Break forth together into singing,
>   you waste places of Jerusalem;
> for the LORD has comforted his people,
>   he has redeemed Jerusalem.
> The LORD has bared his holy arm
>   before the eyes of all the nations;
> and all the ends of the earth shall see
> the salvation of our God.         *Isaiah 52:7–10*

Into the Perfect Likeness

## Son of God

In the Hebrew tradition many who were seen as God-fearing and righteous were called sons of God. This descriptor was intended to establish an intimate relationship between the person and the will of God. The following quotation from Isaiah points toward the possibility of this kind of intimate relationship between one born of woman and God.

> Therefore the LORD himself will give you a sign. Behold, a young woman shall conceive and bear a son, and shall call his name Imman'u-el.[God is with us] He shall eat curds and honey when he knows how to refuse the evil and choose the good. *Isaiah 7:14–15*

More explicitly the quotation from 2 Samuel establishes this kind of relationship between the offspring of David and their God.

> When your days are fulfilled and you lie down with your fathers, I will raise up your offspring after you, who shall come forth from your body, and I will establish his kingdom. He shall build a house for my name, and I will establish the throne of his kingdom for ever. I will be his father, and *he shall be my son.* When he commits iniquity, I will chasten him with the rod of men, with the stripes of the sons of men; but I will not take my steadfast love from him, as I took it from Saul, whom I put away from before you. And your house and your kingdom shall be made sure for ever before me; your throne shall be established for ever.'" *2 Samuel 7:12–16*

# Jesus as the Messiah of Israel

A son of God is one who acts in accord with the will of God. As such, a son of God has the ability to return the people of God to a state of righteousness. The possibility of being a son of God, therefore, becomes one more important piece of background for the New Testament understanding of the messiah.

## Jesus as a Lens

Each of these themes of an anointed one operated to varying degrees and at varying times in different sects within the Jewish community. Many sects exhibited little emphasis on a messiah. Others saw him as a teacher or prophet or king. Many saw the messiah as one who would conquer the oppressing nations, whether they be the Persians or Assyrians or Romans. These themes have great capacity to clarify, either individually or in some combination. Their ultimate power, however, comes from a synthesis that cannot be provided from within the Hebrew Scripture itself. There is a need for some kind of lens through which to view these themes to give them concrete meaning.

A lens has three kinds of functionality. It can clarify for those who do not see very well, it can magnify for those who are far away; and it can focus light in such a way as to turn defuse light into a strong hot focal point. In some sense Jesus functions in this way for Christians. He focuses the diverse beams of the various messianic themes and manifests them in one person; he clarifies by showing how all the themes inform one another; and he magnifies by elevating all of those themes into a picture not just of a person with exceptional qualities but of one who is indeed God incarnate.

Seen through the lens of Jesus Christ, all the themes, including those of prophet, priest, and king, come together in one person. For Christians, the messiah is the one who is sent by God—anointed by God—to save us, to protect us, to teach us, to overcome our enemies, to minister to us, to rule over our hearts and minds, and to tell us all truth. But who are we and what is the goal of such a relationship?

# 5
# Who is Man? Who is Woman?

Having talked about God, now let us turn to mankind. There is both good news and bad news. The good news is that we are created in the image of God. The bad news is that we turned away from God and fell flat on our faces from "day one." (Actually, it was about day 9—or something like that.) This chapter is about the good news. We would like to develop our understanding of what it means to be created in the image of God as a foundation for the later development of our understanding of transformation. This is all about the starting materials with which God has to work. Who are we that God might ask of us some form of transformation? And given this understanding, just how radical is that transformation? Is it a transformation *back* into the ones we were intended to be in the first place? Is it a transformation into something new? This is what we are about here, and we must start at the beginning:

> In the beginning God created the heavens and the earth. The earth was without form and void, and darkness was upon the face of the deep; and the Spirit of God was moving over the face of the waters. . . .
>
> Then God said, "Let us make man in our image, after our likeness; and let them have dominion over the fish of the sea, and over the birds of the air, and over the cattle, and over all the earth, and over every creeping thing that creeps upon the earth." So God created man in his own image, in the image of God he created him; male and female he created them.

And God blessed them, and God said to them, "Be fruitful and multiply, and fill the earth and subdue it; and have dominion over the fish of the sea and over the birds of the air and over every living thing that moves upon the earth." . . .

And God saw everything that he had made, and behold, it was very good. And there was evening and there was morning, a sixth day.

*Genesis 1: 1–2, 26–28, 31*

## The Image of God

So, that's how it all started. It all seemed pretty upbeat. But just how upbeat was it? What is this *image of God* business? Whatever it is, it seems to be pretty powerful. To get at some of the implications let's turn away from our Catholic base and look to John Calvin. As a theologian, Calvin offers some deep insights. The Reformation spawned a number of reactions against Catholic practices that even the Catholics corrected. While, some of the theological reactions had profound effects on their implied Christology, much Protestant theology remains consistent with Catholic theology. Let's hear directly from him.

> *1. Man proceeded spotless from God's hand; therefore he may not shift the blame for his sins to the Creator.*
>
> We must now speak of the creation of man; not only because among all God's works here is the noblest and most remarkable example of his justice, wisdom, and goodness; but because, as we said at the beginning, we cannot have a clear and complete

## Who is Man? Who is Woman?

knowledge of God unless it is accompanied by a corresponding knowledge of ourselves. This knowledge of ourselves is twofold; namely, to know what we were like when we were first created and what our condition became after the fall of Adam. While it would be of little benefit to understand our creation unless we recognized in this sad ruin what our nature in its corruption and deformity is like, we shall nevertheless be content for the moment with the description of our originally upright nature. And to be sure, before we come to the miserable condition of man to which he is now subjected, it is worthwhile to know what he was like when first created. Now we must guard against singling out only those natural evils of man, lest we seem to attribute them to the Author of nature. For in this excuse, impiety thinks it has sufficient defense, if it is able to claim that whatever defects it possesses have in some way proceeded from God. It does not hesitate, if it is reproved, to contend with God himself, and to impute to him the fault of which it is deservedly accused. And those who wish to seem to speak more reverently of the Godhead still willingly blame their depravity on nature, not realizing that they also, although more obscurely, insult God. For, if any deficit were proved to inhere in nature, this would bring reproach upon him.

Since, then, we see the flesh panting for every subterfuge by which it thinks that the blame for its own evils may in any way be diverted from itself to another, we must diligently oppose this evil intent. Therefore we must so deal with the calamity of mankind that we may cut off every shift, and may vindicate God's justice from every accusation. Afterward, in the proper place, we shall see how far away men are from the purity that was bestowed upon Adam. . . . But since God not only deigned to give life to an earthen vessel, but also willed it to be the abode of an immortal spirit, Adam could rightly glory in the great liberality of his Maker.[40]

In the beginning God fashioned us after his image that he might arouse our minds both to zeal for the virtue and to meditation upon eternal life. Thus, in order that the great nobility of our race may not be buried beneath our own dullness of wit, it behooves us to recognize that we have been endowed with reason and understanding so that by a holy and upright life, we may press on to the appointed goal of blessed immortality.[41]

This is spectacular writing and full of deep insight. Here Calvin is at the height of his game and is completely orthodox. One sees very clearly a passion for God and a refined intellect of the highest order. What is so interesting about Calvin is how he juxtaposes the height of glory associated with the *image of God* with the utter depravity of the *fall*. It is like he has this tremendous inner struggle that tears at him constantly.

## Image vs. Likeness

Eventually we will deal more explicitly with how we are called to internalize this tension between the magnificence of the free gift and the tragedy of our betrayal of that gift. Now let's turn to

---

[40] John Calvin, *Institutes of the Christian Religion* (Philadelphia: Westminster Press, 1960), Book 1, Chapter 15, 183.
[41] Ibid., Book 2, Chapter 1, 242.

Who is Man? Who is Woman?

the Church Fathers for a very interesting distinction. To do so, we will return to David Yeago.

> Some of the Greek Fathers made a distinction, in their reflection on the creation story in Genesis, between the *image* and the *likeness* of God. The purpose of this distinction was essentially to replicate the relation of created nature and consummating grace. The *image* of God, on this understanding, is the distinctive site of natural capacities with which humans are outfitted in creation: freedom, language, reason, and so forth. This *image* of God makes us possible hearers of the word of grace, which calls us to be transformed into the *likeness* of God. The likeness is the participation in God's own life, the conformity to the Son of God in the freedom of the Spirit, to the glory of God the Father, to which grace calls us and for the sake of which we were created. The distinction between image and likeness has no very strong exegetical foundation in the text of Genesis, but it does make helpfully a theological structure deeply inscribed in the Biblical story.[42]

Well, now we are getting somewhere. There are a number of things going on here. First, he has set up the entire transformational theme. Mankind is created in perfect harmony with God with a life that participates fully in the life of God. Then we blew it, and the rest of the story is how God has worked with us

---

[42] David Yeago, Chapter 9, 17. What he is saying here is that the distinction between *image* and *likeness* cannot be derived from an analysis of the text from which the words come.

through grace to restore us by a radical transformation into what we were intended to be in the first place.

## Doctrinal Development

Second, Yeago implicitly points out the power of *doctrinal development*. As we stated earlier, orthodox doctrine finds its foundation in apostolic traditions and beliefs as rooted in Scripture. The history of the Church, however, has revolved around clarifying that meaning through a long process of discussion, disputation, convocation, and elaboration—what we call *doctrinal development*.

This distinction between *image* and *likeness*, one could say is irrelevant because it is not strictly scriptural. However, the truth of the transformational theme is completely scriptural, and the distinction while not explicitly stated, may be and possibly should be considered not only consistent with Scripture, but also compellingly enlightening. This is why our relying on "orthodox doctrine" can be a powerful guide to our journey rather than our trying to reinvent the wheel directly from Scripture alone. This is why orthodox doctrine is not *sola Scriptura*.[43]

## The Grace of God

Yeago also discusses the role of *grace* in our transformative journey. He shows how mankind is chosen to have a special place in the purpose of creation. Humanity is chosen to participate in a story with God. The image of God is the nature of mankind that allows humanity to participate in this story. This gift of

---

[43] Understanding *sola Scriptura* is itself tricky, because it could simply mean "based on scripture." Catholics would assert that all their teachings are based on Scripture. Tradition is simply the process by which the Church has interpreted Scripture. It turns out that what is or is not "scriptural" is a judgement call. And so, we go back and forth.

## Who is Man? Who is Woman?

his image is the first example of God's *grace, the gift freely given.*

> There is an old theological axiom which describes the *structure* of this story which leads from creation to fulfillment by way of the generous gift and call of God's grace: *grace does not destroy nature, but elevates and perfects it.*[44]

Yeago thus shifts the emphasis toward the nature of mankind found in the *image* and the role of the *grace of God* in mankind's recovering that *likeness*. Not only did God, through the amazing generosity of grace, bestow on mankind the gift of his own image, but he also offered us his grace throughout our journey back to the *likeness* that God intended for us at the beginning. This likeness is much more than merely a capacity to be in relationship with God, but the actual degree to which we are "like" God—in other words, the degree to which we love like God, live into the God's truth, are merciful like God, are compassionate like God, and so forth.

Let me offer a clarifying analogy. To put out a fire we need four things: A source of water or fire hydrant, water pressure that makes the water abundantly available, a hose to transfer the water to the fire, and most importantly a coupling that makes the hose compatible with the fire hydrant. Let's say that I am the building on fire, and it is my own hose that will be used to put out the fire. We might say that God is the source of life-giving water, and the hose is the extension of me that is reaching out to God. It is the *coupling*, the compatibility of hydrant and hose, of the giver and the receiver that makes the flow of water possible. It is that image of God, a kind of compatibility between God and

---

[44] Ibid., 18.

humanity that makes the offering and receiving of grace possible.

Yeago has an interesting comment on the emphasis shown by his own Protestant tradition.

> But the Protestant neglect of the nature–grace theme has had considerable costs: an exclusive emphasis on sin and forgiveness can lead to an understanding of grace in almost wholly *negative* terms, as the divine generosity that takes away the threat of hell. We need to recover the nature–grace theme, so that we can learn to understand the grace of God not only in negative terms, as liberation from evil, but in positive terms, as the fulfillment for the sake of which we were created as the particular creatures we are.[45]

In other words, God has provided a means for our return to that original state of "uprightness." It is grace. Just as the coupling was essential for the fire hose to connect to the hydrant, allowing the water to flow from hydrant to house, putting out the fire and allowing the house eventually to return to a state of wholeness, the image of God allows the grace to flow from God to humanity making our return to the likeness possible. How that grace is manifested will be clearer when we start to talk about Jesus. There are, however, some subtle traps that we must avoid, and I cannot speak to these better than Yeago can himself.

> At the same time, grace elevates created human nature. And this "elevation" is not simply some sort of organic flowering, a self-realization of what was

---

[45] Ibid., 16.

always already there within us, of our "human potential." The elevation of nature by grace means that something *new* and unforeseeable opens up for us by the surprising generosity of God. The God who created us new *speaks to us once again*, and what he promises in his work of grace could never simply have been extrapolated from creation. No examination of our nature or our relation to God's creatures in the abstract would reveal that our destiny is to share the inner life of the blessed Trinity, to be sons and daughters of the Father in communion with his only-begotten Son.

This is what Henri de Lubac has called *the Christian paradox of the human creature*: the authentic realization of our nature—the "likeness" which perfects the "image"—is a goal which our nature as such has no power to reach. Thomas Aquinas puts the point with spare precision: *"Although the human creature naturally inclines to that goal, yet it is not capable of attaining it naturally, but only by grace; and this is on account of the excellence of that goal."*[46]

## More on the Image

What does New Testament Scripture say about this image? Paul, as possibly the first Christian systematic (and sometimes not so systematic) theologian, uses the concept repeatedly to articulate fundamental relationships between God the Father, Jesus the Son, and ourselves. Consider the following passages:

---

[46] Ibid., 19 (Aquinas quotation from *The Mystery of the Supernatural*, p. 152; Yeago's translation).

## Into the Perfect Likeness

> He [Jesus] is the image of the invisible God, the firstborn of all creation; for in him all things in heaven and on earth were created, things visible and invisible, whether thrones or dominions or rulers through him and for him. He himself is before all things, and in him all things hold together. He is the head of the body, the church; he is the beginning, the firstborn from the dead, so that he might come to have first place in everything. For in him all the fullness of God was pleased to dwell, and through him God was pleased to reconcile to himself all things, whether on earth or in heaven, by making peace through the blood of his cross. *Colossians 1:15–20*

> In their case the god of this world has blinded the minds of the unbelievers, to keep them from seeing the light of the gospel of the glory of Christ, who is the image of God. For we do not proclaim ourselves; we proclaim Jesus Christ as Lord and ourselves as your slaves for Jesus' sake. For it is God, who said, "Let light shine out of darkness," who has shone in our hearts to give the light of the knowledge of the glory of God in the face of Jesus Christ.
> *2 Corinthians 4:4–6*

For Paul, we are drawn back to our intended state by the power of Jesus, who shows us the image and likeness of God.

> Thus, it is written, "The first man, Adam, became a living being"; the last Adam became a life-giving spirit. But it is not the spiritual that is first, but the physical, and then the spiritual. The first man was from the earth, a man of dust; the second man is from

> heaven. As was the man of dust, so are those who are of the dust; and as is the man of heaven, so are those who are of heaven. Just as we have borne the image of the man of dust, we will also bear the image of the man of heaven. *1 Corinthians 15:45–49*

> For those whom he foreknew he also predestined to be conformed to the image of his son, in order that he might be the firstborn in a large family.
> *Romans 8:29*

Here Paul is weaving our relationship to Jesus into all these "images." Clearly, he is not articulating systematic doctrine, since he has not explicitly dealt with the Hebrew Scripture statement of our own image and likeness. He has left that up to the Church to sort out the details, which of course she did in grand style. Consequently, we now have a clear track from our own image of God, through Jesus' image and likeness of God, to the possibility of renewal of our own likeness of God. This is called Christian transformation.

## The Transformation of Women and Men

Now let me deal with a difficult passage from Paul. This is not only what makes Paul a challenge, but also points out the essential role of the Church in sorting out the important doctrine from a host of details.

> For if a woman will not veil herself, then she should cut off her hair; but if it is disgraceful for a woman to be shorn or shaven, let her wear a veil. For a man ought not to cover his head, since he is the image and glory of God; but woman is the glory of man. (For man was not made from woman, but woman from

> man. Neither was man created for woman, but woman for man.) That is why a woman ought to have a veil on her head, because of the angels. (Nevertheless, in the Lord woman is not independent of man nor man of woman; for as woman was made from man, so man is now born of woman. And all things are from God.) Judge for yourselves; is it proper for a woman to pray to God with her head uncovered? Does not nature itself teach you that for a man to wear long hair is degrading to him, but if a woman has long hair, it is her pride? For her hair is given to her for a covering. If any one is disposed to be contentious, we recognize no other practice, nor do the churches of God.
> *1 Corinthians 11:6–16*

This gives us an opportunity to show a stunning example of how the Church has, over the last 2000 years, informed the interpretation of Scripture. We would call that—you got it—doctrinal development. Paul is making a strong statement about men being the image and reflection of God. This is good stuff. When he makes the distinction about women, he is interpreting the meaning and significance of Scripture, as *someone* must ultimately interpret meaning and significance. It is well known that women up until recently in both the Anglican and Roman Catholic Churches wore hats or veils in church, and still in the Roman Catholic Church, women are not able to become priests.

These practices probably flowed at least to some extent from this and other passages from Paul. Here we might make a distinction between cultural norms or even religious practices and orthodox doctrine. Paul is arguing from a particular cultural position. As cultural practices and understandings change, we might expect certain religious cultural manifesta-

## Who is Man? Who is Woman?

tions to change. Here is the critically important point: orthodox transformational doctrine makes no distinction between the transformation that is available to women and that which is available to men. While we may argue intensely about the differences between men and women, and their relationship to one another and to God, for our purposes here it is essential that we make clear that there is no distinction concerning the level of transformation offered to each of us.

We can see the Church in action in continually refining doctrine, not revising Scripture, but developing an understanding of the truth that is consistent with Scripture's larger meaning and intent. This is the kind of work the Church has done repeatedly in the Ecumenical Councils concerning the critical and delicate doctrinal points about who Jesus was and is, as well as a host of other issues including the role of men and women in the Church—and this work will continue. Furthermore, we see Paul offering some wiggle room as he argues against contentiousness and characterizes his thinking as a "practice." He seems to be saying that, while this is his personal "doctrine," it has not reached the state of Church doctrine, if you could even talk of such a thing at this point in the early history of the Church, and certainly would not be considered essential dogma. In other words, even he is acknowledging that some things he says are essential and other things are just his best opinion.

So in conclusion, we need to assert the orthodox essentials concerning who we are as primitive human beings. As Yeago stated: "This image of God makes us possible hearers of the word of grace, which calls us to be transformed into the likeness of God. The likeness is the participation in God's own life, the conformity to the Son of God in the freedom of the Spirit, to the glory of God the Father, to which grace calls us and for the sake of which we were created."[47] It doesn't get any more succinct than that. We are created in the image of God, with the capacity to grow into the likeness of God. Jesus is the image and likeness of God. He has, as a human being, the capacity to reflect the likeness of God to humanity. As the Son of God, he shows us what the likeness to which we aspire looks like. In other words, to be transformed into the likeness of God is to be transformed into the likeness of Jesus and vice versa. And this transformation is available to all of us through God's generous free gift of grace.

---

[47] Ibid., 17.

# 6
# Transformed from What?

In the last chapter we discussed the creation of mankind in the image and likeness of God. This is the good news. Unfortunately, there is some bad news—some awful news. We messed it up. The story in Genesis of what we in the Christian tradition call *the fall* of Adam and Eve is one of the keystones of the arch called Christianity. There are many stones in many arches, but we must see the story of the fall as an essential piece of the puzzle on which all the others rest. It sets up the whole basis for the continuing involvement of God in the story of our journey back to God. Back from what? Back from *the fall*.

## The Fall
So, here is the story, or at least the important chunks:

> The LORD God took the man and put him in the Garden of Eden to till it and keep it. And the LORD God commanded the man, "You may freely eat of every tree of the garden; but of the tree of the knowledge of good and evil you shall not eat, for in the day that you eat of it you shall die."
> Then the LORD God said, "It is not good that the man should be alone; I will make him a helper as his partner." *Genesis 2:15–18*
>
> So the LORD God caused a deep sleep to fall upon the man, and he slept; then he took one of his ribs and closed up its place with flesh. And the rib that the LORD God had taken from the man he made into a

woman and brought her to the man. Then the man said, "This at last is bone of my bones and flesh of my flesh; this one shall be called Woman for out of Man this one was taken."

Now the serpent was more crafty than any other wild animal that the LORD God had made. He said to the woman, "Did God say, 'You shall not eat from any tree in the garden'?" The woman said to the serpent, "We may eat of the fruit of the trees in the garden; but God said, "You shall not eat of the fruit of the tree that is in the middle of the garden, nor shall you touch it, or you shall die.' " But the serpent said to the woman, "You will not die; for God knows that when you eat of it your eyes will be opened, and you will be like God, knowing good and evil." So when the woman saw that the tree was good for food, and that it was a delight to the eyes, and that the tree was to be desired to make one wise, she took of its fruit and ate; and she also gave some to her husband, who was with her, and he ate. Then the eyes of both were opened and they knew that they were naked; and they sewed fig leaves together and made loincloths for themselves.

They heard the sound of the LORD God walking in the garden at the time of the evening breeze, and the man and his wife hid themselves from the presence of the LORD God among the trees of the garden. But the LORD God called to the man, and said to him, "Where are you?" He said, "I heard the sound of you in the garden and I was afraid, because I was naked; and I hid myself." He said, "Who told you that you were naked? Have you eaten from the tree of which I commanded you not to eat?" The man said, "The

Transformed from What?

woman whom you gave to be with me, she gave me fruit from the tree, and I ate." Then the LORD God said to the woman, "What is this that you have done?" The woman said, "The serpent tricked me, and I ate."
*Genesis 2:21–3:13*

Oops! Well, you can read *the rest of the story*, but the net result was a great chasm between God and humanity. The perfection of mankind has been corrupted by his and her willfulness, by their pride. They thought they knew more than God. This is what has been called *the fall*. But how are we to understand the meaning of this story?

## Many Levels of Meaning

Because the story is so important, we need to take a moment to discuss the many levels on which this story can be understood. Each denomination and each member of each of those denominations will take a slightly or drastically different approach than another. Some will take the story as a set of historic facts, namely, that once upon a time, approximately 6000 years ago (figured from genealogies given later in Genesis), there was an individual man, named Adam, and an individual woman, named Eve, and a real place on the map, named the Garden of Eden. The story becomes a kind of documentary.

Some will see the story as an action in history, but take the players and the setting as symbolic. Others will see the story as an allegory about mankind's prideful nature and the consequences of that nature. Still others will see it as a myth that may or may not be factually true but captures the profound truth about the relationship between God and humanity right now. For our present purposes, what is important is not the historicity of the story, but the orthodox doctrinal result—the reality of the chasm between God and humanity. In other words, no matter how you get there, the result is a huge gap between who God intended us to be and who we are in the here and now. We call this chasm *sin*.

## What is Sin?

The Greek word for sin is *hamartia*, which means to miss the mark. But what is the mark? We must generally say that the mark is the will of God for each of us. But then, what is that? If we are to understand the process of transformation, we must spend some time understanding the state in which we find ourselves—the state of *sin*.

Let's look at some scriptural references that should shed some light on the characteristics of sin.

> For there is no distinction, since all have sinned and fall short of the glory of God ...    *Romans 3:23*

The first characteristic of sin is that, in some way, we are all stuck in it. The orthodox understanding would go further and state that, because of the sin of Adam and Eve we have built into us the inability not to sin. This particular brand of sin is known as *original sin*. It is passed down, according to the early Church Fathers such as Augustine of Hippo, through hereditary means and is a basic part of our humanity. Another word that is associated with original sin is *concupiscence*, the tendency to sin as a result of our humanity. In other words, without some help, we are stuck in sin. Yet this doesn't mean that we are without hope. This hope is precisely what energizes our journey, but our starting point is that of "sinner."

Now there are some schools of thought that suggest that this situation is so unattractive that we should make up some "translational" or more comforting story called "new age" or "creation theology" or some other thing that makes us feel better—that

## Transformed from What?

basically does away with the whole concept of original sin. But the fact is that orthodox Christianity takes this sinful state as a given. At least the story of Adam and Eve indicates to us that sin is a given problem for all of us.

> If we say we have no sin, we deceive ourselves, and the truth is not in us.     *1 John 1:8*

This passage reinforces the idea that sin is a given in our lives. But if this is the case, where is the hope? How can we understand these passages in such a way that we see a way out?

### Descriptive v. Prescriptive

We already pointed out the distinction between *translation* and *transformation* as a way to clarify the difference between the good and the best. We will keep coming back to this distinction as an important tool of our efforts to understand our Christian journey. Another distinction that may be equally important is the distinction between *descriptive* and *prescriptive* statements in Scripture. When we read Scripture, we need to ask whether the author is being descriptive of something that happens to be true or prescriptive of something that needs to be true. Is she describing an illness or prescribing the cure? Is he *describing* a situation or story that is true but is not intended as a model for our behavior, such as the story of Moses killing one of Pharaoh's soldiers? Or is the author *prescribing* a kind of behavior that is, in fact, intended to be a model for us, as in the case of Jesus' Sermon on the Mount?

Here we need our orthodox doctrinal development to address this question. The clear implication of this statement in 1 John taken out of context (not just local scriptural context, but also the larger context of the whole of apostolic teaching) is that we are all stuck forever, and that there is no hope. Through doctrinal development, the Church has asserted that this statement is meant to be descriptive. Yes, in fact, if I were to say that I have no sin, I would be deceiving myself. This would also be true for all the rest of the folks I know. It is, however, not *prescriptive*. As we will see, Jesus gives us a way out of this depressing situation. But what does this "situation" actually look like?

**Characteristics of a Sinner**
How do we recognize our own sinfulness? What are the characteristics of a sinner?

> They were filled with every kind of wickedness, evil, covetousness, malice, full of envy, murder, strife, deceit, craftiness, they are gossips, slanderers, God-haters, insolent, haughty, wasteful, inventors of evil, rebellious toward parents, foolish, faithless, heartless, ruthless. Though they know God's decree that those who do such things deserve to die, they not only do them but approve those who practice them.
> *Romans 1:29–32*

Yikes, this is depressing to think that we might find ourselves in this list. And yet, all I have to do is get in my car and some level of craftiness, foolishness, and ruthlessness erupts. All I have to do is look at a new Lamborghini Testarossa and the envy kicks in. All I have to do is encounter someone less intelligent or less refined than myself and the haughtiness starts to break forth. So, we all do it, and we can, if we take a moment, make a list of our own. But why are we stuck?

> . . . everyone who commits sin is a slave to sin.
> *John 8:34*

## Transformed from What?

Now what is this *slave* business? We had the emancipation proclamation, didn't we? (I know there are many subtleties I am overlooking here, but my point is simple.) How can we be slaves? What does it mean to be a slave to *something*? Well, look around you: your house, your car, your family heirlooms, your favorite hunting rifle, your child, your job, your "persona," and on and on. To be a slave to something is to be controlled by it. We call this *attachment*.

**Attachment**
This is another very important distinction: whether we are *attached* to or *detached* from the things we hold dear. To be attached to something is to view that thing as being directly related to our own personal well-being. How do you know if the dog is attached to the tennis ball in his mouth? Just try taking it away from him. How do you know if the baby is attached to the "blankie?" Just try taking it away. We are the same way with many aspects of our own lives. We are, thus, slaves to those things to which we are *attached*.

We know where sin started, but where does this attachment to sin come from?

> You are from your father the devil, and you choose to do your father's desires. He was a murderer from the beginning and does not stand in the truth, because there is no truth in him. When he lies, he speaks according to his own nature, for he is a liar and the father of lies. *John 8:44*

Now it is getting interesting. Where do attachments come from? As we said, attachments are based on an understanding of the fundamental things that we hold to be *true*. In other words, they come from those things that *we think* give us "life." Therefore, all attachments are based on some *lie* that the "serpent" (or whatever you want to think of as the source of lies) tells us about the importance of certain things in our lives—things that, in truth, are really *not* important. Therefore, very early on in our own struggle with sin, we are confronted with the issue on which everything turns: What is the truth and what is its value to us?

In the above passage, the devil is equated with all untruth. Conversely, God must be equated with truth. So, what we have is the serpent telling Eve a lie, and Eve falling for it. And then she passes it on, and Adam not only falls for it again, but also compounds the lie by suggesting that it is good to blame Eve, another lie. So, what is this business about the serpent or demons or the devil or Satan? How do they or him or it fit into our understanding of sin?

## Satan

Our understanding of sin always carries with it at least some connotation of something that is not good—a falling short of some ideal. Carried further, it points toward something that is evil. Because we tend to think anthropomorphically, we tend to personify a wide range of non-human entities by applying human characteristics to them. In the case of evil, we personify it in the shape of the Devil or Satan. But where dies this personification come from?

## The Accuser

The word "satan" means accuser or adversary. In the biblical case, Satan is an angel, created by God with a specific responsibility. In general, our first encounter with Satan is in the book of Job:[48]

---

[48] There actually is one other reference in 1 Chronicles 21:1.

## Transformed from What?

> And the LORD said to Satan, "Have you considered my servant Job, that there is none like him on the earth, a blameless and upright man, who fears God and turns away from evil?" Then Satan answered the LORD and said, "Does Job fear God for no reason? Have you not put a hedge around him and his house and all that he has, on every side? You have blessed the work of his hands, and his possessions have increased in the land. But stretch out your hand and touch all that he has, and he will curse you to your face." And the LORD said to Satan, "Behold, all that he has is in your hand. Only against him do not stretch out your hand." So Satan went out from the presence of the LORD. *Job 1:8–12*

Here we see Satan as an angel who began as the tester or accuser of Job to see if his faith in God was genuine or simply a product of his prosperity. In a broader interpretation, we might say that Satan's original job was to come into the lives of humans and give them challenges in order to bring them closer to the will of God.

**The Battle between Satan and Michael**
At some point, however, Satan decided he didn't need God anymore and decided to "go out on his own" and, in so doing, became the enemy of God. Here is the next part of the story.

> And war broke out in heaven; Michael and his angels fought against the dragon. The dragon and his angels fought back, but they were defeated and there was no longer any place for them in heaven. The great dragon was thrown down, that ancient serpent, who is called the Devil and Satan, the deceiver of the

# Into the Perfect Likeness

> whole world—he was thrown down to the earth, and his angels were thrown down with him.
>
> *Revelation 12:7–9*

So, he is down here. Oh, great! Thanks a lot. No matter how you take the story, the point is that Satan is the personification of evil. We have drawn Satan in all sorts of ways throughout history. The most common image has him with a red suit, a pointy tail, and horns.

## The Power and Traps Associated with the Image

In reality, however, we don't know any more about what Satan looks like than we know about what God looks like. We might like to think of God as an old man up in the sky with a white beard, but we must realize that an image is only a tool, one that may or may not help us in our spiritual journey. Michelangelo's image of God and Adam on the ceiling of the Sistine Chapel is an incredibly powerful and helpful image, if we understand its limits. The same thing is true about our image of Satan. It may be useful to think of Satan as a guy with a red suit and horns, or a big huge ugly dragon, or a sleazy lawyer bent on corrupting souls,[49] but if we get stuck there, our images may also limit us.

## Geraldine

Flip Wilson was a wonderful comedian who had in his repertoire a character named Geraldine. Whenever Geraldine was discovered in some transgression, her stock response was, "De Devil made me do it." Now here is the point. If we define Satan as the cause of all our own personal sin, that is perfectly orthodox. However, if we always look for that cause outside ourselves as

---

[49] As in the movie *The Devil's Advocate*, Warner Brothers, 1997.

## Transformed from What?

some agent over which we have no control, now we have derailed. We have fallen into a gaping trap. Satan becomes active when invited in, fattened up, and given dominion over some aspect of our lives. To see how this works we should look at a work by C. S. Lewis. He did the Christian world a great service when he wrote the book entitled *The Screwtape Letters*.

**Screwtape**
In the book he personifies the Devil as a personage named Screwtape. He is the boss of an array of minions, one of whom is a novice demon, named Wormwood. In these imaginary letters, Screwtape is advising Wormwood how to draw Christians, over which he has responsibility, away from "the Enemy." Of course, "the Enemy" to Screwtape is God. Here is an excerpt from Letter XIV.

> You must therefore conceal from the patient the true end of Humility. Let him think of it not as self-forgetfulness but as a certain kind of opinion (namely, a low opinion) of his own talents and character. Some talents, I gather, he really has. Fix in his mind the idea that humility consists in trying to believe those talents to be less valuable than he believes them to be. No doubt they *are* in fact less valuable than he believes, but that is not the point. The great thing is to make him value an opinion for some quality other than truth, thus introducing an element of dishonesty and make-believe [lie] into the heart of what otherwise threatens to become a virtue.
>
> The Enemy wants to bring the man to a state of mind in which he could design the best cathedral in the world, and know it to be the best [truth], and

> rejoice in the fact, without being any more (or less) or otherwise glad at having done it than he would be if it had been done by another. The Enemy wants him, in the end, to be so free from any bias in his own favour [truth] that he can rejoice in his own talents as frankly and gratefully as in his neighbor's talents—or in a sunrise, an elephant, or a waterfall.[50]

This gives you an idea of Lewis's approach. Here he shows the relationship between the untruth of Satan and the truth of God and shows how our own sinfulness results from our buying into the former. We are constantly being beguiled by the lie. What is interesting is that Screwtape works through our own thinking. It all has to do with what we *think* is the truth.

If we looked carefully at this passage, and the whole book for that matter, we would see that Satan acts anytime we become captured by some untruth, some lie. In other words, it is a bald-faced lie that my deep wellbeing has anything whatsoever to do with the Lamborghini, or the big house, or the country club. Lies, lies, lies. These accoutrements are not to be taken as bad in and of themselves. It is all about how we *think* about them and, of course, how our actions are predicated on those assumptions.

To place this inclination we have toward untruth in some context, we might look at some of the ways we address the problem of sin. Are there levels of sinfulness or untruth? What are the challenges associated with these levels? Are there points of no return?

---

[50] C. S. Lewis, *The Screwtape Letters* (New York: Macmillan, 1966), 63–5.

Transformed from What?

## Possession, Therapy, and Exorcism

When we talk about being "captured by untruth," we could also use the idea of being "possessed" by that untruth. Now, interest in Satan and possession has gained newfound life since the movies *The Exorcist*,[51] *Exorcist II*,[52] *Exorcist III*,[53] and *Exorcist: the Beginning*.[54] I would like to clarify some terminology that may come in handy later—the distinction between *therapy* and *exorcism*. If we think of possession as a process of being captured by the untruth in our lives, then to some degree we are all "possessed." There are parts of our lives that are predicated on something that is not true and that influence our behavior.

Now, imagine that you are talking with a friend who is expressing his delusional attitude toward the addictive nature of excessive alcohol use that has clearly gotten him into deep trouble. He thinks he is fine; you know he is not. You would say that his flawed understanding is clearly *a lie*. Therapy is when your friend has enough truth in himself to do his own work to climb out of the hole created by the lie. A friend or even a professional psychologist as *therapist* is simply facilitating the process. In this case, your therapeutic response might be something like, "That is quite interesting. Have you considered the possibility that your recent problems might be related to your attitude toward alcohol?"

On the other hand, what about those times when your friend doesn't have enough truth in himself to do his own work. This is an important distinction, because the assumption here is that such a situation might require a response all the way from "BALONEY!" to some form of *radical intervention*. These kinds of response can be seen as varieties of exorcism. If we

---

[51] Warner Brothers, 1973.
[52] Warner Brothers, 1977.
[53] Morgan Creek Productions, 1990.
[54] Morgan Creek Productions, 2004.

follow this line of reasoning, we see that possession exists on a continuum from mild delusion to hard-core refractory possession. Consequently, the more extreme the possession, the more radical the response, from mild therapeutic cajoling to some deliberate form of exorcism. In the extreme, we might even see the possible need for the Roman Catholic Rite of Exorcism requiring priests, crosses, holy water—the works. But it is all on a continuum of lie. One might call it the slippery slope of sin.

By the way, we can now define being "lost" as not having enough truth for God, through the "exorcist," to grab onto. It is as if we have fallen into quicksand. Therapy is when someone can talk us out of it, exorcism is when someone must reach in to grab us, and being lost is when we become totally submerged in the quicksand of lie and there is no truth at all to grab onto.

## A Call to the Journey Back

So that is the bad news. We have fallen—and we need to return to that condition we experienced before we fell. This journey from innocent purity to a state of separation from God and back again is the context for our understanding of the centrality of Christian transformation in the life of the Church. We were created in the image and likeness. We have lost the likeness and must regain it. Let's use Calvin to tie these themes together.

> But that primal worthiness cannot come to mind without the sorry spectacle of our foulness and dishonor presenting itself by way of contrast, since in the person of the first man we have fallen from our original condition. From this source arise abhorrence and displeasure with ourselves, as well as true humility; and thence is kindled a new zeal to seek God, in

## Transformed from What?

whom each of us may recover those good things which we have utterly and completely lost.[55]

Although Calvin tends to be very pessimistic regarding our plight on earth, here he clearly alludes to a journey back to our "primal worthiness." But is that really the question? Are we simply called to return or are we called into something even more? If our journey "back" involves Jesus, does that journey simply take us back to the innocence of the Garden of Eden or is there more? It is the answer to this question that we are seeking, so let's forge ahead.

---

[55] *Institutes*, Book 2, Chapter 1, 242.

# 7
# Transformed into What?

What is it that we are called to be transformed into? This theme may seem like jumping the gun, since it looks a lot like the punch line of our whole effort. But here we will lay out the scriptural references that point us toward some kind of transformation. There are two things to keep in mind. First, much of what Jesus said is *prescriptive* in that it prescribes for his followers what they are to look like or how they are to act and think. Second, in addition to this large body of prescriptive language, there exists the doctrine of the Church that has grown up around the teachings of the Apostles concerning the person of Jesus and the relation of that person to our own transformation. In this chapter, we will deal with the former and create the basis for the fundamental doctrinal questions that we address in the next few chapters.

## The Sermon on the Mount

First, let's consider the Sermon on the Mount:

> When Jesus saw the crowds, he went up the mountain; and after he sat down, his disciples came to him. Then he began to speak, and taught them, saying:
> 
> "Blessed are the poor in spirit, for theirs is the kingdom of heaven.
> 
> "Blessed are those who mourn, for they will be comforted.
> 
> "Blessed are the meek, for they will inherit the earth.

# Transformed into What?

"Blessed are those who hunger and thirst for righteousness, for they will be filled.

"Blessed are the merciful, for they will receive mercy.

"Blessed are the pure in heart, for they will see God.

"Blessed are the peacemakers, for they will be called children of God.

"Blessed are those who are persecuted for righteousness' sake, for theirs is the kingdom of heaven.

"Blessed are you when people revile you and persecute you and utter all kinds of evil against you falsely on my account. Rejoice and be glad, for your reward is great in heaven, for in the same way they persecuted the prophets who were before you.
*Matthew 5:1–12*

Of course, there are books written on the meaning of these statements and the rest of the sermon found in the following two chapters of Matthew. There are four concepts that are of particular interest to us here: the idea of being *blessed*, the reference to the *kingdom of heaven*, the idea of being *filled*, and the possibility of becoming *children of God*. What do these mean? They are certainly intended to paint a radical picture of what happens to and for those who follow these precepts, but what exactly do they mean in the context of our understanding of transformation?

What does it mean, for example, to be "blessed?" The word has a complex etymology, but in common usage, ties together the ideas of the worship and the praise of God and the good that results. We could say that to be blessed is to be the beneficiary of a good gift from God. The doxology, "Praise God from whom all blessings flow" captures this idea.[56] In fact, the word beneficiary has as its root the Latin word *bene*, meaning "good." Jesus seems to be saying that if one has these characteristics, they are the recipient of good gifts from God, and to desire these gifts, is to desire to be changed into one with whom God is well pleased. In other words, to desire to be blessed by having these characteristics is to desire to be changed or transformed. Because the Sermon on the Mount is a central statement by Jesus of who we are called to be, we must conclude that transformation into one with these characteristics is the essential point of our spiritual journey. Let's look at a few more consequences of these characteristics.

The goal or destination of this journey is clarified by Jesus' reference to a place of perfection—the kingdom of heaven. To pray for our transformation in this life on earth is really the same thing as to pray for the kingdom of God to be manifest on earth. We see this clearly in the first part of the Lord's Prayer:

> Our Father, who art in heaven,
> hallowed be thy Name,
> thy kingdom come,
> thy will be done,
> *on earth as it is in heaven.*     Matthew 6:9-10

To pray this prayer is to ask for the perfect will of God that exists in the "dwelling place" of perfection (Whatever you take that to mean, the shorthand for it is the word "heaven.") to be manifest here on earth. We are asking for our world to be transformed into a place where the will of God reigns and where all creatures are

---

[56] This particular doxology or praise of God, sung to the tune of *Old Hundredth*, can be found at
https://hymnary.org/text/praise_god_from_whom_all_blessings_ken.

## Transformed into What?

in harmony with that will. For individuals to be blessed by the gift of the kingdom of heaven is to be blessed with that which allows God to rule our lives—where God is king. The logical conclusion has to be that God wants us to be changed or transformed into individuals who are in harmony with his will. But how do we know what that looks like? Well, as Christians we have a model for one who was perfectly in harmony with the will of God—and our model for that harmony is Jesus Christ.

To be "filled" is another gift, but to be filled with what? We are left with a question here, but we might assert that we will be filled with what God wants us to be filled with. While the passage is not at all clear, the simple logic seems to say that, if you thirst for righteousness, you will be filled with righteousness or right relationship to God. In other words, you be transformed into one in right relationship or harmony with God—and our model for that is Jesus. The word does not refer to a degree of change, but to a completion. To be filled is to have no more room for anything else—maxed out. In other words, Jesus seems to be saying that he wants us to be changed completely.

To be "children of God" is to be the recipient of the gift of intimate or offspring-like connectedness to God. But what is the connection to making peace? We will talk much more about the importance of peace as a rationale for our transformative journey, but suffice it to say, that peace is one essential component of that journey. To be a peacemaker is to be one who brings peace—not just any peace, or worldly peace between non-belligerent nations, but the peace of God. To be called a child of God implies that one is worthy of an intimate relationship with God. Not disowned. The implication is that one is in the will of God if one brings the peace of God, the parent, and that to be in the will of God is to be operating as his offspring. As a child of God, one is taken to be an heir of all that God wishes to give his children. Again, this all implies a transformation that brings us into accord with the will of our Father, parent, in heaven.

## The Model is Jesus

In other words, all of these statements imply something about being transformed into ones who are in harmony with the will of God—and our model for that transformation is Jesus. For Christians, these qualities can have no concrete meaning apart from our understanding of Jesus. It is Jesus who shows us what it is like to be totally *blessed*. It is Jesus who shows us what it is like to be a *child of God*. It is Jesus who is the one who shows us what it looks like to be perfectly *filled*. It is Jesus who shows us what it looks like to live in the *kingdom of heaven* on earth. This is why we must answer the central Christian question: *Who was Jesus?*

Now that we have established the general line of thinking, let's just put out on the table a number of additional pieces of Scripture that point toward transformation.

> No one has ascended into heaven except the one who descended from heaven, the Son of Man. And Just as Moses lifted up the serpent in the wilderness, so must the Son of Man be lifted up, that whoever believes in him may have *eternal life*. *John 3:13–15*

> All need to be made right with God by his grace, which is a free gift. They need to be made *free from sin* through Jesus Christ. *Romans 3:24*

> We know that our old self was crucified with him so that the body of sin might be destroyed, and we might

Transformed into What?

> no longer be enslaved to sin. For whoever has died is *freed from sin.*                        Romans 6:6–7

> ... for you are *children of light* ...
>                                         1 Thessalonians 5:5

We could go on and on. The point here is the same as above. The one who shows us what it looks like to live eternal life right here on earth is Jesus. The one who shows us what it looks like to be free from sin or not enslaved to sin is the one who was fully human and yet without sin, Jesus. The one who shows us what it looks like to be a child of light is Jesus. But one nagging question still lingers: How are we to think about what separates us from all these possibilities? How are we to think about the grasp that sin has on us?

## Freedom from Sin

It is important to emphasize that Paul seems to think freedom from sin has been offered to us. If Jesus shows us what it looks like to be free from sin, and Paul calls us to be free from sin, then *you* put it together—just as the Church Fathers did. In some profound way we are to become as Jesus. I know we haven't quite pushed our likeness to the point of some kind of identity but stick with me. At least we can say unequivocally that Jesus is intended to be the model for our lives—lives that are lived without that which separates us from the will of God—in other words, with lives that can be lived with the possibility of being without sin.

> Thus it is written, "The first man, Adam, became a living being"; the last Adam became a life-giving spirit.                              1 Corinthians 15:45

## Into the Perfect Likeness

Paul is making it clear that, if Adam was the original model of righteousness before the fall, then Jesus shows us what that righteousness looks like after the restoration. In other words, Jesus is the model for our lives. We look to him for every measure of our relationship to God, light, heaven, etc.

Again, Jesus is the beginning and the end, the all in all.

> I am the Alpha and Omega," says the Lord God.
> *Revelation 1:8*

We need look no further for our exemplar, our model, our yardstick. In everything, we should compare ourselves to Jesus. As we do that, we should look more and more like him. The question is: How much *like* him are we called to look? I don't want to keep you in suspense. The orthodox answer is *exactly*, completely, perfectly. We are called to be indistinguishable from him.

## Indistinguishable

These are bold words. What in the world are we saying? If you are living the life that has been offered to you by and through Christ, and you walk into the room, those in the room should not be sure, if they had not known either you or Jesus personally, that you are not Jesus himself. Remember we are talking about the power of the image. Of course, we cannot be another individual. We always retain our individuality just as Jesus retained his own personal individuality. But consider the possibility that you might be mistaken for him by your actions, you demeanor, your very being—that the spirit of Christ dwells in you to such a degree that you look and act like him. Well, now the cat is out of the bag.

Let me put it another way based on Jesus' instruction to the twelve apostles:

## Transformed into What?

> As you go, proclaim the good news, 'The kingdom of heaven has come near.' Cure the sick, raise the dead, cleanse the lepers, cast out demons.   *Matthew 10:8*

What I am trying to say is this. If Jesus were standing on one corner of an intersection curing the sick, raising the dead, cleansing the lepers, and casting out demons, and you were standing on the other corner curing the sick, raising the dead, cleansing the lepers, and casting out demons, and I walk along and look at you both, *I cannot tell the difference*. To me you and Jesus are *indistinguishable*. And Jesus is tickled. Pleased as punch. That is what he intends for us by way of transformation. Consider one further tantalizing possibility: I come along, see Jesus and you, who happen to be a woman, and I say to myself, "But I thought Jesus was a man." I am confused. Ha! Now *that* is the point. Although we will support this idea later, it may be important to put it out on the table early, so you can pay attention as we go along and watch how orthodox doctrine is developed and is grounded mightily in Scripture.

### A Caveat

Now, we have said that Jesus is the model for every aspect of our lives and that we should compare ourselves to him in everything that we think, feel, and do. Let me give you a little heads up about what to expect when you start to do this, and especially when you start to verbalize that comparison to others. People will be put off, even irritated. How dare you be so audacious as to compare yourself to Jesus? Here is an example. Say that you have stood up in a meeting at your church and have pointed out some problem with their self-centered argument for not expanding the outreach program, or something like that. Someone says that you are being disruptive. You respond that Jesus was disruptive sometimes (actually he was earth-shakingly disruptive most of the time). Well now, you had better duck, because here it comes: "Well, Jesus was God, and you're NOT." I want you to understand that such a comment is wholly without merit—if one has the least understanding about the kind of transformation that Jesus not only offers, but also calls us into. We are *supposed* to compare ourselves to him. *He is the model for our lives.* In other words, your disruption must be evaluated on its merits and cannot simply be dismissed simply because it is disruptive.

## Trying on Jesus

While the Church fathers are replete with radical transformational language that we will get to later, let's look at how C. S. Lewis treats this call to see Jesus as the model for our lives. He gets about as close as any contemporary writer to the call for radical transformation.

> Its very first words are *Our Father*. Do you now see what those words mean? They mean quite frankly, that you are putting yourself in the place of a son of God. To put it bluntly, you are *dressing up as Christ*. If you like, you are pretending. Because, of course, the moment you realize what the words mean, you realize that you are not a son of God. You are not being like The Son of God, whose will and interests are at one with those of the Father: you are a bundle of self-centered fears, hopes, greed, jealousies, and self-conceit, all doomed to death. So that, in a way, this

## Transformed into What?

> dressing up as Christ is a piece of outrageous cheek. But the odd thing is that he has ordered us to do it.[57]

Now isn't that last statement interesting. Have we been *ordered* to dress up like Jesus? Let's focus for now on clarifying how Lewis sees the radical call to transformation.

> He is beginning to turn you into the same kind of thing as Himself.
>
> And now we begin to see what it is that the New Testament is always talking about. It talks about Christians "being born again" [John 3:410]; it talks about them "putting on Christ" [Romans 13:14]; about Christ "being formed in us" [Galatians 4:19]; about our coming to "have the mind of Christ" [Philippians 2:5].[58]

Before we go on, maybe this would be as good a place as any to make a distinction between what we mean by the name *Jesus* and the name *Christ*. As we said in Chapter 5, the Greek word *christos,* or Christ, means the same thing as the Hebrew word *mashiach,* or messiah. It means the chosen one of God, the anointed one. When we speak of Jesus here, we are referring to the man who lived over 2000 years ago and died on a cross in Jerusalem in about A.D. 33. When we, in general, speak of the Christ here, we are referring to a broader spiritual reality that includes both the incarnate Lord and the Second Person of the Holy Trinity. Certainly, we as Christians believe that that man

---

[57] C. S. Lewis, *Mere Christianity* (New York: Macmillan Publishing Company, 1952), 159.
[58] Ibid., 162.

on the cross was the Christ, the Messiah, the savior of the world. But as you will see in Lewis, we also believe that the Christ, as the second person of the Trinity, lives on in our lives.

The emphasis in this book is on Jesus, because it was Jesus who was the Incarnation of God on earth—God in human flesh. We are talking about the man Jesus, because there are so many ways to soften and avoid certain aspects of doctrine regarding the call to radical transformation, if we dwell only on the more spiritual and less earthly name of Christ. But as Lewis states, it is the Christ who abides with us day by day and through whom the grace of God flows so that our transformation can take place. To focus on Jesus is to focus on the nature of that transformation, not on how it takes place, at least not just yet. We will deal with that later.

> Put right out of your head the idea that these are only fancy ways of saying that Christians are to read what Christ said and try to carry it out—as a man may read what Plato or Marx said and try to carry it out. They mean something much more than that. They mean that a real person, Christ, here and now, in that very room where you are saying your prayers, is doing things to you. It is not a question of a good man who died two thousand years ago. It is a living man, still as much a man as you, and still as much God as He was when He created the world, really coming and interfering with your very self; killing the old natural self in you and replacing it with the kind of self He has. At first, only for moments. Then for longer periods. Finally, if all goes well, turning you permanently into a different sort of thing; into a new little Christ, a being which, in its own small way, has

the same kind of life as God; which shares in His power, joy, knowledge and eternity.[59]

Now, there is much in this section that is food for discussion. When Lewis uses diminutive words like "little" and "small," he is implying something about the amount of transformation that he believes has been offered to us here and now. We will clear up some of these subtle points as we go along. The point here is that he is recognizing the connection between the scriptural call for transformation and the person of Jesus.

## The Incarnation as the Model

While it is important to understand the role of Christ in our transformation, it is the concrete historical man Jesus who is the model for that transformation. For the next few chapters, we will be doing the essential work of trying to understand who this man was. Notice that I say *was*, not because he does not live on as the Son of God, the Second Person of the Holy Trinity, but because the Incarnation *was* in fact an historical event in space and time. The Jesus of the Incarnation *was*.[60] There was a beginning to the Incarnation—

> And she gave birth to her firstborn son and wrapped him in bands of cloth, and laid him in a manger ...  *Luke 2:7*

---

[59] Ibid., 162–3.
[60] Actually, this is a more complicated discussion than I have indicated here. There is a deeper sense in which the Incarnation is just as present now as when Jesus accomplished his earthly ministry. This is Christology on the highest order and is beyond the scope of this book. We will however try to be careful about the words we use in order to be consistent with the best orthodox Christological traditions.

# Into the Perfect Likeness

—and an end—

> When Jesus had received the vinegar, he said, "It is finished"; and he bowed his head and gave up the spirit.  *John 19:30*

There is much more to the story, but it is critical for us to understand that the model for our lives on earth showed us this model only during his lifetime on earth.

# 8
# Who Was Jesus? Divine vs. Human

We now start the essential work of describing who Jesus was when he walked with us in his earthly ministry. From the earliest years of the Church through the eighth century, there had been lively debate concerning the nature of Jesus. Although Scripture paints a picture of his active ministry, which lasted about three years, there was plenty of room for controversy. For the next few chapters, we will be dealing with the major issues that had to be resolved and the final dispositions that became *Christological doctrine*—a fancy way of saying the Church's understanding of *who Jesus was*.

## The Incarnation

This chapter focuses on the way in which the Church came to understand the relationship between Jesus' humanity and his divinity. This relationship is captured in the idea of the *Incarnation*. The Incarnation of the Son of God is the way in which the Son became human—became enfleshed. To start to grasp the importance and meaning of the Incarnation, we need to get oriented on the meaning of this divine-human issue before we start to sort out the different positions and the outcome of the debates.

From the Apostles' point of view, Jesus was clearly a man like they were. Especially at first, they had a difficult time grasping the possibility that there was any more to it. The Christ or the Messiah in Jewish terms was not necessarily intended to indicate someone who was himself God. The role of the savior was to lead the people out of bondage as Moses led the people out of bondage in Egypt. This is pretty much all they had to go on, except the prophetic literature of people like Isaiah. It certainly wasn't clear to them how to interpret the passages we quoted in Chapter 4 that many Christians today take for granted as clearly pointing toward Jesus. Consider, however, the following Scripture:

> Now when Jesus came into the district of Caesare'a Philippi, he asked his disciples, "Who do men say that the Son of man is?" And they said, "Some say John the Baptist, others say Eli'jah, and others Jeremiah or one of the prophets." He said to them, "But who do you say that I am?" Simon Peter replied, "You are the Christ, the Son of the living God." And Jesus answered him, "Blessed are you, Simon Bar-Jona! For flesh and blood has not revealed this to you, but my Father who is in heaven. *Matthew 16:13–17*

While the first part is where Peter declares the most striking announcement of who Jesus was, it is Jesus' response that is so often overlooked. What he seems to be saying is that the physical man standing before you, one of flesh and blood, cannot, in itself, reveal the whole truth. The full revelation is one of faith revealed by "my Father who is in heaven." This may be the most powerful pointer we have that the relationship between Christ's humanity and his divinity are not at all clear cut. While his humanity is manifest in flesh and blood, his divinity is revealed through faith. It is this challenge that we will be addressing in this chapter.

Given this kind of difficulty, we need to cut the first century Jews a little slack here. If it took a resurrection to get the point across to some of those closest to Jesus, think how hard it was for the average Jew to get it. Furthermore, we might be even more tolerant of them, since there are many Christians even today who still don't *get it*, as you will see from the following discussion.

## Human Characteristics

The struggle to understand this mystery began with the early Church and continues today. For our purposes, we will be drawing heavily on a little book by C. Fitzsimons Allison entitled *The Cruelty of Heresy*.[61] The strength of this book is that it is a succinct summary of the doctrinal struggles of the early Church, their roots, their potential traps, and the way the Church resolved them.

Before we get started, however, let's put out some different pieces of Scripture that point to the humanity of Jesus.

> Why do you call me good? No one is good but God alone. *Mark 10:18*

> The Father is greater than I. *John 14:28*

> Jesus wept. *John 11:35*

> ... "I thirst." *John 19:28*

> And Jesus cried again with a loud voice and yielded up his spirit. *Matthew 27:50*

> And the child grew and became strong in spirit. *Luke 1:80*

---

[61] C. Fitzsimons Allison, *The Cruelty of Heresy* (Harrisburg, Pennsylvania: Morehouse Publishing, 1994).

> And Jesus increased in wisdom and in stature.
> *Luke 2:52*

One of the earliest questions in the Church, and one that persists even today, concerns the humanity of Jesus. Was his humanity just like yours and mine or was it a special kind of humanity? Did he just act human or were his human characteristics genuine? Did he really think that the goodness of the Father was greater than his own or was he obliquely pointing to his own divinity? Did he weep because he felt a deep sadness just like the rest of us feel at times or did he just pretend to be sad for the sake of those who truly did mourn the loss of Lazarus? Was he really thirsty because his body was requiring the same sustenance that we all need, or was he alluding to a spiritual thirst? Did he really die? I mean "dead as a door nail," just like Grandmother and Grandfather Fletcher, and of course all of your ancestors as well, or did he just act dead and then get up after three days to fake out the Apostles—and everyone else? These may seem to be trivial questions that only distract from the central theme of Jesus salvation work, but the early Church clearly didn't think so. Neither should we.

## Divine Characteristics

Before we address these questions, let's look at the other side of the coin. What about his divinity?

> "But who do you say that I am?" And Peter answered, "The Christ of God." *Luke 9:20*

> He who has seen me has seen the Father. *John 14:9*

> In the beginning was the Word and the Word was with God and the Word was God. *John 1:1*

# Who Was Jesus? — Divine versus Human

> He is the image of the invisible God, the first born of every creature.
> *Colossians 1:15*

> Thomas answered him, "My Lord and my God!"
> *John 20:28*

Do these statements contradict Jesus humanity? Was he truly God? Was he simply God walking around in a special theophany? (A theophany is any physical manifestation of God, like the burning bush in Exodus 3.) Did he just appear to be Godlike because we wanted him to be? Was it wishful thinking on the Apostles' part? If we say that Jesus *was God*, just exactly what do we mean? Again, the Church has struggled with these questions throughout its entire existence, so it would be good to set out the boundaries of the playing field before we see what happened in this sort of Christological jousting match.

## The Endpoints

It is clear that there are two ends of the Christological spectrum. The one end is the idea that Jesus was only human, and any sense of his divinity comes from an array of possible mechanisms. On the other end of the spectrum is the idea that Jesus was only divine, and that the appearance of "humanity" again comes from an equally creative array of mechanisms. Now that we have nailed down the end lines of the playing field, here are some of the sticking points that formed the set of possible strategies in the "game." We will articulate some of the rules in a bit.

1. Jesus was God and was born uniquely of the Virgin Mary, or Jesus was human and had a normal birth by Mary and Joseph just like the rest of us.

2. Jesus was God, so he was omnipotent and therefore only appeared to exhibit human weaknesses, or Jesus was not God and was therefore limited by his humanity just like you and me, and only appeared to have divine characteristics.
3. Jesus was God who "came down from heaven" with a complete understanding of his "job description" or Jesus exhibited the same kind of natural human "ignorance" as the rest of us and struggled just like the rest of us as he grew into his own understanding of his role as savior and Messiah and his nature as Son of God.
4. Jesus was only divine and did not sin because he was not of this world and could not sin or Jesus was just as much a part of this world as you and I, and struggled with the same temptations as you and I do.

Given what appear to be diametrically opposed and mutually exclusive characteristics, how did the Church sort all this out?

## The Early Heresies

Here is a simplification of some of the positions that arose in the early Church and continue to give us trouble. The early *Docetists* said that Jesus was divine and consequently he only appeared to exhibit human characteristics.[62] This idea got pitched out. The *Gnostics* thought that he was only divine and that he exhibited special divine knowledge that he made available only to a select set of initiates.[63] This also got pitched out. The *Ebionites* rejected his divine status and believed he was simply the son of Joseph

---

[62] From the Greek word *dokein*, meaning to appear or to seem. Note that there is considerable overlap in these categories.

[63] From the Greek word *gnosis*, meaning knowledge.

## Who Was Jesus? — Divine versus Human

and Mary upon whom the Spirit of God descended at the time of his baptism.[64] Out! *Adoptionists* were those who believed that Jesus was divine by adoption by God due to his exemplary behavior. Jettisoned! Allison therefore sets the extremes to be the *Adoptionists* at one end of the spectrum and the *Docetists* at the other. And in fact, the Church tried to find the ground that was not either human or divine, but both human and divine. This was a difficult task.

These different schools of thought that got pitched out were called *heresies*, and those who committed them were called *heretics*, which simply referred to something that was contrary to the teaching of the Church. It is important for us to realize that, as we proceed on our journey toward a fuller understanding of Jesus, we cannot really commit heresy or be heretics. A heretic is one who has formulated a doctrine that contains either no truth or only part of the truth. Historically heresies were formulations that took a part for the whole. They left out something or distorted something that was essential. We don't know enough at this point to be worried about being heretics. We are just asking questions and learning.

## Some Basics of Orthodoxy

Well, maybe this is enough to chew on for now. Here are some of the boundaries of the playing field that must be satisfied by any *orthodox* Christology.

1. Jesus was fully human, was tempted just as we are, and yet he was without sin. (Hebrews 4:15)
2. Jesus grew in wisdom and understanding. (Luke 2:52)
3. Jesus struggled. (the Garden of Gethsemane. Matthew 26:36–41)

---

[64] Allison, 31.

4. Jesus could do nothing on his own authority. (John 5:30)[65]

So how was the game played? In other words, how did the Church sort out all these different concepts? How did they arrive at what we now call orthodoxy? Well, they argued and wrote, and convened an ecumenical council,[66] and argued some more; and the most powerful side would gain the upper hand; and more writing, and more arguing, and then the majority would formulate a principle and some would be excommunicated and others would be un-excommunicated. Then it would start all over—write, argue, convene, argue, formulate, excommunicate, un-excommunicate. Sometimes the Roman Emperor exerted influence. Sometimes powerful bishops exerted influence. And more writing, arguing, convening, formulating, and so on.

The whole point is that it wasn't easy. And they made mistakes. But they kept coming back to the drawing boards, hammering out the details of what we know today as orthodox doctrine.

## The Nicene Creed

One of the most important of these formulations was that of the Council of Nicaea held in A.D. 325, a formula that was eventually refined at the Council of Constantinople in A.D. 381. We know this formulation today as the Nicene Creed, which Roman Catholics, Eastern Orthodox, and Anglicans (Episcopalians in the US) see as foundational to their faith. Let's have a look.

---

[65] Especially the RSV translation.
[66] An ecumenical council would be one that included all the Christian churches. It just happened that in the early days we were one big Church.

Who Was Jesus? — Divine versus Human

We believe in one God,
> the Father, the Almighty,
> maker of heaven and earth,
> of all that is, seen and unseen.

We believe in one Lord, Jesus Christ,
> the only Son of God,
> eternally begotten of the Father,
> God from God, Light from Light,
> true God from true God,
> begotten, not made,
> of one Being with the Father.
> Through him all things were made.

For us and for our salvation
> he came down from heaven;
> by the power of the Holy Spirit
> he became incarnate from the Virgin Mary,
> and was made man.

For our sake he was crucified under Pontius Pilate;
> he suffered death and was buried.
> On the third day he rose again in accordance with the Scriptures;
> he ascended into heaven and is seated at the right hand of the Father.

He will come again in glory to judge the living and the dead,
> and his kingdom will have no end.

We believe in the Holy Spirit, the Lord, the giver of life,
> who proceeds from the Father and the Son.
> With the Father and the Son he is worshiped and glorified.
> He has spoken through the Prophets.
> We believe in one holy catholic and apostolic

> Church.
> We acknowledge one baptism for the forgiveness of sins.
> We look for the resurrection of the dead, and the life of the world to come.[67]

Now, it would be nice if this creed solved all the problems, but even though many use it, the Church struggled on to patch some of the more subtle but critical holes in the dyke. Let me point out a couple of issues. The creed assumes that everyone has an understanding of what it means to be *incarnate*—to be "made man." Later councils struggled with questions concerning his nature (the monophysite controversy) and his will (the monothelite controversy). The history of these problems and how they were resolved is a complex one and more than a bit dizzying. We will try to keep it as simple as possible.

One can just hear the debates that concluded in a certain "watering down" of the language in order to be acceptable to a range of positions and factions. The Council of Nicaea, as well as later councils, in which creedal formulations arose, were conducted by human beings with egos, vested interests, power bases, political affinities, and constituent influences, and any resulting formula had to have been some sort of compromise. No one got everything he wanted.

## The Chalcedonian Formula

Since we are most concerned with the nature of Jesus in his earthly ministry, we will spend some more time on the Incarnation. The need for carefully crafted language is made even clearer in the formula that was developed at the Council Chalcedon held in A.D. 451. Here is the text:

---

[67] *The Book of Common Prayer*, 326–7.

## Who Was Jesus? — Divine versus Human

Therefore, following the holy fathers, we all with one accord teach men to acknowledge one and the same Son, our Lord Jesus Christ, at once complete in Godhead and complete in manhood, truly God and truly man, consisting also of a reasonable soul and body; of one substance (homoousios) with the Father as regards his Godhead, and at the same time of one substance with us as regards his manhood; like us in all respects, apart from sin; as regards his Godhead, begotten of the Father before the ages, but yet as regards his manhood begotten, for us men and for our salvation, of Mary the Virgin, the God-bearer (Theotokos); one and the same Christ, Son, Lord, Only-begotten, recognized in two natures, without confusion, without change, without division, without separation; the distinction of natures being in no way annulled by the union, but rather the characteristics of each nature being preserved and coming together to form one person and subsistence, not as parted or separated into two persons, but one and the same Son and Only-begotten God the Word, Lord Jesus Christ; even as the prophets from earliest times spoke of him, and our Lord Jesus Christ himself taught us, and the creed of the Fathers has handed down to us.[68]

Now this one is loaded. Let's see if we can translate and distill some of it to answer some basic questions. One of the contributions that this statement makes concerns the relationship between Jesus and us. He is not only of "one substance" with the Father as regards his divinity ("Godhead"), as is explicitly stated

---

[68] *The Book of Common Prayer*, 864.

## Into the Perfect Likeness

in the Nicene Creed, but he is also of "one substance" with us as regards his manhood. The real problem that is not explicitly addressed regards what exactly did the Apostles see. Recall the words of Jesus and Peter: "Flesh and blood has not revealed that (my divinity) to you but my Father in Heaven." What this implies is that what the Apostles saw and experienced—what was manifest to them—was his humanity. In other words, the challenge for us is to understand what this formula means when it says he was "complete" in both divinity and humanity.

From this formula or definition, we also get some critical terminology—the distinction between person and nature. While the subtleties are considerable, suffice it to say that orthodox belief would assert that Jesus is one divine person with two natures, human and divine, while the Godhead is three persons (the Trinity) with one and the same divine nature. Luckily, we don't really need to unpack this here. We will see that the critical piece for us is the question as to what exactly was manifest in his life and ministry on earth. The key phrase here is, "like us in all respects, apart from sin." It should be clear what the challenge is for us. We must understand what this means. We will try to clarify this statement as we proceed.

Another compelling challenge posed to the early Church regarded the meaning of "one substance." When they talk about being of "one substance" and use the Greek word *homoousios*, they are alluding to a controversy that arose as to whether Jesus was of the same substance as the Father or simply of *like* substance. The Greek word for having a substance that is *like* the Father is *homoiousios*. Notice that the difference is that little "i" in the middle; the Greek letter is an *iota*. Now here is a little cocktail party tidbit. When someone says that something doesn't make one iota's difference, they are unknowingly referring to this controversy in the fifth century concerning the nature of Jesus. Actually, that one little iota made *all the difference* in our

## Who Was Jesus? — Divine versus Human

understanding of Jesus. The Chalcedonian Formula could not have made those bold statements about the Son's divinity if the iota had been allowed to remain.

One final point that comes out of this statement is that *Jesus was human*—period. And *Jesus was divine*—period. In the above words, the distinction in natures is in *no way* annulled by the union. We do not have to say that Jesus was *fullyhumanandfullydevine* as if they had to be fused together. They both are true, but the Chalcedonian Formula insists that one does not in any way qualify the other. They are both true, just as if you were a woman and a doctor, you don't need to say I am *fullydoctorandfullywoman* (This is a very limited analogy that cannot be pressed too far.). Each of those characteristics can stand alone and still be completely true. Here is the point. The people who cannot separate them fall into one of the classic traps about Jesus—that Jesus was some sort of "combo" man who combined both divine and human characteristics such that he was neither "fish, fowl, nor good red herring" as the folks in Maine might say—he was neither truly ("fully") human nor truly ("fully") divine.

At this point we all may be thoroughly confused about what it all means. What we know is that Jesus was human just like you and me, and he was God just like, well, God. But he struggled, and wept on the one hand, and he cleansed the lepers and cast out demons, and healed the sick and raised the dead on the other. He bled, and suffered, and died on the one hand, and he walked on water, and turned water into wine and was resurrected from the dead on the other. If the former set of characteristics are clearly related to his humanity and the latter set clearly relate to abilities that are outside normal human behavior, how do we reconcile the two sets of characteristics:

First, the Church early on, related the second set to his intimate relationship to his Father. Gradually this intimate relationship was seen as reflecting the nature of God himself. We call the nature of God which includes the Son and the Holy Spirit, Trinitarian theology. In this way of thinking, if God, by definition, is divine, then the Christ, who is the second person of the Trinity is divine. But how can Jesus be both human and divine?

## Kenosis – the Blind Trust

In order to make sense out of this, Paul is of tremendous help here.

> Let the same mind be in you that was in Christ Jesus, who, though he was in the form of God, did not regard equality with God as something to be grasped, but *emptied himself*, taking the form of a slave, being born in human likeness.
> And being found in human form, he humbled himself and became obedient to the point of death—even death on a cross. *Philippians 2:5–8*

This *emptying* is the key that unlocks the whole *Incarnation*. It is so important that the Greek word for the "emptying," *kenosis*, is still in use among theologians to discuss this issue.

Our understanding of the *kenosis* or emptying is important for two reasons. First, it tells us that there were certain qualities of God of which the Son emptied himself or gave up temporarily, and second, it tells us what happened to those qualities while Jesus was in his earthly ministry. This again is one of those critical areas of doctrinal development that had to be shaped and honed in order to arrive at a clear understanding of Jesus. If the divinity of Jesus participated in all the qualities of the Godhead, then these qualities would include omnipotence, omniscience,

## Who Was Jesus? — Divine versus Human

and omnipresence. But if he was fully human and was not simply pretending to be limited by that human nature, then the *kenosis* is the key. How can he both have his cake and eat it too?

A good way to think of this emptying process is to think of what happens to a wealthy industrialist when he or she accepts an appointment into public office. To avoid the possibility of a conflict of interest, the appointee must put her stocks into "blind trust." She still owns the stocks, but during the time in office, she has no use of them, no control over them. This is the idea behind the *kenosis*. Jesus possesses all the qualities of the Godhead, but during his ministry on earth (the Incarnation), he has no ability to use them (on his own authority). To be very specific, Jesus was not superman. He could not leap tall buildings at a single bound. He could not stand at one end of the basketball court (if there had been one) and turn around, close his eyes, throw the ball over his shoulder backwards and make a basket, "nothing but net." If golf had been around, he could not have made a hole-in-one every time he hit the ball. He had the same human limitations as you and I have. This is orthodox doctrine.

So, if this is true, how did he do all the miracles? How did he walk on water? How did he raise Lazarus from the dead? Remember our guideline: he was human just like you and me except for sin. Using this rule, we have two choices. One is that he really didn't do the miracles. Many liberal writers today would assert this. The stories are nice fairy tales that reinforce our delusion about a nice God who only wants to comfort us. A second is that you and I are intended, in our humanity, to do those same miracles. Remember, Peter walked on water until his faith started to wain (Matthew 14:29–30) and raised Dorcas from the dead (Acts 9: 36–43). The answer is the latter, but we will spend much more time on this later. Consider the following:

> "Truly, truly, I say to you, he who believes in me will also do the works that I do; and greater works than these will he do, because I go to the Father."
>
> *John 14:12*

This is just one more pointer that binds Jesus and his words to us. Clearly, he intends for us to look and act like he did. But how did he act. Or, more precisely, how did he *function*? The important thing is to know that the incarnate emptied Jesus operated just as he said he did.

> "I can do nothing on my own authority; as I hear, I judge; and my judgment is just, because I seek not my own will but the will of him who sent me."
>
> *John 5:30*

> "The words that I speak I do not speak on my own authority; but the Father who dwells in me does his works."
>
> *John 14:10*

While in his earthly ministry, he does everything through the authority of the Father. It is not simply that he *does* nothing but he *can do* nothing on his own authority. It is not only that he speaks words and does works but that it is the Father who speaks and does. It is not easy to fit all this together neatly, but what we can say, at this point, is that there is an essential collaboration between Father and Son that allows the Son to operate outside the bounds of normal human behavior. In other words, if the Father wants the basketball to travel around the world twice and then go through the basket, nothing but net, and if Jesus is a willing, obedient instrument of the Father, then orthodox doctrine says *nothing but net*. This we would call a *miracle*. If he were playing golf, he couldn't even hit the green if he hadn't practiced—unless the Father wanted that ball to go in the hole in one stroke through the Son and the Son were the willing, obedient instrument of the will of the Father, then the ball would go in the hole every time, and that's called, you guessed it, a *miracle*. There are certainly confusing passages of Scripture that imply that Jesus could do whatever he wanted on his own independent authority. This is why doctrinal development has to clarify some things. The central question before us, however, is how does this collaboration take place?

## Prayer

One of the most interesting, compelling and often overlooked aspects of Jesus was his prayer life. The Church has always been challenged to understand his intimate relationship to his Father and how this could have resulted in extraordinary knowledge and miraculous activity. Thomas Aquinas postulated that Jesus experienced a perpetual state called the *beatific vision*, which gave Jesus an immediate face-to-face access to the Father—the kind the rest of us will have in heaven. Unfortunately, many consider such a capability to be outside the bounds of normal human behavior. That leaves us with three choices: accept it at face value and simply ignore the inherent problems it raises, discount it outright, or adjust the meaning of the beatific vision to suit a more humanly compatible understanding. There is, however, another approach that is centered on the prayer life of Jesus. The following Scripture is important:

> But he withdrew to the wilderness and prayed.
> *Luke 5:16*

> Then Jesus went with them to a place called Gethsem'ane, and he said to his disciples, "Sit here, while

I go yonder and pray." And taking with him Peter and the two sons of Zeb'edee, he began to be sorrowful and troubled. Then he said to them, "My soul is very sorrowful, even to death; remain here, and watch with me." And going a little farther he fell on his face and prayed, "My Father, if it be possible, let this cup pass from me; nevertheless, not as I will, but as thou wilt." And he came to the disciples and found them sleeping; and he said to Peter, "So, could you not watch with me one hour? Watch and pray that you may not enter into temptation; the spirit indeed is willing, but the flesh is weak." Again, for the second time, he went away and prayed, "My Father, if this cannot pass unless I drink it, thy will be done." And again, he came and found them sleeping, for their eyes were heavy. So, leaving them again, he went away and prayed for the third time, saying the same words.
*Matthew 26:36–44*

Rejoice always, *pray constantly*, give thanks in all circumstances; for this is the will of God in Christ Jesus for you. *1 Thessalonians 5:16–18*

While the last passage is from Paul admonishing the Thessalonians to pray constantly, we can assume that Jesus himself would not have fallen short of this standard. If we combine these three pieces of Scripture with the two above, we get a clearer picture of how Jesus *functioned*.[69] Consequently, we can assert unequivocally that he prayed constantly, went away sometimes

---

[69] At this point we might want to be so bold as to suggest we are developing what we might call a "functional Christology"—one that relates intimately the way Jesus functioned to the way he calls us to function.

## Who Was Jesus? — Divine versus Human

to pray without distraction, and prayed always to discern the will of his Father. In other words, we can ascribe to the will of the Father any extraordinary knowledge or miraculous capabilities displayed by the Son.

Here is the key. While me might assert that the Son *possessed* all of the divine characteristics, he had use of them only in as much as they were in accord with the will of the Father. Notice that he says here that he "can" do nothing on his own authority. In other words, he is limited as you and I are unless the Father wishes him to transcend those limitations. We call these instances *miracles*.

There is one important distinction we might want to make here. While many might think that all authority was given to Jesus at conception, or birth or at baptism, after which time he really operated autonomously,[70] we would like to assert here a different model that we will call *dynamic obedience*. In this concept, Jesus is in continual intimate relationship with his Father through prayer, listening for his will, and operating accordingly. Most of the time, and this is really important, he is operating out of his own human limitations. Most of the time, the Father says to the Son, "Play the Game." This is precisely what the Father says to the Son in the Garden of Gethsemane. Play the cards that were dealt you as a human being subject to the very same fear and frustration and pain and suffering as the rest of your human brethren would experience under the same circumstances.

Finally, we should assert that the particulars of the exchange between Father and Son are certainly unique and a pure mystery. While we assert that the prayer is of the same nature as our own

---

[70] We actually have the following Scripture passage that points specifically in that direction: "And Jesus came and said to them, "All authority in heaven and on earth has been given to me" (Matthew 28:18). This is one more example of why doctrinal development is so important.

prayer, that it functions exactly as our prayer functions, the content of that exchange is the very nature of the mystery of the Incarnation. In fact, we might say that we have simply shifted the mystery in such a way that we relate more intimately to the way he functioned without removing the fundamental mystery of his relationship to his Father.

## Free Will, Temptation and Sin

Here is another important point. Jesus struggled just like the rest of us. Here we are guided by an important piece of Scripture:

> For we have not a high priest who is unable to sympathize with our weaknesses, but one who in every respect has been *tempted as we are, yet without sin.*
> *Hebrews 4:15*

In our discussion of sin we started with the definition as being based on the Greek word hamartia—to miss the mark. In this context we should understand temptation as being pulled from the mark and sin is the process of yielding to that pull. Think of a circular weight scale. One may grab the scale and gradually pull the needle off of the zero mark and then let go, at which point the needle returns to zero. This would be our metaphor for temptation. If we were to plop a stone in the scale and the needled off the zero mark and stayed there, that would be our metaphor for sin. The question we are asking is twofold: Was Jesus tempted as we are, did he sin, and what is the role of free will in the process?

The first thing we should say unequivocally is that Scripture and orthodox Christology asserts that he was indeed tempted as we are. We see this in the desert after his baptism and we see the struggle in the Garden before he was crucified. He was pulled by hunger and he was pulled by the dread of a hideous death. The second thing that we see is that he did not yield to these temptations. He did not sin. What we need to understand about all this is that, because of the continuum of temptation and sin, he does understand sin. Remember this, if someone offers you a cow pie to eat, you are not tempted. You are only tempted by those things that some part of you is crying out for. In other words, if you were to tell him of the trouble you are having with sin, he would know exactly what you are talking about. That is the profound importance of this bit of the Letter to the Hebrews. In fact, the Catholic Church has morphed this statement into an even more radical one that we will see later: "like us *in every way*, yet without sin." If this is indeed true that he must make decisions while being tempted, we need to understand the role that free will played in that process.

This process of being tempted and making a choice not to yield implies that he had free will, just like the Father and just like you and me. Therefore, he could have said "no" to his own call to be the savior of the world. In the scene in the Garden of Gethsemane, he struggles with the prospect of a painful sacrifice. If he could not have said "no," his "yes" would have been meaningless. In other words, he could have said, "I think this is just too hard and too painful. I think I will do something else." But how he chose to live his life was in the perfect service to the will of the Father.

While all orthodox theologians would agree that Jesus had free will, some would argue, and I think rightly, that he "could not" have said "no" because it was contrary to his nature. What we mean by "could not," however, needs to be nuanced. Just as you or I "could not" commit some heinous crime that is totally contrary to our personality or values, Jesus operated within a framework that guided his thoughts, words and actions. This framework, as it should be for us, is predicated on the will of the Father. If you or I were to describe some awful crime that would make your skin crawl, we would say that it is not "in us" to do that—and I hope we would be right. But we are still *free* to. It is that kind of fundamental freedom that God has, that Jesus had, and that we have. Our consent to the will of the Father always is offered in the context of a possible refusal. It is that latter possibility that give meaning to the former.

While we have been talking mainly about Jesus' power and the nature of physical miracles, there is another whole issue concerning his knowledge that must be addressed.

## Ignorantists

In addition to the issue of omnipotence, we are challenged by the issue of omniscience. The question this raises is whether Jesus knew everything because he was God. Early in the debate concerning the nature of the Incarnation was the problem of Jesus' ignorance. Many who tended toward the divine (docetic) side of the equation had a hard time thinking of Jesus as being ignorant about anything. Others felt that his humanity demanded a certain level of natural ignorance. Certainly, there are plenty of incidents in which he exhibits unusual knowledge, especially in the following passage when he is talking to the Samaritan woman at the well.

> Jesus said to her, "Go, call your husband, and come back." The woman answered him, "I have no husband." Jesus said to her, "You are right in saying, 'I have no husband'; for you have had five husbands, and the one you have now is not your husband. What you have said is true!" The woman said to him, "Sir, I see that you are a prophet." *John 4:16–19*

Here it appears that Jesus is all knowing, but what may be going on is that his extraordinary knowledge comes from the Father.

In other words, this is a *miracle* that takes place by the will of the Father and the willingness of the Son.

Those who believed that Jesus' humanity implied a certain level of human ignorance were disparagingly called *ignorantists*. Consider, however, the following:

> "But concerning that day and hour no one knows, not even the angels of heaven, nor the Son, but the Father only.
> *Matthew 24:36*

Clearly the Son is saying that there are things that even he does not know. Today orthodox doctrine would insist on this kind of ignorance. In other words, we orthodox Christians are *ignorantists*. Jesus did not know what an integrated circuit was; he didn't know anything about World War II or the atomic bomb or computers or the internet or smart phones. Now he certainly did know human nature and about the propensity of humanity to create amazing things and to get itself into deep messes. In that sense he was not only the Son of God, but he was the greatest of all prophets. In other words, many Jews are correct in saying that Jesus was a great prophet. This is true. What we as Christians believe, however, goes far beyond that. The way toward that understanding has everything to do with the nature of the Holy Spirit.

## The Holy Spirit

The role that the Holy Spirit played in the life of Jesus is one of the ongoing conundrums regarding *who Jesus was* and *how he functioned*. In fact, these two questions may have quite different answers. They center around the difference between Trinitarian theology and Incarnational Christology. We can thank one of our past US presidents for saying that everything in question hinged on "what the meaning of *IS* is."[71] This is actually very true. Unfortunately, the verb *to be* is so very versatile that it can be confusing as to just exactly what we mean when we use it. We might say that who Jesus *was* is related to where he came from, how he was "constructed," what was his purpose, and how he operated. The Church has focused on the first three and has left the fourth as a kind of mystery. In the previous section on Prayer, we talked about this question explicitly and suggested that he operated through an intimate prayer relationship to his Father. Here we are concerned about the role of the Holy Spirit in his life.

First, we should point out one particular challenge. If Jesus was fully divine and possessed all the characteristics of his divine nature but was limited in their utilization, what was the need for the Holy Spirit? This question is really easy to ignore because we already have a sense of our own indwelling of the Holy Spirit. We talk about Christians being "Spirit Filled" and have no particular trouble intuiting the meaning. In the controversies of the early Church, however, it became important to assert that Jesus was not simply *filled with the Holy Spirit* as the prophets were. It was important to state that what was going on with Jesus was more than that. On the other hand, we have Scripture that points directly to some sort if indwelling. Here are some important pieces of Scripture in this regard:

> And Jesus, full of the Holy Spirit, returned from the Jordan, and was led by the Spirit for forty days in the wilderness, tempted by the devil. And he ate nothing in those days; and when they were ended, he was hungry. *Luke 4:1–2*

---

[71] Bill Clinton during interviews regarding sexual impropriety.

## Who Was Jesus? — Divine versus Human

> In those days Jesus came from Nazareth of Galilee and was baptized by John in the Jordan. And when he came up out of the water, immediately he saw the heavens opened and the Spirit descending upon him like a dove; and a voice came from heaven, "Thou art my beloved Son; with thee I am well pleased."
> *Mark 1:9–11*

> Jesus said to them again, "Peace be with you. As the Father has sent me, even so I send you." And when he had said this, he breathed on them, and said to them, "Receive the Holy Spirit. If you forgive the sins of any, they are forgiven; if you retain the sins of any, they are retained."   *John 20:21–23*

What we will suggest here is that there is a difference between who Jesus was and how he operated. Who he was was the Second Person of the Holy Trinity who assumed a human nature and took on human flesh. That is pure orthodoxy. On the other hand, how he operated was as a human being. How can we make sense of this? One way is to see the indwelling of the Holy Spirit as a model for the relationship between his own divinity and his own humanity. We will see more on this in the next chapter. Suffice it to say that he is *functioning* just exactly like he expects you and me to function. He prays in the Spirit just like he expects you and me to pray in the Spirit. His obedience to the Father is a result of allowing the Spirit to function within him just like he expects us to allow the Spirit to function within us. How that actually worked for him *in its essence* is clearly a mystery, but what we can depend on is that he is *functioning* just exactly how he expects us to function. The product of the Spirit's functioning within him as the Son of God may be uniquely related to his role as Son and Savior, but the mechanism is the same as it is for the rest of us. In other words, if he is functioning in a way that is essentially different from the way we function, the way we function is not saved. We will see how this works next.

## Traps

Why are these points important? What you will find from a detailed study of the history of the doctrinal debates is that great issues turned on some very subtle points, like the iota. What the Church Fathers found was that, if some of the suggested ideas had been adopted and carried to their logical conclusion, what you ended up with was something that was clearly contrary to apostolic teaching. In other words, there were traps lurking beneath the surface of each of the early heresies. The Church Fathers could see the implications of hedging, for example, on Jesus' humanity. Their formula was summed as follows:

> *Quod non est assumptum, non est sanatum.*
> **Jesus cannot save what he has not assumed.**[72]

In other words, he cannot be the savior of humanity unless he is human himself. This is a powerful guideline and has led the Church through many sticky issues. To suggest that Jesus was not fully God is to suggest that there was more than Jesus—that Jesus was not the full story. As Christians, this would be a vast inconsistency. How can we say that Jesus is the perfect model for humanity, the final answer, the only savior of the world, and at the same time imply that there might be something better or different? On the other hand, to suggest that he was not fully human, implies that he really does not relate to us. The whole

---

[72] This is essentially the argument of St. Anselm in "Cur Deus Homo." The Latin is literally, "What is not assumed, is not healed." It is from Gregory of Nazianzus.

## Who Was Jesus? — Divine versus Human

point of the Incarnation is that "he became man." He became one of us to show us what we were supposed to look like.

Finally, it might be instructive to quote one of the clearest statements of the way Jesus functioned. It comes from the *Catechism of the Catholic Church*:

> The Son of God. . . worked with human hands; he thought with a human mind. He acted with a human will, and with a human heart he loved. Born of the Virgin Mary, he has truly been made one of us, like to us in all things except sin.[73]

It is so very easy to drift into docetism as we start to think of Jesus acting independently from the will of his Father. This quotation is rather radical in its clarity.[74] But according to everything we have said so far, this is the very definition of orthodoxy. During the Incarnation, Jesus worked through his humanity. The individual Peter saw in front of him was a man—flesh and blood.

Having stressed the implications of Jesus' humanity in this chapter, in the next chapter we will spend much more time on the question of Jesus' divinity.

---

[73] *Catechism of the Catholic Church* (Vatican City: Libreria Editrice Vaticna, 1997), Paragraph 470, 119 (quotation from Austin Flannery, O.P., ed. *Vatican Council II, Volume 1, The Conciliar and Postcondiliar Documents* (Northport, New York: Costello Publishing Company, 2004), *Gaudium et spes*, paragraph 22:2, 923).

# 9
# How Was Jesus God?

While we have been discussing the way in which Jesus was both fully human and fully divine, up to this point we have been stressing his humanity as something that is not well understood. Now let us turn to his divinity. It was clear from the Nicene Creed and the formula of the Council of Chalcedon that orthodox Christians are to believe explicitly that *Jesus was God*—more specifically God incarnate. In other words, Jesus as the Son is the second person of the Trinity, which expresses the true nature of the Godhead. Again, we are faced with the topic of the Trinity, about which a great deal has been written and around which much controversy has swirled. We can at least assume that it is one of the great mysteries and treasures of the Christian faith. How, then, can we get to the core of Jesus' "divinity," without getting tangled in the complexity of Trinitarian theology? Let me approach it this way. Take the following phrase from the Nicene Creed:

> For us and for our salvation
> he came down from heaven:
> by the power of the Holy Spirit
> he became incarnate from the Virgin Mary,
> and was made man.

We often might try to think about some decision-making process that took place in heaven. The directional reference seems to lead to this question. In reality, we don't know exactly how it took place in the *mind of God*. What the *kenosis* says, however, is that once the Son "became incarnate," he had access to his divine characteristics in a very different way. He no longer was all powerful, God's omnipotence, and no longer had access to the mind of God, God's omniscience. What this state of affairs leads us to is one of the most puzzling questions that has challenged Christians from very early on. What did Jesus understand about himself?

More specifically we would like to know whether Jesus was fully aware of his own divinity. This is actually a good question. If by "fully" you mean that he understood his divinity as the Father, who was and is omniscient, understood it, then the answer has to be *no*. He "gave up" the omniscience of the Son by the *kenosis,* which was the basis of the *Incarnation.* But let's be clear, he knew all that was possible for a human to know and still not have the perfect and all-knowing *mind of God.* So, what did that look like? To answer this, we should look at some of the scriptural passages that relate to what Jesus said about himself and what he allowed others to say about him while he was in their presence. This is important, because we are about to make a strong distinction between what was said and thought *by* Jesus and what the Apostles and the later Church said and taught *about him* after he was physically gone.[75]

## What Jesus Said About Himself
Clearly, the question concerning what Jesus said about himself and what he meant by what he said are two different questions.

"The Father and I are one." *John 10:30*

---

[75] Remember, we are taking Scripture at face value—that it is true, at least at some level. There is a huge debate regarding how much of New Testament Scripture is historic fact and how much is simply a reflection of a belief system that grew up around an historic figure.

"I am the resurrection and the life. Those who believe in me, even though they die, will live, and everyone who lives and believes in me will never die."
*John 11:25–26*

"Before Abraham was, I am." *John 8:58*

"I am the light of the world. Whoever follows me will never walk in darkness but will have the light of life."
*John 8:12*

"If I am not doing the works of my Father, then do not believe me." *John 10:37*

"Do you not believe that I am in the Father and the Father is in me? *John 14:10*

"I am the way, and the truth, and the life; no one comes to the Father, but by me." *John 14:6*

Again the high priest asked him, "Are you the Christ, the Son of the Blessed?" And Jesus said, "I am; and you will see the Son of man seated at the right hand of Power, and coming with the clouds of heaven."
*Mark 14:61–62*

Thomas answered Him, "My Lord and My God!"
*John 20:28*

All of these statements imply a profound knowledge of who he was. Even though there are all sorts of ways to explain these in terms of a Jewish understanding, there is no question that he knew enough to do the work he was given to do. For Jesus to call

## How Was Jesus God?

himself the Son of Man, or the Son of God, implies an extremely intimate relationship with both humanity and the Father. For him to say that he is "one with the Father" in the Hebrew sense of the atonement or at-one-ment, is precisely what all Jews sought. Where is he stating something that is so clear as to be only interpreted as his saying, "I am God." The most compelling is, "Before Abraham was, I am." It cryptically refers to the name of God—I am who I am—to refer to himself. This has to mean that he had some deep level of understanding of his relationship to the Father. How did he know all this? Again, we must assert that he knew this because it was revealed to him through his intimate prayerful relationship to his Father. Remember what happened at his Baptism:

> And when Jesus was baptized, he went up immediately from the water, and behold, the heavens were opened and he saw the Spirit of God descending like a dove, and alighting on him; and lo, a voice from heaven, saying, "This is my beloved Son, with whom I am well pleased." *Matthew 3:16–17*

If we read this carefully, we see that this revelation is not to everyone present at Jesus' baptism but to Jesus himself. As far as we know this was a private revelation. As such, it must be seen as a model for all revelation from his Father concerning his divinity and his call. If this is indeed true, we have a model for all of his knowledge about himself. He knows as much as the Father wants him to know. In other words, we are not burdened with the need to construct a complex speculative Christology that explains his knowledge. As a model for you and me, Jesus seeks the will and knowledge of the Father and waits in obedience for that which the Father wants to impart.

This all seems pretty straightforward, but where is the wiggle room. Consider the following:

> You heard me say to you, 'I go away, and I will come to you.' If you loved me, you would have rejoiced, because I go to the Father; for the Father is greater than I. *John 14:28*

All of a sudden, we have some tension between statements that drive his understanding of his divinity to the highest level and then a statement that subordinates himself to the Father. What is going on? For our own purposes, we must make a distinction between Trinitarian theology and Incarnational Christology. The former addresses the relationship of the Son to the Father within the Trinity and the latter addresses the relationship of the Son to the Father during the Incarnation. Orthodoxy asserts that the Son and Father are coequal within the Godhead. At the same time the Son, during the Incarnation, is obedient to the Father. Somehow the Church had to sort out which statement went to which doctrinal system. Without this distinction, we would have had a complete muddle.

The one statement that is unquestionably the most powerful statement in all Scripture is made by the one who doubted. Thomas gets a bad rap sometimes because he needed proof that the man before him was indeed the risen Lord. But even in the context of this doubt, he is also the only one who speaks the powerful words, "My Lord and my God." Thomas gets it in a way that no one else articulates. What we get from this statement is that at some point in the early Church, it became abundantly clear, whether from the lips of Thomas or otherwise, that Jesus was to be taken as God.

But let's be clear about the circumstances surrounding this statement. It takes place after the resurrection, when Jesus is in some form that allows him to transcend some of his purely human limitations. He is in transition. Before the resurrection he is still limited by the *kenosis*. He is still fully human. This is the Jesus we are most concerned with here. As far as Jesus is concerned, he is indeed the Son of God whose intimate relationship with the Father allows him to operate within the perfect will of the Father. As we have already said, he performs miracles not on his own authority but as the perfect instrument of the will of the Father. This he understands clearly and articulates repeatedly.

Before we go any further, notice the source of all but two of the quotations sited above. They are all from the Gospel of John. The power of this Gospel is that its author is describing a dimension of Jesus that the others did not fully articulate. John takes us to a much deeper level in our understanding of the divinity of Jesus. Certainly, there are scholars who would argue that Jesus never made the statements attributed to him in John. This really doesn't matter to us here, because we are assuming whatever the Church asserts. If John says that Jesus said it, then we will go with that.

Finally, we see that Jesus is saying some very radical things about himself, and of course upsetting a bunch of people in the process. You can imagine, if you were a pastor and some guy showed up saying "I am the way," the pastor would probably be both troubled and threatened. The obvious conclusion would be that at least this person was disruptive, speaking utter blasphemy, and probably delusional. It is no wonder that the Pharisees were worried. We might ask precisely the same question the Pharisees asked, "Where do you get off saying these things?"

## A Speculation

Here I am going to postulate something that I think is perfectly in accord with orthodoxy, as we will see in a minute. Imagine that you are born with a special purpose, as we all are. It just happens that your purpose is to be the savior of the world. You are not all-knowing, so you have to work out your own calling, just as all we humans have to work out our own special calling. (We will come back to this theme again in the next chapter.) You look around and see that the world is in a mess. You struggle mightily with the monumental possibility that you have a unique calling. As we all do, with all the best-intentioned humility, you too deny it, and push it away, and make excuses. You say to yourself that this simply cannot be true.

But God keeps tugging at you. God keeps prodding you and poking you. And finally, you come to the crystal-clear God-given conclusion that *you are the one*. You don't *have* to be the one. It would be wonderful if there were another, but there isn't. By the way, you come to this conclusion in your thirtieth year. If you had come fully to this conclusion earlier, the disruption you will cause would have started earlier. But it took thirty years either for this clarity to crystalize or (which may be the same thing) for you to hear the clear message from the Father that "now" is the time.

So you step out in faith. To others it looks like immense ego to say the things about yourself you do, but you say them because you believe them to be true. As you step out, it becomes clearer and clearer. The words of the prophets of old are coming true simply because what the prophets spoke was the truth, not some forecasting of something that will happen in the future, but a truth that has always been true before the foundations of the world. As you live into your purpose, as you surrender every fiber of your body and mind and soul, amazing things start to happen; the raising of the dead, the walking on water, the healing of the sick. You see that what is going on through you is in fact the salvation of the world. And yet, even in the Garden of Gethsemane, you struggle with the ultimate call, the ultimate fulfillment of your purpose. But you know that the path you began, based upon the call of the Father, is the only path you can take now. To deny that path is to die the horrible death of separation from God. So, you place one blessed foot in front of another to complete the work that has been prepared for you to do.

Now, granted, this is all speculation. But I contend it is orthodox speculation. Everything he said and did was consistent with this imaginary story. Everything the Church asserts about him is consistent with this story. Now let's look at some other statements made *about him*.

## What Was Said About Him

Note that the first pieces of Scripture were the letters to the Gentile communities written by Paul. Then the Gospels were written. In other words, the letters of Paul and the Gospel of John are written from a vantage point that is somewhat removed from the actual events themselves. The writers, consequently, have the advantage of some time to process and formulate an understanding of the Christ event that the Apostles, as they were living it, did not. We might expect, therefore, a more refined understanding, and that is what we get. So, what is said *about* Jesus often takes a leap from what he said about himself. At least it takes his pointers and develops them more fully. Here are some passages:

> In the beginning was the Word, and the Word was with God, and the Word was God. He was in the beginning with God; all things were made through him, and without him was not anything made that was made. In him was life, and the life was the light of men. The light shines in the darkness, and the darkness has not overcome it. *John 1:1–5*

## Into the Perfect Likeness

> Therefore God has highly exalted him and bestowed upon him the name which is above every name, that at the name of Jesus every knee should bow, in heaven and on earth and under the earth, and every tongue confess that Jesus Christ is Lord, to the glory of God the Father. *Philippians 2:9–11*

> No one has ever seen God; the only Son, who is in the bosom of the Father has made him known.
> *John 1:18*

> Who, though he was in the form of God, did not count equality with God a thing to be grasped, but emptied himself, taking the form of a servant, being born in the likeness of men. *Philippians 2:6*[76]

I had a conversation with a friend some years ago who had been troubled considerably about the validity of his faith. He said that he had come to the conclusion that the Church had *made* Jesus God, as if to say this somehow invalidated the divinity of Jesus. In all honesty, I think to some extent he is correct. Yet at the same time, I believe he has misconstrued the power of the Church as the body of Christ to continue the work of Christ, including the clarification of the meaning of Jesus himself. As we see from the passages above, "John"[77] and Paul both take their

---

[76] This particular quotation, from the RSV, translates the Greek word "harpagmon" (related to "snatching") as "grasped," (or snatched at) This is a much better rendering of the idea of attachment than the NRSV word "exploited," which seems a bit too rational and loses its spiritual content.
[77] I have put quotation marks around the name John, because the authorship of most of the Gospels is considered by most scholars to be often complex. It is of no particular consequence here except that we may want to recognize ever so slightly that we understand this fact.

understanding of the Christ event to new depths. This, in fact, is the first instance of *doctrinal development*. From the perspective of the life, death, resurrection, and ascension, the Church has continued to develop its understanding of just what it meant by saying that Jesus was God incarnate.

To illustrate how difficult it has been for the Church to clarify the meaning of the statement "Jesus was God," I would like to discuss briefly a couple of valiant attempts.

## The Human Face of God

The first is by a bishop of the Church of England, John A. T. Robinson, who was considered by many to be rather heretical in his efforts to demystify Christology for the average Anglican. The second is by Philip Turner, a professor of ethics at General Theological Seminary, an Episcopal seminary in New York City. One of the reasons why we are looking at Anglican writings is that Anglicans are not "constrained" by a unified understanding of orthodoxy. In other words, they feel more comfortable thinking outside the box—a box we would call traditional historic orthodox doctrine.

Robinson's main Christological work was entitled *The Human Face of God*. The first valuable thing he does is to set out the issues he is addressing and, in doing so, establishes the importance of doing the work of Christology. Knowing who Jesus was is central to our work as Christians. Then he tries to put what he is going to say in some perspective.

> Churchmen and professional theologians who know what they are looking for will be ready with their stickers to label my position 'reductionist,' 'adoptionist,' 'humanist' and the rest. I believe in fact that they will be wrong and that it is none of these

things. For I fully share their concerns—yet doubt if these can be matched by the old orthodoxies.

On the other side there will be incredulity that serious men can still spend their time grubbing around the old holes. The question is not so much, *How* do we speak today of 'the humanity and divinity of Christ', or his historicity, his sinlessness, his uniqueness, his finality, or his 'full, perfect and sufficient sacrifice, oblation and satisfaction for the sins of the whole world'?,[78] as *Why*?[79]

... Christians must, as I see it, be prepared to work through and out the other side of the traditional questions, if they are to be liberated to contribute Christologically to the secular debate—if they are not, that is, to be hung up with quite inadequate Christ-answers to the great human questions of our day. For if they are so hung up, they will not be able to be more than humanists or theists who insist on 'bringing in Jesus', rather than men who see all things, political, aesthetic, scientific and the rest, in Christ and through Christ.[80]

I give you this so that we can be fair to him. He is clearly concerned about the same things that Jesus was concerned about. "How do I tell the *good news* of the Kingdom of God in a way that the people I am talking to will understand?" But right off the bat we see the tension in Robinson's own mind between the "old

---

[78] This can be found in the Episcopal *Book of Common Prayer* (1979) on page 334.
[79] John A. T. Robinson, *The Human Face of God* (Philadelphia: Westminster Press, 1973), viii-ix.
[80] Ibid., ix.

orthodoxies" and the "traditional questions" over and against the need for a contemporary language that has the power to draw us back to the true Christ. Of course, let me assert here that what we are about is demonstrating that those "old orthodoxies" are still the foundation of our faith. We just haven't understood them clearly. But this is getting ahead of ourselves.

Robinson's Chapter 7 is entitled "Man for All." Here he brings together his central thesis that Jesus is for us the representative of God on earth. Here is how he develops this idea.

> According to the New Testament Jesus is the man of God, the son of God, God for us, precisely as he is not the man for himself, but the man for others, the man for all: he is the representative man, who dies—and lives for all [2 Corinthians 5:14ff]. He is the universal man, the final man, the man for all space and all time.[81]

So far this is wonderful, powerful language that is certainly true. Let's see where he goes with it.

> [We discussed previously] how fundamental to Jesus' vocation and how firmly grounded in the gospel tradition is his claim, not indeed to replace God, but to represent him, and that it is this relationship, rather than any divine blood in his veins or peerless human perfection, that constitutes his claim to uniqueness. Yet Jesus is not exclusively the Christ, as if he personally and individually constituted the entire 'Christ-event'. For the New Testament indeed he is unrepeatable: there is no other foundation. Like God

---

[81] Ibid., 212.

he cannot be replaced, but like God he can—and must—be represented. For just as God is to be seen, known and received in those who represent him, whether in the disciples who act in his 'name' or in his nameless brothers. For, in words attested in varying forms in the strongest possible combination of gospel sources. . . 'He who receives you (or, whom I send, or one of these little ones) receives me, and he who receives me receives not me but him who sent me' [Matthew 10:40]. By this identification Jesus makes himself as dependent on them as God has made himself dependent on Jesus. For this is what incarnation means: 'God' is en-manned, represented by man. And the double pattern of representation shows that this is not finished and over with, but a continuing reality.[82]

For Robinson, Jesus was the human face of God, God's representative. Well, that is true, at least. He is clearly concerned that our contemporary understanding of Jesus is inadequate to the task of his being a powerful transformative force in our modern society. This is probably true, *de facto*. But unfortunately, he ascribes this inadequacy to "old orthodoxies," or old ways of thinking about the meaning of Jesus. Orthodoxy certainly would support Robinson's contention that "representation" is something that happened in the Incarnation. And he is correct in suggesting that the Incarnation is something that happened in history. As we have said, "Jesus was." But he seems to be missing the fact that orthodox Christology goes much further. He may be missing some "ontological" issues (having to do with *being*) that orthodoxy contains. I would suggest here that it is Robinson's

---

[82] Ibid., 213–4.

understanding of orthodoxy that may be incomplete. But he does point us in an interesting direction when he says, "Jesus is not exclusively the Christ." Unfortunately, the way in which this might be construed to be true is not at all clear. If he is not to be dismissed and treading on very dangerous ground, he would have to offer a much more in-depth treatment of just what he means. In any case he has taken his best shot at making the Incarnation central to one's Christian beliefs, and for this he is admirable. Many of us are content to settle for ignorance in place of risking the almost inevitable mistakes associated with striving for new insights. His book could be a prime example of fools rushing in where angels fear to tread. If we can treat Robinson with some generosity, it may be the very same generosity with which we are called to treat Paul, Augustine, Kazantzakis, and especially Fletcher.

## The Deep Structure of God

Another attempt to clarify the nature of Jesus in contemporary terms is Philip Turner. In his book *Sex, Money & Power*, Turner looks at the "deep structure" of society, God, and Jesus. What he identifies as this deep structure concerns the concepts of *love* and *gift*.

> Perhaps the universal phenomenon of gifts points to what we can dare call both a law of our nature and a law of society. In both an individual and communal sense, to *be* is to *give*, *receive* and *return*; not to be is to refuse such engagements.[83]

---

[83] Philip Turner, *Sex, Money & Power* (Cambridge, Massachusetts: Cowley, 1985), 16–7.

Through the life, death and resurrection of Christ, Christians believe God has made known not only how he is related to the world, but also who he is. Christ makes manifest not only the nature of God's activity, but also the nature of God's inner life. In the terms of classical theology, in Christ both an economic[84] and ontological[85] Trinity are revealed. In Christ we believe God to be Father, Son, and Holy Spirit, One God, in himself and in relation to the world. Since Christians believe that all people are created in the image of God, the revelation of God's inner life is of first importance if human nature is to be adequately understood. The key to an adequate anthropology lies in what has been made known about divine nature. What Christians believe to have been revealed about God's life is summed up in the doctrine of the Trinity.[86]

Unlike Arius, Athanasius thus believed dependency to be a part of the divine life. This dependence, however, is not one of imperfection—it is "begotten" by love, and in love the dependent Son gives back all that he is given to the Father. All that is given is returned. God thus [loves][87] and is love. His inner life eternally is one of giving, receiving and returning,

---

[84] How it reveals itself in history.
[85] What it is in its very being.
[86] Ibid., 17.
[87] The text uses the word "lives." I think it must be a misprint, if the sentence is to be consistent with Turner's theme.

and all this takes place in and through the Spirit. Between Father, Son, and Spirit there is coinherence, a total presence, a giving, receiving, and returning.[88]

The deep structure of God—Father, Son, and Holy Spirit—is the gift of love expressed in a perfect presence and a complete giving of the gift of self, a total receiving of the total gift, and a complete returning of that gift. This is reflected in the relationship between the three persons of the Trinity and is reflected in the life of Jesus and his relationship to the Father. According to Turner, Jesus shows us the "deep structure" of God and in so doing shows us the activity as well as the inner life of God. In the Hebrew sense, he could therefore be called a son of God, implying that he finds his source in and is shaped by God. But not only does he show us something by his actions as a son of God, but we believe as Christians that it is his nature to do so as the unique "only begotten" Son of God. Turner sees in the Christ event the fact that the Father gives of himself to his Son, Jesus receives that gift from his Father and then returns it to the Father through his love and obedience. Thus, for Turner Jesus *is* God, not only because of orthodoxy, but also because Turner sees in the life of Jesus the deep structure of God as Turner has defined that deep structure.

Both of these authors have tried very hard to give Jesus meaning for a cynical and skeptical world, and they have shed some valuable light. Robinson saw Jesus as one who showed us the face of God's love, mercy, and compassion through his humanity. Turner went a bit deeper and saw how the very nature of God in the Trinity has the deep structure of giving, receiving and returning and saw that same deep structure not only in how Jesus related to his Father but also how he related to us. If our search

---

[88] Ibid., 18–9.

for orthodoxy has any significance at all, we should assert that any attempt such as these must be grounded in orthodoxy. This is crucial. It is certainly true that Jesus is "the human face of God." And it is certainly true that he also exhibits and embodies the "deep structure" of God. The question is whether these explanations are sufficient in and of themselves. We all need to be well grounded in our "old orthodoxies" if we are to gain value from such thoughtful and often very helpful fresh looks at the nature of Jesus and specifically what we mean when we state without any glibness that "Jesus was God."

## The Meaning

If we are to understand better the meaning of the statement that Jesus was God, we must look carefully at a little exchange between Jesus and other Jews that follows his description of the "Good Shepherd."

> "My sheep hear my voice. I know them, and they follow me, I give them eternal life, and they will never perish. No one will snatch them out of my hand. What my Father has given me is greater than all else, and no one can snatch it out of the Father's hand. The Father and I are one.
>
> The Jews took up stones again to stone him. Jesus replied, "I have shown you many good works from the Father. For which of these are you going to stone me?" The Jews answered, "It is not for a good work that we are going to stone you, but for blasphemy, because you, though only a human being, are making yourself God." Jesus answered, "Is it not written in your law, 'I said, you are gods'? If those to whom the word of God came were called 'gods'—and the Scripture cannot be annulled—can you say that the

## How Was Jesus God?

one whom the Father has sanctified and sent into the world is blaspheming because I said, 'I am God's Son'? If I am not doing the works of my Father, then do not believe me. But if I do them, even though you do not believe me, believe the works, so that you may know and understand that the Father is in me and I am in the Father." *John 10:27–38*

This passage is typical of many such passages that the writer of John uses to express a deep understanding of the intimate relationship between Jesus and the Father. It is really to John that we owe the emphasis on and clarification of this relationship. First, Jesus is asserting to the Jewish leadership his authority to give eternal life. (That must have gotten them going!) They know that only God can give eternal life. Then he really drives home the relationship between himself, his followers, and the Father. If one were really paying attention, as certainly the temple leaders were, it would be noted that he slides seamlessly back and forth between his "hand" and the Father's "hand." This disturbing intimacy was clear enough right from the start, but then he really frosts the cake by stating unequivocally, "The Father and I are one." This drove them berserk. Picking up stones, they intended to kill him for a second time.

It would be useful again to emphasize what the Hebrew meaning of "oneness" was. To do this let me refer to Martin Scorcese's film rendering of Nikos Kazantzakis' novel *The Last Temptation of Christ*.[89] In it Scorcese has Jesus saying, "I and the Father are one and the same." Oops! This is certainly not what Jesus said, as stated in Scripture, and certainly not what he

---

[89] Martin Scorcese, director, *The Last Temptation of Christ*, Universal Studios, 1988, based on Nikos Kazantzakis, *The Last Temptation of Christ*, Simon and Schuster, 1960.

meant. In Judaism, "oneness" was the goal of all Jews' relationship with their God. The holy day called the Feast of the Atonement was simply the day in which good Jews reoriented their lives toward the life of God in order to return to a relationship of oneness with God. For a Jew, oneness meant to be "in accord with."[90] If this was the goal of all Jews, to be at one with God, then why should they be totally derailed by Jesus saying that he was in that relationship. They too should have been in that relationship. Somehow, they sensed he was saying more—much more. Or it could be, as we even find today among Christians, that they had lost the deep understanding of their own faith.

Finally, we see that Jesus was assuming a Hebraic understanding for this radical relationship with the Father. Here he was referring to Psalm 82:6, which some modern translations render as "judges" of Israel. The actual term used is *elohim*, which is another word for divine beings, gods, or God. The idea was that those who were tasked with the responsibility of speaking in God's stead or, in other words, pronouncing the "word of God," were called divine, or gods. What was meant was not "gods" in the Greek sense, but more of the idea of oneness with God.[91] So Jesus is reminding the Jews that they already have a precedent for such an intimate relationship. He asserts that his language is not blasphemy, if the things that he has done and the words he has spoken have indeed been "of" the Father.

---

[90] This whole discussion is centered on the Jewish celebration of Yom Kippur, what we translate to be the Day of Atonement. Clearly the intention of this day was to repair the relationship between man and God. More can be found on the importance of this concept at https://www.hebrewversity.com/deeper-hebrew-meaning-yom-kippur/.

[91] More on the use of the word *elohim* can be found at http://bibleq.net/answer/6730/.

## How Was Jesus God?

There is an interesting shift here, however. They are criticizing him for "making himself God" while he says that he is calling himself "God's Son." It seems clear that they equated the two. To be the Son of God was to *be* God. I am sure they had not worked out the theological implications of these statements. All they knew was that he was going too far.

It is clear that Jesus intended for us to understand several things about himself:

1. He was at one with the perfect will of the Father.
2. Therefore, He did nothing on his own authority, but from the authority of the Father who sent him.
3. When you saw what he did and heard what he said, you saw the actions and heard the words of the Father.
4. Given this intimate relationship with the Father, it follows from the Hebraic understanding that Jesus was "God's Son."
5. While he was not continually stressing his uniqueness, the Gospel writers, Paul and the Church, through a process of doctrinal development, clarified, tightened, and narrowed the meaning from God's Son in its broadest sense to "the only begotten Son" and further to an essential aspect of God in the Trinity, and ultimately to, well, God.

It is important that we understand that both Scripture and tradition are essential to our understanding of Jesus. We have two parts to consider. First, whom did Jesus think and say he was, and second, whom did others —including the Church — think and say he was. When we say, "Jesus was God," we are plumbing the depths of the mind of God, and no one on earth is able to do that completely, not even the incarnate Jesus. What we do know is that the way Jesus was God is not trivial. It is the great mystery of the Incarnation. And while we certainly have not done the topic justice in this chapter, I hope I have opened up some wondrous possibilities.

# 10
# Who Was Jesus? Particular vs. Universal

We have discussed Jesus' humanity and his divinity, and we have tried to create some clarity concerning the relationship between the two. I want to return to his humanity in this chapter and discuss two important aspects of that humanity that we need to get straight. Jesus was a particular man in a particular time, and yet we say that we are called to be like him in some way. Therefore, we need to make a distinction between the "particulars" concerning this particular man and the universal characteristics of this man that are available to all of us. What I want to do first is to consider a host of hypothetical "particulars," so we are well grounded in the idea that Jesus was indeed a "particular" man.

## Jesus – a Particular Man
We might start by giving some scriptural passages that point to some particular qualities.

> ... the thong of whose sandal ... *John 1:27*

> Jesus looked ... *John 1:38*

> "Is this not Jesus, the son of Joseph, whose father and mother we know?" *John 6:42*

> Jesus began to weep. *John 11:35*

# Into the Perfect Likeness

> ... he stretched out his hand and touched him ...
> *Matthew 8:3*

All of these references point to a particular man with particular attributes. What size were his feet? What shape? What color were his eyes? Could they have been hazel, like mine? Did he have "perfect" vision—20/20? Did he look like his mother? How did he weep? Like me? What were his hands like? Could they have been like mine? These questions prime the pump, one which can tap into an entire wellspring of unanswerable questions, but questions that have the potential of drawing us closer to him—much closer.

Now we can outline a few additional particular things that we know about him. First, he was a man. This is the best and most obvious example of a particular. He was Middle Eastern so he probably was of dark complexion with dark hair. Because folks back then were not as tall as we are today, in general, he probably was not tall by today's standards, maybe 5 ft. 4 in. He was a carpenter, so his hands probably were thick, muscular, and probably rough, at least until he began his ministry.

We don't get many "personality" traits, but we might make up some that would be consistent with someone whose very nature was to give themselves totally to us. He was probably delightful to be around—not dour. Thoughtful and certainly prayerful, but not introspective in the sense that those around him felt cut off from him. He was bright, but we don't know his IQ. Let's say it was 125. We might assert this because we want to make sure we proclaim that one does not have to be a genius to be perfectly one with the Father. His feet probably were not large, but because he did not have the benefit of orthopedically designed shoes, his feet were probably wide from all the walking around, let's say a 7E if he were being fitted today in the United States.

# Who Was Jesus? — Particular versus Universal

**A Meditation**
Now that we have begun to be a bit fanciful, let's imagine for a moment that we were talking to Peter about him. What might Peter have said?

> Do I remember? How could I forget one tiny detail of his being. It is funny you should ask, because no one usually is interested in such details. But I remember. He had a great smile, but it was a little crooked, especially when he lost control in laughter. I remember once we were walking toward Galilee, and he stubbed his toe on a rock. We had just been talking about how God was protecting us all from harm, and then he kicked this big stone. Instead of being angry, he began to laugh as he hopped around on one foot holding the other. As we all started to laugh too, we started one by one to sink to our knees in hysteria. I don't think we ever laughed as hard as we did that day. I don't know what it was, but it was like we all were washed by the wonder of truth and love. We also used to kid him about being a bit knocked kneed. So was Matthew, so they would defend each other, saying that it was an advantage for cracking nuts or some foolishness.
>
> Sometimes in the evening if we were alone some would start to toss around a small stone. Gradually this would develop into a kind of game to see how long we could keep it going without dropping it. He wasn't very good at it and would often be the first to drop the stone, but he was great fun to play with. He always loved it when one of us would make a particularly spectacular catch. Oh, how we would laugh when we would play that silly game with no particu-

lar point. I also remember that he was quite a scrapper, and would try his best, often sacrificing his body to try to make a good catch. A couple of times we all were a little worried that he had hurt himself, but he would jump up, brush himself off and be back at it—full bore. The only time I saw a frown on his face was when someone would start to get selfish and the tenor of the game would start to change. We knew that *he knew* that something precious was slipping away from us, and he would not let that happen.

He had short stubby fingers, not very pretty as hands go, but their touch was, well you probably already know something about that. He had a great appetite, but he was pretty lean. He must have had a pretty high metabolism because when the rest of us would be putting on weight, he would stay as slim as ever. Food? Well, he didn't care for what I think you call Brussels sprouts. Every so often someone would cook up a mess of sprouts just to see him squirm. He never complained, but we chuckled as he grimaced ever so slightly as he mixed them in with the other food on the plate. We also knew that James couldn't stand them either, so we would give both of them a big serving until we got a good reaction, and then someone would have mercy on them and take part of their share.

Of course, you could go on and on. Writing this little piece was actually a wonderful experience, as it resulted in a feeling of intimacy that we often miss in our Sunday or daily worship. You should try it. Just put yourself in one of the apostle's place and write away. The point is that Jesus was a real person with a complete complement of particular attributes just like you and me.

# Who Was Jesus? — Particular versus Universal

**The Last Temptation of Christ**
One of the most interesting attempts to fill in some of the blanks about Jesus is the book by Nikos Kazantzakis, *The Last Temptation of Christ,* to which I referred in the last chapter. Just as the exercise above in our little imaginary conversation with Peter had the potential to be quite fruitful, Kazantakis, in his Prologue, relates the same kind of experience. For us to appreciate what is going on in his story about the struggle of Jesus, we first need to appreciate the deep Christian spirituality that was driving the author.[92]

> The dual substance of Christ—the yearning, so human, so superhuman, of man to attain to God or, more exactly, to return to God and identify himself with him—has always been a deep inscrutable mystery to me. This nostalgia for God, at once so mysterious and so real, has opened in me large wounds and also large flowing springs.
>
> My principal anguish and the source of all my joys and sorrows from my youth onward has been the incessant, merciless battle between the spirit and the flesh.
>
> This is the Supreme Duty of the man who struggles—to set out for the lofty peak which Christ, the first-born son of salvation, attained. How can we begin?

---

[92] In fact, Kazantzakis, a Greek Orthodox, was excommunicated for this work, which was also banned by the Roman Catholic Church. I hope you might see the precious value in this devout Christian's effort, however flawed, to paint a stunningly real picture of a particular man's struggle with his universal "calling" to be the Savior of the world.

> If we are to be able to follow him we must have a profound knowledge of his conflict, we must relive his anguish: his victory over the blossoming snares of the earth, his sacrifice of the great and small joys of men and his ascent from sacrifice to sacrifice, exploit to exploit, to martyrdom's summit, the Cross.
>
> I never followed Christ's bloody journey to Golgotha with such terror, I never relived his Life and Passion with such intensity, such understanding and love, as during the days and nights when I wrote *The Last Temptation of Christ*. While setting down this confession of the anguish and the great hope of mankind I was so moved that my eyes filled with tears. I had never felt the blood of Christ fall drop by drop into my heart with so much sweetness, so much pain.[93]

Now I am not suggesting that Kazantzakis is a model of orthodoxy. If his story had been a Christological treatise, he would have had to have been a little more careful, or at least include a few explanatory notes. There are two things that we want to get from his testimony. First, we can trust that the author is a devout Christian with a deep spiritual yearning. Second, he is willing to step out on a limb in terms of *particulars* in order to experience more deeply the *universals*. He is bold, but not necessarily unorthodox. He was highly criticized when the book first came out, but he may merit our own generosity—he was courageously tackling a daunting challenge.

---

[93] Nikos Kazantzakis, *The Last Temptation of Christ* (New York: Simon and Schuster, 1960), 2. Used by permission, Simon and Schuster, New York. All rights reserved.

## Who Was Jesus? — Particular versus Universal

Here are a couple of passages that can serve as an example for us. Let me warn you that this may seem very foreign to you. It is certainly not a rehash of Scripture. As you read, think of your own struggles and then try to imagine what kind of monumental struggles the Son of God must have experienced. We are talking about the struggles of the Savior of the world. Kazantzakis is trying to express this amazingly powerful, earth-shattering, foundation-shaking struggle.

> He sat up on the wood shavings and propped his back against the wall. A strap studded with two rows of sharp nails was hanging above his head. Every evening before he slept he lashed and bled his body so that he would remain tranquil during the night and not act insolently. A light tremor had seized him. He could not remember what temptations had come again in his sleep, but he felt that he had escaped a great danger. "I cannot bear any more; I've had enough," he murmured, raising his eyes to heaven and sighing.[94]

The picture of a young man struggling in such a strange way with the demons that attack him relentlessly is not exactly orthodox, but what is interesting is how any of us might try to express Jesus' wondrous struggle. Could it be that what he saw as a struggle against sin, (which is the way Kazantzakis puts it) was in fact the perfect will of the Father? Can you imagine telling Jesus of your struggle against sin and have him look at you blankly and say he really couldn't relate? He is the one who relates to our struggles at a deeper level than any other person. How does one understand how he gets there? This is what Ka-

---

[94] Ibid., 13–4.

zantzakis is dealing with here, and if you allow him some doctrinal latitude, he writes an incredibly bold meditation on the unknowable particulars concerning the Son of God.

    Jesus took a long stride and entered the house. He saw Matthew next to the lamp, still holding the open notebook on his knees. He stopped. Matthew's eyes were closed; he was still submerged in all that he had read.
    "Matthew," said Jesus, "bring your notebook here. What do you write?"
    Matthew got up and handed Jesus his writings. He was very happy.
    "Rabbi," he said, "here I recount your life and works, for men of the future."
    Jesus knelt under the lamp and began to read. At the very first words, he gave a start. He violently turned the pages and read with great haste, his face becoming red and angry. Seeing him, Matthew huddled fearfully in a corner and waited. Jesus skimmed through the notebook and then, unable to control himself any longer, stood up straight and indignantly threw Matthew's Gospel down on the ground.
    "What is this?" he screamed. "Lies! Lies! Lies! The Messiah doesn't need miracles, He is the miracle—no other is necessary! I was born in Nazareth, not in Bethlehem; I've never even set foot in Bethlehem, and I don't remember any Magi. I never in I my life went to Egypt; and what you write about the dove saying 'This is my beloved son.' to me as I was being baptized—who revealed that to you? I myself didn't hear clearly. How did you find out, you, who weren't even there?"

"The angel revealed it to me," Matthew answered, trembling.

"The angel? What angel?"

"The one who comes each night I take up my pen. He leans over my ear and dictates what I write."

"An angel?" Jesus said, disturbed. "An angel dictates, and you write?"

Matthew gathered courage. "Yes, an angel. Sometimes I even see him, and I always hear him: his lips touch my right ear. I sense his wings wrapping themselves around me. Swaddled in the angel's wings like an infant, I write; no, I don't write—I copy what he tells me. What did you think? Could I have written all those miracles by myself?"

"An angel?" Jesus murmured again, and he plunged into meditation. Bethlehem, Magi, Egypt, and "you are my beloved son": if all these were the truest truth . . . If this was the highest level of truth, inhabited only by God . . . If what we called truth, God called lies . . .

He did not speak. Bending down, he carefully gathered together the writings he had thrown on the ground and gave them to Matthew, who wrapped them in the embroidered kerchief and hid them under his shirt, next to the skin.

"Write whatever the angel dictates," Jesus said. "It is too late for me to . . ." But he left his sentence unfinished.[95]

I don't know what you think about this, but I think this is precious—almost too holy for us to appreciate without a lot of help from the Holy Spirit. Like so much that is holy, we need

---

[95] Ibid., 391–2.

to *handle with care*. He has in a few lines addressed one of the most puzzling paradoxes of the Christian faith. Where did the information come from that formed the basis of the Gospel writings, information that was not witnessed directly by the writers? Again, let me stress that Kazantzakis knows what he has written is not "true" in a worldly factual sense. What he has written is a meditation on Scripture that is full of magnificent tension, struggle, spirituality, enlightenment, absolute commitment to the "truth" in an eternal sense, and a wondrous willingness to see the truth of God as transcending the truth of the world.

**Just as We Struggle**
He paints a picture of Jesus as one who is pulled by facts just as you and I are, yet is supple in the arms of God's often paradoxical truth as you and I are called to be. To get to the place where there was no untruth in him he had to struggle just like you and I struggle, first to identify the truth in a world full of untruth, and then to surrender to that truth and all the consequences that accompany that surrender. All we have to do is look at our own lives and see the many times each day we hedge on the truth to please a boss or friend, or the many times we participate in the untruth of the world simply because it is easier.

As we start to recognize these slips, we also start to appreciate just how hard the struggle can be to be fully in the truth. What we must see is that, if Jesus were here talking with us today, and if we alluded to our struggles, he would not look at us blankly as if he were totally puzzled. We have to believe that he would say, "Yes, I know exactly what you mean." This is orthodox Christology—and it is crucial that we get it.

**Trying and Choosing**
There are two aspects of any individual human being's behavior that are useful to be pointed out in the case of Jesus, since they are usually overlooked: trying and choosing. What, you say?

## Who Was Jesus? — Particular versus Universal

Yes, I said, *trying* and *choosing*. Let's take *trying* first. We all try to do things. We try to open the pickle jar. If it is hard to open, we turn it over and bang the lid on the counter. Can you imagine Jesus doing that sort of normal, everyday trying? We try to remember where we left the keys and ask if anyone has seen them. Can you imagine Jesus doing that sort of normal, everyday trying? We try to scratch an itch right in the middle of our backs and ask someone to scratch it for us. Can you imagine Jesus saying to Peter, "Peter, can you give me a scratch right in the middle there? Ah, yes, a little higher, yes, ah, right there. Ahhhh. Perrrfect. Thanks a lot."

In addition, let's consider the possibility that Jesus might actually play a game. In our little meditation above, this scenario was actually painted. How could he try his best in a game, if simply by wishing something to be done, it was automatically done? There has to be room for trying to do his best in a game without omnipotence getting in the way. In other words, we are asserting that most of the time the will of the Father is, "Play the game." Open the jar with the normal strength you have, try to remember with the normal memory capacity you have, scratch the itch with the normal arm length you have and play the game with whatever normal athletic ability you have. If these kinds of exercises are totally foreign to you, as they probably are for most folks, you probably have not really come to terms with his real, normal, everyday humanity with all the particular characteristics that we all have.

The second challenge is one of *choosing*. We somehow get the picture from Scripture that Jesus has made up his mind about what to do and when to do it without any real effort. It almost looks like he is a kind of autonomous miracle worker—until we get to the Garden of Gethsemane. Recall the passage from Matthew in the section on Prayer two chapters ago. In it, clearly Jesus is struggling mightily first to discern the will of his Father and then to submit to the horrific consequences of the decision

## Into the Perfect Likeness

to follow that will. We have other instances where choice seems to pop up. At the wedding at Cana, Jesus is talking with his mother about the need for more wine:

> On the third day, there was a marriage at Cana in Galilee, and the mother of Jesus was there; Jesus also was invited to the marriage, with his disciples. When the wine gave out, the mother of Jesus said to him, "They have no wine." And Jesus said to her, "O woman, what have you to do with me? My hour has not yet come." His mother said to the servants, "Do whatever he tells you." Now six stone jars were standing there, for the Jewish rites of purification, each holding twenty or thirty gallons. Jesus said to them, "Fill the jars with water." And they filled them up to the brim. He said to them, "Now draw some out, and take it to the steward of the feast." So they took it. When the steward of the feast tasted the water now become wine, and did not know where it came from (though the servants who had drawn the water knew), the steward of the feast called the bridegroom and said to him, "Every man serves the good wine first; and when men have drunk freely, then the poor wine; but you have kept the good wine until now." This, the first of his signs, Jesus did at Cana in Galilee, and manifested his glory; and his disciples believed in him. *John 2:1–11*

What is interesting about this passage is the exchange between Mary and Jesus in which he actually changes his mind. He has a choice to make, and he waffles. If our model of prayer is accurate, he is in the process of discerning the will of his Father and comes to the conclusion that the will is to change the water into wine. If we extrapolate this kind of situation to every miracle he does, what we see is a man constantly making choices based on his understanding of the will of the Father. But recall one important aspect of this process: most of the time the Father tells the Son, "Play the Game." Make choices based on love and truth but make them without any extraordinary input from the Father or extraordinary access to your own divine characteristics.

We have been a bit bold in our speculations concerning the particular aspects of a Middle Eastern man who live a real life in what we now call the first century. Whether or not what I or Kazantzakis wrote is historically factual, the sum total of the message is profound. We all must be willing to couch Jesus' story in a host of particulars in order to get at a host of universals. We must be willing to be bold in our insistence on a picture of Jesus that is not fuzzy and fluffy, but rather one that is concrete and real. A picture of a man who would have talked with you, and walked with you, and shared his life with you as he allowed you to share your life with him. A man who is so concrete to you, you can start on the journey to *be transformed into the likeness of him* for others. We start with a highly particular crystal-clear picture of a particular man so that we might distill from that picture the universal qualities that have been made available to all of us. What are those qualities? Where do we look for them?

## Jesus – the Universal Man

This, in a sense, is the easiest and at the same time the most difficult part to write. We all know that Jesus was loving and kind, strong and brave, etc. What is challenging is to say something that is not trivial. What I want to discuss are a few characteristics that we may not associate with him, but which may be keys to our understanding of his overall character and the challenges we face to be like him. Here we will assert that he was transparent, self-giving, truthful, and therefore, totally loving in ways that were certainly confusing to those who encountered him.

**Transparent and Self-giving**
First, let us recall another phrase that Flip Wilson as Geraldine used to say: "What you see is what you get." I think that Jesus would say, "What I am is the perfect truth, I show it all to you, and I give it all to you." In other words, "What you see is what you get, and I give it all to you." When he says, "I am the way, the truth, and the life," what he is saying, in essence, is, "I will show you the truth, and this is the way of life. I will hold nothing back from you. I will show you all of who I am, and I will give you all of who I am."

This essential connection between transparency and gift tells us much about the human possibility. What would it look like for us to be completely transparent? As we will see later, there is some good news and some bad news. The good news is that transparency makes possible precious encounters with other folks that both delight and bless. The degree to which we are willing to show ourselves may be the degree to which we allow others to show themselves to us. This kind of transparency is tied directly to an ability to trust others and to make it possible for others to trust us. This trust, that becomes a foundation for transparency, results, by its very nature, in a gift of self.

We may spend much of our lives in some form of relationship with those around us, but it is only as we enter into trusting, transparent relationships that we begin actually to offer ourselves to others. If there is one characteristic that we Christians would all attribute to Jesus it is that he offered himself to those around him. It is hard to see this in the particulars of his daily life, because we just don't have any clear evidence, but his death on the cross has become the ultimate symbol of a gift of self.

## Who Was Jesus? — Particular versus Universal

> Greater love has no man than this, that a man lay down his life for his friends. *John 15:13*

This willingness to suffer for others to the point of death offers us an indelible image of a total gift of self, but the link with trust and transparency may be more important to us in our daily lives. Since few of us will be called freely to make the ultimate sacrifice, we will depend on a more accessible understanding of the self-gift. The day-to-day opportunities we have to be transparent must be modeled on what we believe was a universal characteristic of Jesus as he interacted with the Apostles and with others with whom he came in contact.

Here we might make an important distinction between *doing* for others and *being* for others. The first sense is usually what we associate with servanthood, a willingness to spend our time, energy and other resources in the service of others. But Jesus goes much further than this. His very being is an offering for us. It is for us that he exists, that his very being becomes the model for our lives. We often think of the daunting task of doing for others all the time. Those who spend their entire lives in this way often do this out of some form of unhealthy obsession. In fact, we should spend some time doing for ourselves—eating, sleeping, playing, studying, sunbathing, etc. It is the second sense in which we are called, just as Jesus was called, to *be* for others—to have a posture that is constantly open to others and offers others who we are in relationship, with a full measure of transparency and good will.

This gift of self and the willingness to receive the same gift from others is so fundamental to our Christian journey it must be elevated to an essential universal characteristic of Jesus. As Turner might say, this giving, receiving, and returning of self is the deep structure of God. It is also the deep structure of Jesus Christ. It is only by participating in the life of Christ that we learn how this universal characteristic can be reflected in our own lives.

**Truthful and Loving**
What does it mean for Jesus to live in the truth and be the man of love at the same time? First let me assert a relationship between truth and love. Jesus said the two great commandments were:

> "'You shall love the Lord your God with all your heart, and with all your soul, and with all your mind.' This is the greatest and first commandment. And a second is like it: 'You shall love your neighbor as yourself.' On these two commandments hang all the law and the prophets." *Matthew 22:37–40*

I contend that there is a flipside to the love commandments that takes you to the same place. If love of God has to do with loyalty and obedience, then the way of truth, that itself is of God, is precisely the way that is in accord with the will of God—a way of loyalty and obedience. In other words, Jesus could have just as easily said, "Do not lie and do not participate in the lies of others. These are the two great commandments. On these hang all the law and the prophets." The point here is that there is no love without truth, and there is no truth without love. A "fact" spoken in self-serving anger is not truth from God's perspective. "Love" applied in the context of "lie" is not true love from God's perspective. So the Kingdom of God is the place where truth and love are not only *indistinguishable,* but also are *the same thing*. If you have trouble grasping this possibility, you are in good company. We are talking about God here, and paradoxes and puzzlements are common fare.

Let me relate a little story to illustrate. One day I was talking with the branch manager of my bank when the new-accounts manager, Margaret, came up and offered us some candy. She was a wonderfully generous ample black woman who clearly enjoyed her food. The branch manager thanked Margaret for her generosity, but I, with a wry smile, suggested that Margaret was not being generous; she just wanted an excuse to eat some candy herself. At that point we all started to laugh almost hysterically. Margaret first knew that I adored her (both she and I thought she was my second mother), and second, that what I had said was absolutely true. In that brief moment, the Kingdom of God touched down in that place, sort of like a little funnel cloud. At that moment love and truth merged, and the utter joy of the experience was clear to the three of us.

So, Jesus is the one who lives a life in which love and truth are inseparable. When he is denouncing the Pharisees or in the Temple chasing off the moneychangers, this is clearly truth, but it is also profound love. As we grow in our understanding of how Jesus shows us how love and truth work themselves out in his life, we learn how love and truth can work themselves out in our own lives.

There is a funny movie that came out in 1979 with Peter Sellers and Shirley MacLaine entitled "*Being There.*" It is about this simple-minded gardener (Sellers) named Chance who all of a sudden finds himself on the street after his employer and guardian dies. Through the course of events, he reaches a high and revered status as a close friend of a very wealthy industrialist's wife (MacLaine). She has the amazing ability to see what she wants to see and ignore all the signals that point to Chance's true character. She wants to see a towering intellect of kind and gentle nature, and she does. When he tells her blandly that his name is "Chance the gardener," she assumes that he is saying "Chauncey Gardiner." The whole hilarious movie is an endless series of these flips in interpretation.

There are two characteristics of Chance, however, that speak to our subject. First, he is totally transparent. What you see is exactly what you get. Second, he lives completely in the truth, as he is able to see it. There is a complete absence of guile. These are *universal* qualities available to us all. What is absolutely stunning is the scene at the end of the movie. (I hate to give away the punch line.) As he is being mentioned as a possible presidential candidate (the height of absurdity), he blandly (as always) walks to the edge of a pond on the Industrialist's estate (staged at the Biltmore Estate in Ashville, North Carolina), gently ministers to a sagging pine sapling (he is a gardener, remember), and proceeds to *walk out on the water*.[96] What in the world? What does that mean?

We are left with a stunning question for the author, Jerzey Kosinski. Was he telling us that Chance was not as dumb as we were led to believe, or was he saying that perfect wholeness and integrity (we call this the Christ) is reflected in the one who is fully transparent and lives completely in the truth—and it has nothing whatsoever to do with one's IQ. As Kazinsky states at the end of the movie: "Life is a state of mind." If we are right, that state of mind has something to do with transparency and truthfulness—and not IQ. If this is, indeed, true, then Chance has a stunning lesson for us. The nature of Jesus is available to all of us no matter how "simple" we might be from a worldly perspective. God is using a totally different set of measures. Consequently, Chance, the complete dope, may be perfectly Christ-like by God's measures. What Chance shows us is that the life of truth does not depend on one's stature, accomplishments, or intellect. Rather, the life of truth is accessible to anyone, at any time—even Chance.

**Tough Love**
There is one thing about love that we can point out here that is not always obvious until we look at Jesus. It has to do with what

---

[96] *Being There*, United Artists, 1979.

we now call "tough love." We think that tough love was invented as a modern response to alcohol and drug dependency as a way for parents and friends to deal lovingly but effectively with the particularly refractory problem of addiction. In fact, God has used tough love on his people from the very beginning, and there is no better example of this brand of love than many of the things that Jesus said and did. The temple scene is a prime example.

> Then Jesus entered the temple and drove out all who were selling and buying in the temple, and he overturned the tables of the moneychangers and the seats of those who sold doves.  *Matthew 21:12*

An important response to the question, "Did Jesus love the moneychangers?" is "Of course he did!" He knew that their true life depended on his driving out the untruth that was associated with their activities. Another example is the "woe to you speech" when he rails at the Pharisees.

> "Woe to you, scribes and Pharisees, hypocrites! For you lock people out of the kingdom of heaven. For you do not go in yourselves, and when others are going in, you stop them. Woe to you, scribes and Pharisees, hypocrites! For you cross sea and land to make a single convert, and you make the new convert twice as much a child of hell as yourselves.
>
> "You snakes, you brood of vipers!
> *Matthew 23:13–15, 33*

Ouch! The exclamation points in the quotations above clearly indicate that the translator thought he was railing. This tirade goes on for the entire chapter—39 verses of blasting. Is this love? Yes. He knows that as long as the Pharisees are captured by the untruth reflected in their attitudes and practices, they do not have access to the life of God. What we find is that, if we really want to know what the universal quality of love looks like, we need to look at Jesus. Sometimes love will look warm and generous, and sometimes it will look aggressive and confrontational. The challenge for us is to find and express the love of God at the core.

This love is not necessarily easy to define, let alone live out, but it clearly has to do with a willingness to give and receive trust, to offer and receive real transparency, and to live into the truth wherever it may lead. As Jesus admonished us many times, the world will not always understand the nature of this love and will often be intolerant of its message and its effects, but the transformation into one who reflects the transparency, truth, and love of Christ is the only agenda for Christians.

# 11
# How Does Jesus Open the Door for Transformation?

We have discussed the fall of humanity from innocence as represented in the story of Adam and Eve. The apostolic tradition establishes the fundamental problem of our life here on earth as one of separation from what we were intended to be—from the very beginning. However you interpret the story, we are still left with the same result—we spend the majority of our lives in modes of behavior and thinking that take us nowhere but into further confusion and disconnectedness. We have assumed to this point that God's nature and Jesus' Incarnation have had something to do with the solution to this dilemma. Our first assumption is that we could not solve the problem by ourselves. We needed some form of intervention (recall the difference between therapy and exorcism in Chapter 6) by God to help us return to God.

## Formulas of Salvation

The Church has developed over the last two millennia a number of formulas that address the solution, all of which involve the salvational work of the man Jesus of Nazareth. What we call the Good News in Jesus Christ is precisely the idea that, through Jesus, the fracturedness originally created at the *fall* is mended in Jesus. Just exactly what the Church says about the mechanism for this mending is the subject of this chapter.

The salvation formulas that have been developed are based on the understanding of the Apostles and the resulting biblical writings, which open the door for us to move from a state of separation from God to a state of oneness with God. Let's start

## Into the Perfect Likeness

with some scriptural passages that will point us in the right direction.

> But he was wounded for our transgressions.
> *Isaiah 53*

> "Here is the lamb of God who takes away the sin of the world!" *John 1:29*

> ... God put forward as a sacrifice of atonement ...
> *Romans 3:21–26*

> In him we have redemption in his blood.
> *Ephesians 1:3–14*

> ... without the shedding of blood there is no forgiveness of sins. *Hebrews 9:22*

> ... ransomed ... with the precious blood of Christ ...
> *1 Peter 1:18–21*

> But if anyone sin, we have an advocate with the Father ... *1 John 2:1–6*

> ... through him God was pleased to reconcile to himself all things ... *Colossians 1:15–20*

> Therefore, just as one man's trespass led to condemnation for all, so one man's act of righteousness leads to justification and life for all. *Romans 5:18–19*

How Does Jesus Open the Door for Transformation?

> For since death came through a human being, the resurrection of the dead has also come through a human being.
> *1 Corinthians 15:21–22*

> Though he was in the form of God, did not regard equality with God as something to be grasped, but emptied himself, taking the form of a slave, being born in human likeness. And being found in human form, he humbled himself and became obedient to the point of death—even death on a cross.
> *Philippians 2:6–8*

There are two themes expressed here: one explicit and one implicit. In the first, the sacrifice of Jesus on the cross is seen in the same way that all sacrifices were viewed in the Hebrew context. Such sacrifices were made to *atone* for some transgression against God, in other words *sin*. Here the Good News is that the reparations have been made for our sins so that our relationship with God might be restored. The other implicit theme is the *Incarnation* as reflected in Paul's amazing understanding of Jesus in Philippians. Here Jesus is seen as the God-man, the very manifestation of restored humanity. He brings to us the reality of that restoration at the moment of his conception. One is restoration by his *action* that culminates in the Crucifixion, and the other is restoration by his very *being* that is the very nature of the Incarnation. Of course, the first is meaningless unless the second is true. And one might even say that the second is meaningless unless the first is true. In other words, one cannot separate the *Incarnation* from the *Cross,* or the *Cross* from the *Incarnation*.

What are some of the words we use to describe this saving work? Some have slight shades of meaning that can help to inform our understanding of some of the subtleties of how the Church has understood this work of Jesus. *Redemption* means the same thing that it means to the pawn broker. If I pawn my watch because I need some money, I can redeem my watch, or get it back, if I pay the money back and clear the debt. Through the death and resurrection of Jesus, we are *redeemed* by the God-man Jesus back to God by the payment of the debt incurred by the fall. *Salvation* implies that we are in a sorry state, and the work of Jesus is to rescue us from that state, in exactly the same way a lifeguard might save someone who is drowning. *Atonement* is simply the result of being restored to a life of oneness with God that was intended for us in the beginning.

It is interesting to consider the difference between the emphasis placed on one or the other of these themes by the Latin (Roman Catholic) traditions as contrasted with the Greek (Eastern Orthodox) traditions. Consider Figure 1.

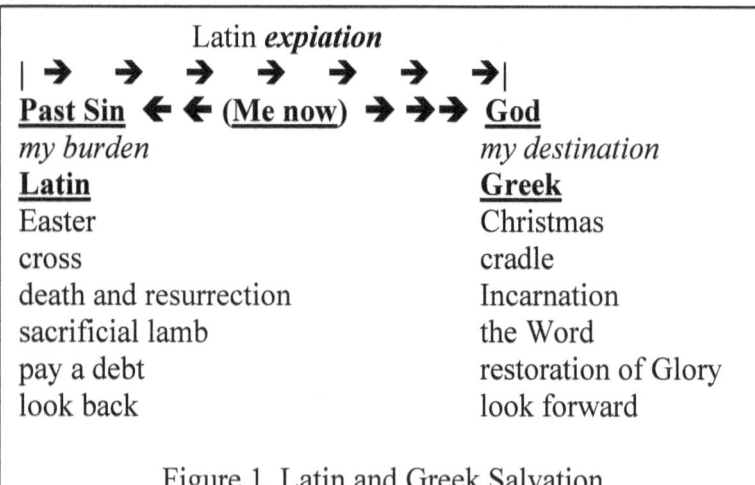

Figure 1. Latin and Greek Salvation

Please know that this is a huge simplification that I hope will at least encourage us all to see how these two themes relate to one another. In the Latin tradition, out of which arose the

How Does Jesus Open the Door for Transformation?

Protestant understanding, Easter is the central salvational event. Paul stresses the importance of the cross.

> For Christ did not send me to baptize but to proclaim the gospel, and not with eloquent wisdom, so that the cross of Christ might not be emptied of its power.
> For the message about the cross is foolishness to those who are perishing, but to us who are being saved it is the power of God.
>
> ... but we proclaim Christ crucified, a stumbling block to Jews and foolishness to Gentiles, but to those who are the called, both Jews and Greeks, Christ the power of God and the wisdom of God.
> *1 Corinthians 1:17–18, 23–24*

For Paul the crucifixion of the Messiah is the central aspect of God's loving act of redemption. Here, Paul and the Latin tradition that flows from his Christology would say that Jesus is the perfect *expiation* for our sins. In other words, he has mended the chasm between ourselves and God incurred by our guilt. As the diagram implies, the Latin tradition would stress the idea that I must go back and take care of past sin before I can move toward the life God intends for me. Since I cannot accomplish this on my own, Jesus' death on the cross becomes the sufficient payment or expiation for that past sin.

Another idea is that my past sin has angered God and, in order for me to make up for this error, I must find some way to make God happy. I must find some way to appease God. This is what we mean when we say that Jesus was the perfect *propitiation* for our sins. Here the sense is that, through Jesus' death on the cross, God's anger is satisfied. All of these ideas indicate that the Latin tradition tends to place a bit more emphasis on Easter.

The Greek emphasis, as the figure implies, is more forward looking and considers the very life of Jesus as a restoration. The Greek emphasis is more on the Incarnation as a manifestation of the Word, the Logos of God, that itself represents the reconciliation between God and humanity. Philosophers would say that the very *being* of Jesus as the God-man, ontologically (having to do with *being*) addresses the separation of God and man, as represented by the fall of Adam. We might expect the Greeks, therefore, to place somewhat more emphasis on Christmas. These are of course gross generalizations, but you can see how it would be easy to slide in one direction or the other. I recall one priest I knew said that he was an "Easter" Christian. He was actually a Baptist who had converted to the Episcopal Church. What he said was perfectly consistent with his own personal evolution as a Christian. Unfortunately, it does not reflect an orthodox balance.

## Three Meditations

Let me assert that the orthodox doctrine of salvation is a perfect balance between the Incarnation and what is known as the Pascal Mystery,[97] the death and resurrection of Jesus Christ—between the "cradle" and the "cross." In temporal terms, the cradle preceded the cross. In eternal terms, there is no cradle without the cross, and there is no cross without the cradle. Let me offer three meditations that were written for a day of silence at my church

---

[97] The Pascal Mystery is named for the sacrifice of the lamb during Passover, known as the pascal lamb. In the Hebrew Bible, the blood of the lamb was sprinkled on the door posts of the Israelites so that God would "pass over" those houses and spare the first born of that family as he slayed the first born of the Egyptians. It is a foundational story of all Jews and represents God's saving mercy during their exodus from Egypt.

How Does Jesus Open the Door for Transformation?

right before Christmas, a time traditionally called Advent. They were meant to encourage us to consider how these two salvational events are intertwined.

**Cradle or Cross-I**
By Kathryn Larisey

Prepare the Way of the Lord. Make his paths straight.

Advent.
A time of preparing and waiting.
A time of planning and reflecting.

Preparing the Way of the Lord.

I go inside myself and I can picture the circumstances of these weeks. The sounds and sights, the sensations of the Advent season wash over me:
   the green of evergreen branches
   the pinks and lavenders of the Advent candles
   the Giving Tree with its many-colored symbols
   caroling, mittens, winter coats, and wool hats
   the soft lights of children's pageants
     "homey" smells of cookies baking
   gifts under the tree
   mistletoe, tinsel, and eggnog
   snowflakes that glitter like stars when they fall
     through the light of the street lamps
   cider simmering
   violet vestments
   fires rippling in the fireplace
   stockings hung by the chimney

## Into the Perfect Likeness

Preparing the Way of the Lord . . . Making his paths straight.

My thoughts wander to the shepherds and their flocks, pastured near Bethlehem:
    Heaven's star shining brightly overhead
  Angels bending over them
  harps of gold
  anthems of praise, gladness, and celebration
  intense light
  good tidings . . .
  Tidings of comfort and joy, comfort and joy
  O tidings of comfort and joy

Preparing the Way of the Lord . . . Preparing the Way . . .

And then there is the Manger Scene, the soft velvets of a crèche under a tree:
  sleepy cows and a donkey
  oxen and the sweet smell of hay
  the lowing of the animals
  Joseph close by
  the softness and the radiance of Mary
  the warm swaddling clothes
  the gentle, rhythmic breathing of the baby,
  lying in the manger,
  sleeping in Heavenly Peace

Preparing the Way of the Lord . . .

"You are what I am waiting for!" my heart cries out.

How Does Jesus Open the Door for Transformation?

"You are the one I am preparing for!"
"You, little baby,
  the Prince of Peace,
  my Jesus,
  fast asleep on the hay."

Prepare the way of the Lord . . .

But this Jesus says to me,
"Do you think I came to give PEACE on Earth? No,
I tell you, but rather, division! I came to cast fire
upon the earth, and would it were already kindled!!"

"No. No." I say. "Hush. Sing lullaby. Hush lullaby.
Sleep, little baby, in Heavenly peace."

He pushes,
"Foxes have holes, birds have their nests, but the
Son of Man had nowhere to lay his head."

"No. No." I say. "Hush. Silent Night. Holy Night.
All is calm. All is bright."

He challenges me,
"It was the terrain of winter . . . the very dead of
winter . . . the journey from Nazareth to Bethlehem
was hard . . . they had a rough going of it . . . all
eighty miles . . . they came not on holiday, but to be
taxed . . . the town was crowded . . . the atmosphere
was one of fury, bitterness, suspicion, hatred . . .
there was no room for them anywhere . . . the stable
was harsh and bare . . . Mary groaned under her labor contractions, which came with hard, convulsive

regularity . . . Herod plotted and schemed . . . the world groaned under its sin . . ."

"NO! NO!" I say. "Tidings of comfort and joy. Here in the crib, secure from harms, sleep, sleep in your mother's arms."

He says,
"I was despised and rejected. A man of sorrows, and acquainted with grief . . . I gave my back to the smiters . . . I hid not my face from shame and spitting . . ."

"No. No." I say. "Hush, lullaby. Here betwixt ass and oxen
mild, sleep, sleep, sleep our little child."

He asks,
"But who may abide the day of my coming? And who shall stand when I appear? For I am like a refiner's fire . . ."

"No." I say. "Hush. All is calm . . ."

He looks at me and says,
  "And a sword will pierce through your own soul, too."

Advent.
A time of preparing and waiting.
A time of planning and reflecting.

Preparing for what?

How Does Jesus Open the Door for Transformation?

Just what are the full circumstances of this season? Glory or horror? Expectancy or defeat? Tenderness or callousness?

Dear Lord,
Are we making our way to the manger for Birth or for Death?
Are you preparing for us a Cradle or a Cross?

Prepare the Way of the Lord. Make his paths straight.


**Cradle or Cross-II**
by the author

Prepare the Way of the Lord.

Advent.
A time of preparing and waiting.
A time of planning and reflecting.

Preparing the Way of the Lord.

Reflecting.

As I reflect on the manger scene - Joseph, Mary, and the tiny baby—the strobe of my mind flashes. What is it that intrudes my thoughts? I am at the same time engulfed by the peace and hope of the

## Into the Perfect Likeness

moment when God and man became one—and distracted by an intruder. At first it is so brief that I pay no special attention. It's merely my own distraction. Certainly, it is not from God.

I return to the Baby, meek and mild, the warm, gentle, wondering, yearning faces of Mary and Joseph. There it is again. As with old Ebenezer Scrooge, I discount the interruption as something of my own making, but it persists, and I insist on ignoring it, no, submerging it.

But I am disquieted. I am less and less able to bask in the peace. What is this distraction? I start to pay attention and it becomes more sustained and clearer. As I give myself to what was once a nagging distraction, I am able to make it out—the indistinct outline of a cross.

I return to the cradle—the sweetness of that moment in history. Emmanuel, God with us. Think of it.

But this time I don't resist the pull back to the cross. It is larger now and more real.

As I move from cradle to cross, the peace I originally felt returns, but now it's different. It's broader and has to do less with me and more with the world and the larger Truth that is God.

This Baby and God
This Cross and God

## How Does Jesus Open the Door for Transformation?

They just don't seem to fit—impossible! I fight the tension. I resist the apparent conflict. No! No! This is impossible! The world will never understand. I will never understand. I don't want to understand. *I don't want to understand!*

In the silence I am touched by my own willfulness. In the silence I am left with the power of the imponderable.

My Lord and my God.

The wood of the manger that holds you is so solid and well worn. So simple and unpretentious but full of glory for it is the throne of God. How precious is this wood to hold the child of love and truth—the Son of God.

But before my eyes this wood is transformed. Small crossed pieces of the manger change to larger crossed pieces—and larger. A glimpse of horror comes but is quickly dispelled. The cross—simple and unpretentious, and full of glory for it is the throne of God. How precious is this wood to hold the man of love and truth—the Son of God.

Cradle and Cross—they are one.

The straw that surrounds and cushions you, little one. It is not intrusive or harsh but not entirely gentle as its little points touch your soft face. What a privilege it is to touch the face of the Holy one—the Lamb of God.

## Into the Perfect Likeness

But these little bits of straw are transformed. They become longer and more stout. Thorns appear. The horror comes again, and again it is brushed aside. The Crown of Thorns. What a privilege to touch the face of the Holy one—The Lamb of God.

Cradle and Cross—they are one.

My thoughts turn to the swaddling clothes that warm and comfort you. Simple and unpretentious, but full of glory. It is the mantle of the King of Kings. What an honor to adorn the Lord of Lords.

But this same cloth is transformed from coarse white to red—a Centurions robe. Not red but red on red—stained by the blood of Christ. My Horror is pushed aside with more difficulty. But this blood-stained robe is also the mantle of the King of Kings. What an honor to adorn the Lord of Lords.

Cradle and Cross—they are one.

And now you little child are fed—fed with mother's milk, the milk of love. It is so simple and unpretentious and full of glory for it eases the pangs of hunger of the Christ Child. It is sustenance for the Savior of the world.

But this milk too is soon transformed to another drink. It turns clear and full of pain. This drink, the vinegar and gall, eases the pangs of death for the

## How Does Jesus Open the Door for Transformation?

Christ. It too is sustenance for the Savior of the world.

Cradle and Cross—they are one.

Then I look at your tiny hands, so gentle and perfect. They have never felt the hardening of toil or the pain of suffering. They are the hands of surrender. Completely surrendered to all that is larger and more powerful and yet knowing nothing but love, receiving nothing but love, giving nothing but love. These are the hands of God Himself who so loved the world.

Oh no! Not the hands too! Those tiny precious little hands that I adore so much are also transformed. Please, not the nails! Not the blood! My heart is breaking. I can't do this anymore. I can't stand this alone. The pain is just too much.

Then there is a touch, and I am embraced—no enfolded by the presence of love Himself, and He says to me:
There is more—so much more
There is hope
There is new life
There is resurrection

I promise. *I promise!*

He dries my tears and wraps me in a spotless garment.
He lays me down on a bed of great comfort.

## Into the Perfect Likeness

He places my head on a pillow of deep softness.
He feeds me with his own sustenance—with Himself.
And He holds my hands in His.

Cradle and Cross
Peace on earth and suffering
Good will to men and sacrifice
they are one.

**Cradle or Cross-III**
by the author

Prepare the Way of the Lord.

Advent.
A time of preparing and waiting.
A time of planning and reflecting.

Preparing the Way of the Prince of Peace.

I have so much to do.

Christmas cards,
Presents for family and friends,
Doing something for someone less fortunate.

I have so much to do. The "Christmas Spirit" is so elusive.

How Does Jesus Open the Door for Transformation?

Where does it come from? There are plenty of warm feelings surrounding the birth of the Christ child. But why don't they seem to penetrate? Why doesn't the season ever bring the deep joy and peace that is spoken of in the story?

Peace on earth, good will to men.

I have so much to do.

Why can't I ever seem to get the Christmas cards done. I have cards I bought ten years ago and still have never sent. This is my greatest falling short. For a couple of weeks, I have plenty of time—the window of opportunity. I still have some time. I still have a little time. Then all of a sudden the window is slammed shut, and I don't have time. I missed the chance once more. The cards stay in the drawer for one more year gathering dust.

Cradle and Cross—they are one.

So, what is it that this Cradle and Cross tell me about myself. I yearn to share my love with those I care for. I yearn to participate in and enhance the peace of their season, but I am unwilling to suffer, even slightly, so that they might know the love of God a little more. Even slightly! My brother hangs on the cross for me and I am unwilling to put my name on a card, an address and a stamp on an envelope, and walk—not crawl as He did for me—but stroll to the mailbox. Dear God, help me forsake my sins.

## Into the Perfect Likeness

Cradle and Cross—they are one.

But I have so much to do.

I have gifts to buy, but I have plenty of time. I know that if it's to be done right, I must take time and do it prayerfully. The gift I give must be a gift of the heart at least as much as it is a gift of the pocketbook. I still have some time. I still have a little time. Then all of a sudden my back is against the wall, and I rush out to fulfill my obligations. Something for Mom, something for Penny, something for Lee and John and so forth. Ah, only two more gifts to get. I simply fill the air with material goods to satisfy the demands of the culture, to fulfill the obligations of the season. I am left dry and tired and dead.

Cradle and Cross—they are one.

The gift of love and salvation was given to me freely, not grudgingly or of necessity. Freely! And I in return fulfill the obligations of the season. Again I am unwilling to suffer the miniscule pain of carving out time to do it right. I am unwilling to forgo some of the activities thrust upon me in order to live into the promise of the season. Dear God help me forsake my sins.

Cradle and Cross—they are one.

But I have so much to do.

## How Does Jesus Open the Door for Transformation?

And what about those less fortunate? I did take a star from the Advent Giving Tree. It would have been all too easy not to. I had no sense of urgency. But I did take a star. Bob is his name. Bob is an adult who needs jeans and a sweater. I have jeans—six pairs. I have sweaters—about twenty. I have twenty and Bob needs one. What am I doing?

Cradle and Cross—they are one.

Why am I not compelled by a burning desire to act out the sacrifice that was made for me? He gave it all for me, and I am complacent about my meager sacrifice for another. Bob forgive me. Dear God, help me forsake my sins.

Cradle and Cross
Peace on earth and suffering
Good will to men and sacrifice
they are one.

How can I prepare for the coming of the Savior of the World without the Cross? Peace without suffering? Good will without sacrifice? It makes no sense any more.

Is it too late for me this year?

I remember how Ebenezer Scrooge said to the boy in the street, "'What's today?'
'Today!' replied the boy. 'Why, Christmas Day.'

## Into the Perfect Likeness

'It's Christmas Day!' said Scrooge to himself. 'I haven't missed it.'"[98]

What day is it? Is it too late again this year to heed these warnings?

Prepare the way of the Lord.

Cradle and Cross—they are one.

This eternal relationship between the Incarnation and the Pascal Mystery is indeed a mystery, but one would be safe in saying that orthodox Christology would assert that they are somehow intimately related and are both essential to the redemptive work of Jesus.

So here is a list of words we use to point to the work Jesus did to open the door to us for transformation:

> Salvation
> Atonement
> Redemption
> Propitiation
> Expiation
> Deliverance
> Restoration
> Justification
> Sanctification
> Ransom
> Remission of sins

---

[98] Charles Dickens, *A Christmas Carol* (New York: J. B. Lippincott Company, 1976), 139–40.

How Does Jesus Open the Door for Transformation?

Satisfaction
Reconciliation
Victory

The point here is they all point with varying shades of meaning to exactly the same result. Through Jesus, the door is opened to us for our transformation into his very likeness. Now let's look at what two of the Church Fathers had to say about this salvational work.

## A Hebrew Context

One of the most important organizing principles we can apply to our understanding of many of these salvation concepts is their Hebrew context. The whole Christ event arises out of the Jewish traditions in which Jesus was raised. While many of these formulas may appear to relate to what seems to be the petty emotions of the God of Abraham, Isaac and Jacob, they all are connected in a deep way to the history of salvation of the Jewish people. The blood of the Passover Lamb is central. The practices of the Jewish priesthood to make sacrifices for the atonement of the Jewish people is an abiding theme that is carried over into the Christian themes of salvation. In other words, to fail to see this continuity is to fail to understand the headwaters of salvation history that culminates in the Christ event. This is why there really is no such thing as a "New Testament" Christian church. Our whole understanding of the meaning of salvation in Jesus Christ is rooted in the Old Testament understanding of the activity of God in history.

## Irenaeus

Irenaeus was mentioned in the first chapter. He lived from A.D. 125 to 202. One of his major contributions was a work called *Against Heresies*, written as a defense of orthodox doctrine against *gnostic* errors. Remember that the Gnostics believed that Jesus was not really human just like the rest of us but was just pretending to have human limitations. Irenaeus was arguing that this understanding does not work and amounts to throwing the incarnational baby out with the bathwater.

Here is an excerpt from this work that gives some of his thinking on the subject of redemption.

## BOOK V
## REDEMPTION AND THE WORLD TO COME

### Doctrine of Redemption in Reply to the Gnostics

We could in no other way have learned the things of God unless our Teacher, being the Word, had been made man. For none could declare to us the things of the Father, except his own word. For who else has known the mind of the Lord, or who has become his counselor? Nor again could we have learned in any other way than by seeing our Teacher, that we might become imitators of his works and doers of his words, and so have communion with him, receiving our increase from him who is perfect and before all creation.

Redeeming us by his blood in accordance with his reasonable nature, he gave himself a ransom for those who had been led into captivity. Since the apostasy[99] tyrannized over us unjustly, and, when we belonged

---

[99] The word *apostasy* means a "turning away." It is usually used as a pejorative since one would be turning away from the truth. Here "the apostacy" is seen as the agent of heresy.

How Does Jesus Open the Door for Transformation?

> by nature to God Almighty, had unnaturally alienated us, God's Word, mighty in all things, [reclaimed us], making us his own disciples, . . .
>
> So then, since the Lord redeemed us by his own blood, and gave his soul for our souls, and his flesh for our bodies, and poured out the Spirit of the Father to bring about the union and communion of God and man—bringing God down to men by [the working of] the Spirit, and again raising man to God by his incarnation—and by his coming firmly and truly giving us incorruption, by our communion with God, all the teachings of the heretics are destroyed.[100]

In these early writings, Irenaeus and others formulated what we call today "orthodox doctrine" as a result of the struggles of the early Church to keep early Christians from straying from apostolic teaching as reflected in Scripture.[101] This is the beginning of doctrinal development, not to add to or subtract from, but to clarify. This passage gives you a little flavor of the writings that were directed at doing battle with those who even unwittingly would lead the Church down an erroneous path.

## Anselm

The second writing I want to look at is by a later author of the twelfth century. The work is entitled *Cur Deus Homo* or "Why God-man" by Anselm. Anselm (A.D. 1033 to 1109) was born in northern Italy, spent many years as a monk in France, and

---

[100] Irenaeus, *Against Heresies*, found in Richardson, Cyril C., ed. *Early Christian Fathers* (New York, Macmillan Publishing Co., Inc., 1970), 385–7.

[101] Note that Scripture itself was gathered together and authorized as one of the key defenses against heresy.

eventually was appointed by the king of England to the post of Archbishop of Canterbury. This work is considered by many to be one of the most important contributions to the theology of redemption that came out of the Middle Ages. It is in the form of a dialogue between Anselm and a fellow monk named Boso.

### CHAPTER VI
*How no being, except the God-man, can make the atonement by which man is saved?*

*Anselm.* But this [return to perfection] cannot be effected, except the price paid to God for the sin of man be something greater than all the universe besides God.

*Boso.* So it appears.

*Anselm.* Moreover, it is necessary that he who can give God anything of his own which is more valuable than all things in the possession of God, must be greater than all else but God himself.

*Boso.* I cannot deny it.

*Anselm.* Therefore none but God can make this satisfaction.

*Boso.* So it appears.

*Anselm.* But none but a man ought to do this, otherwise man does not make the satisfaction.[102]

This dialogue is remarkably reminiscent of Socrates, although Boso's responses seem a bit self-serving, since Anselm wrote the whole thing himself. Boso is awfully agreeable. We

---

[102] Anselm, *Cur Deus Homo*, found in Deane, S. N., trans., *St. Anselm Basic Writings* (Chicago: Open Court Publishing Company, 1962), 256–9.

How Does Jesus Open the Door for Transformation?

do, however, get exposed to an early and important formula: Only God *can*—only man *ought*. In other words, only mankind has the responsibility for his sin against the infinite God, and only the infinite God himself can pay the price for that sinfulness. Although Anselm has managed to give some rationale for orthodoxy, we should not be enticed into believing that we need any such rationale. All we need to know is that the door has been opened. Why and how are simply reinforcements of the fundamental fact. There is nothing holding us back from the transformation that God intends for us.

## Baptism

The next question we must ask is how do we as Christians appropriate the benefits of Jesus redemption? The orthodox answer is through the sacrament of Holy Baptism. A more Protestant answer might be indicated by the words of Paul: ". . . if you confess with your lips that Jesus is Lord and believe in your heart that God raised him from the dead, you will be saved" (Romans 10:7–9). Let's look at Baptism first.

The doctrine of Holy Baptism, as the central transformational instrument of the Church, began from the earliest times. When John the Baptist connects his baptism by water to the baptism of the Holy Spirit that Jesus will bring, he sets the stage for the central importance of this act. The Church developed its doctrine of salvation side by side with its doctrine of sacraments. These sacraments are the "outward and visible signs of an inward and spiritual grace."[103] These are the actions the Church takes that are outward signs of God's inner work. In the Catholic tradition, the inner work of salvation is thus associated with the

---

[103] Recall that I was writing this as an Episcopalian. The Catholics would add a twist to this definition—that the sacrament is an "efficacious" sign. In other words, the sign actually brings with it the grace.

outward work called Holy Baptism. Other traditions my place more emphasis on a less sacramental and more spiritual baptism. However one views the details, the Church would say that through baptism, one is brought into the body of the Church, and thus the body of Christ, and therefore partakes of all the redemptive work done by Jesus. Thus, we will take orthodox doctrine to assert that after baptism we are saved.[104]

Let me stress just exactly what all this means. By the fall of Adam, mankind became slaves to sin. Augustine called it "Original Sin" and the term stuck. The idea was that the sin of Adam is passed down from human to human through the hereditary process, and none of us escapes its grasp. For those who are not saved, sin is a necessity—an enslavement. Jesus, through his work of salvation, redemption, atonement, etc. crushes that grasp, breaks the chains that bind us to sin. The Church, in the doctrine of Holy Baptism, therefore, asserts that after we are baptized, we are no longer slaves to sin. This does not mean, however, that we no longer sin. It just means that we no longer *have to* sin.[105] We no longer have an excuse. We can no longer say that we sin because we are human. After baptism, we must say that we sin because we *choose to*.

A more Protestant approach puts more emphasis on a more cognitive approach. At some point in our lives we are touched

---

[104] If there is any aspect of this whole discussion that might cause dissent, the way salvation is attained is it. Sacramental theology has been one of the most important points of disagreement in Church history. I hope somehow the broader picture can be maintained.

[105] Now, there is a little concept called *concupiscence* that is the inclination to sin. This is a little complicated but, suffice it to say, concupiscence is always with us as a stain of original sin but can be overcome by the activity of the Holy Spirit that is offered to us through Christ. In other words, Jesus' work of salvation does not lose any of its efficacy, but we may need to encourage the Holy Spirit to work a little harder if we are to avail ourselves of all its benefits.

## How Does Jesus Open the Door for Transformation?

by the Holy Spirit in such a way that we "give our lives to Christ." It could happen at a revival prayer meeting, in an altar call during a church service, or on a hike in the Rockies. At some point we came to the realization that God's answers to us for all our questions about life and love are found in Jesus Christ. However you get there, being saved opens up the pathway back to God.

In other words, Jesus, by his redemption, frees us from the power of sin. However that is manifest, either by sacramental baptism or through some other personal experience of salvation, we now must take full responsibility for our lives and the choices we make. Jesus has kicked the door open for our transformation. Now it is up to us to choose to walk through it or not.

# *12*
# How Does It Look to Be Christ-like?

This is the first of four chapters that try to work out different aspects of what it looks and feels like to be transformed into the likeness of Jesus. In this chapter, we will look at the nature and dimensions of that transformation. In doing so, we will be clarifying our expectations of how such a transformation might be treated or viewed by those around us. Our first challenge is to elucidate what we mean by transformation—transformation into what?

## Christ's Characteristics
Let's now look at how the Church has distilled Jesus' characteristics. Consider the following Scripture.

> To be spiritually minded is life and peace.
> *Romans 8:6*

> Love without hypocrisy … *Romans 12:4–21*

> Bear others' burdens … *Romans 15:1–4*

> … abound in love for one another and for all …
> *1 Thessalonians 3:12*

> … keep away from believers who are lying in idleness … *2 Thessalonians 3:6*

> … mere busybodies … *2 Thessalonians 3:7*

## How Does Jesus Open the Door for Transformation?

... it is required of stewards that they be found trustworthy. *1 Corinthians 4:2*

... so that none of you will be puffed up ... *1 Corinthians 4:6*

... we endure ... *1 Corinthians 4:12*

... we speak kindly. *1 Corinthians 4:13*

Keep alert, stand firm in your faith, be courageous, be strong. *1 Corinthians 4:6*

... to test you and to know whether you are obedient in everything. *2 Corinthians 2:9*

... by purity, knowledge, patience, kindness, holiness of spirit, genuine love, truthful speech ... *2 Corinthians 6:6*

"God opposes the proud but gives grace to the humble." *James 4:6*

If we boil these verses down, what would the list of characteristics look like that we are called to emulate.

Spiritual
Not hypocritical
Willing to bear burdens of others
Loving
Faithful
Willing to labor
Not meddling

Trustworthy
Not puffed up
Enduring
Kind to each other
Alert
Faithful
Courageous
Strong
Obedient
Pure
Knowledgeable
Patient
Holy
Genuine
Truthful
Humble

Well, I don't know about you, but my shoulders are starting to buckle under the weight, and the list could go on and on.

## Dealing with the List

If we were to take on each one of these characteristics, where would we begin? First of all, we would find that some of these virtues look contradictory in some circumstances. How can I be loving and obedient and speak the truth when those I am called to care for are clearly hurt by my openness? How can I be humble and truthful, when the truth is that I have just done something quite spectacular (from someone's perspective)? How can I be patient and courageous, when I am prompted to act decisively? The challenge is to reach a much deeper understanding of what lies behind each of these characteristics.

Usually, as a fallback position, we pick a few characteristics that we think we can handle and try to adhere to them. We try not to tell bald-faced lies concerning how many Olympic gold medals we won, even though we are not an Olympic-caliber athlete. We try not to pick up big heavy objects and hit someone over the head just because they disagree with us. We try to resist thoughts of robbing the bank when we get a little strapped for cash. And we only run red lights when we think they are stuck.

Now this certainly is a start. If the list is too long and too complicated, and we know we can't live up to the list, are we supposed simply to settle for a shorter and less complicated list? Maybe if we pick out the most important ones, the others will fall into place, like when Jesus picked out loving God and loving your neighbor as yourself. We might start with the idea that we need to do all that God desires for us. The Church calls this "the will of God." So, to be obedient to the will of God is at the top of the list.

## Dealing with the Will of God

The problem is that we often have great difficulty discerning exactly what this "will" is. So, we seem to be caught in a bind. If we start with the details, we get frustrated. If we start with the "big picture," we get confused. The question is whether we are missing the point. Lists of characteristics are fine, even important, but they are not enough. Let's look at a couple of authors and see how they approach this dilemma.

### The Imitation of Christ

Thomas á Kempis was a fourteenth century monk who wrote a famous book on the Christian spiritual life, entitled *The Imitation of Christ*. Here is how he begins.

Into the Perfect Likeness

Book One
COUNCILS ON THE SPIRITUAL LIFE
Chapter I
*On the Imitation of Christ*

'He who follows me shall not walk in darkness,' says Our Lord.

In these words Christ counsels us to follow His life and way if we desire true enlightenment and freedom from all blindness of heart. Let the life of Jesus Christ, then, be our first consideration.

The teaching of Jesus far transcends all the teachings of the Saints, and whosoever has His spirit will discover concealed in it heavenly manna. But many people, although they often hear the Gospel, feel little desire to follow it, because they lack the spirit of Christ. Whoever desires to understand and take delight in the words of Christ must strive to conform his whole life to Him.

Of what use is it to discourse learnedly on the Trinity, if you lack humility and therefore displease the Trinity? Lofty words do not make a man just or holy; but a good life makes him dear to God. I would far rather feel contrition than be able to define it. If you knew the whole Bible by heart, and all the teachings of the philosophers, how would this help you without the grace and love of God? 'Vanity of vanities, and all is vanity,' except to love God and serve Him alone. And this is supreme wisdom—to despise the world, and draw daily nearer the kingdom of heaven.

It is vanity to solicit honors, or to raise oneself to high station. It is vanity to be a slave to bodily desire,

## How Does Jesus Open the Door for Transformation?

and to crave for things which bring certain retribution. It is vanity to wish for long life, if you care little for a good life. It is vanity to give thought only to this present life, and to care nothing for the life to come. It is vanity to love things that so swiftly pass away, and not to hasten onwards to that place where everlasting joy abides.

Keep constantly in mind the saying, 'The eye is not satisfied with seeing, nor the ear filled with hearing.' Strive to withdraw your heart from the love of visible things, and direct your affections to the invisible. For those who follow only their natural inclinations defile their conscience, and lose the grace of God.[106]

He starts out pointing toward the "spirit of Christ"—the kind of transformation we have been talking about. He hints at something larger than a list of specific qualities but does not really pursue it. Consequently, the most powerful part of the entire book is the title—*The Imitation of Christ*. In this, he captures the essence of our journey. What is even more interesting is that instead of talking about Jesus, he proceeds to create a long *list*. Here are some of the chapter headings.

On Personal Humility
On the Teaching of Truth
On Prudence in Action
On Reading the Holy Scriptures
On Control of the Desires

---

[106] Thomas á Kempis, *The Imitation of Christ* (New York: Penguin Books, 1952), 27–8. Reprinted by permission, Penguin Group, London. All rights reserved.

# Into the Perfect Likeness

On Avoiding Vain Hope and Conceit
On Guarding Against Familiarity
On Obedience and Discipline
On Avoiding Talkativeness
On Peace, and Spiritual Progress
On the Uses of Adversity
On Resisting Temptations
On Avoiding Rash Judgments
On Deeds Inspired by Love
On Bearing with the Faults of Others

Wow! Now *this* is a list. I am not saying that this is not a valuable source of incredibly rich insights into the spiritual life that is part and parcel of the transformation process. But for now, there is one thing that is important. The imitation of Jesus is not just following a list or measuring up to some scale associated with each element on the list. The transformation process we are talking about *results* in the characteristics on the list, but is not necessarily *achieved* by checking off each of these characteristics. We must be assured, however, that this transformation process has intimately related to the spirit of Jesus, the spirit of God, the work of the Holy Spirit. More on this later.

## Just Like Jesus

As we look for some further insight, let us consider the work of a contemporary author. Max Lucado is unquestionably one of the most popular Christian writers today. He comes from the Protestant evangelical tradition and is strictly orthodox in the major premise in his book, *Just Like Jesus*. Here is part of the first chapter.

How Does Jesus Open the Door for Transformation?

## A HEART LIKE HIS
*What if, for one day, Jesus were to become you?*

What if, for twenty-four hours, Jesus wakes up in your bed, walks in your shoes, lives in your house, assumes your schedule? Your boss becomes his boss, your mother becomes his mother, your pains become his pains? With one exception, nothing about your life changes. Your health doesn't change. Your circumstances don't change. Your schedule isn't altered. Your problems aren't solved. Only one change occurs.

What if, for one day and one night, Jesus lives your life with his heart? Your heart gets the day off, and your life is led by the heart of Christ. His priorities govern your actions. His passions drive your decisions. His love directs your behavior.

What would you be like? Would people notice a change? Your family—would they see something new? Your coworkers—would they sense a difference? What about the less fortunate? Would you treat them the same? And your friends? Would they detect more joy? How about your enemies? Would they receive more mercy from Christ's than from yours?

And you? How would you feel? What alterations would this transplant have on your stress level? Your mood swings? Your temper? Would you sleep better? Would you see sunsets differently? Death differently? Taxes differently? Any chance you'd need fewer aspirin or sedatives? How about your reaction to traffic delays? (Ouch, that touched a nerve.) Would you still dread what you are dreading? Better yet, would you still do what you are doing?

Would you still do what you had planned to do for the next twenty-four hours? Pause and think about your schedule. Obligations. Engagements. Outings. Appointments. With Jesus taking over your heart, would anything change?

Keep working on this for a moment. Adjust the lens of your imagination until you have a clear picture of Jesus leading your life, then snap the shutter and frame the image. What you see is what God wants. He wants you to "think and act like Christ Jesus" (Philippians 2:5).

God's plan for you is nothing short of a new heart. If you were a car, God would want control of your engine. If you were a computer, God would claim the software and the hard drive. If you were an airplane, he'd take his seat in the cockpit. But you are a person, so God wants to change your heart.

"But you were taught to be made new in your hearts, to become a new person. That new person is made to be like God—made to be truly good and holy" (Ephesians 4:23–24).

God wants you to be just like Jesus. He wants you to have a heart like his.

I'm going to risk something here. It's dangerous to sum up grand truths in one statement, but I'm going to try. If a sentence or two could capture God's desire for each of us, it might read like this:

How Does Jesus Open the Door for Transformation?

> *God loves you just the way you are, but he refuses to leave you that way. He wants you to be just like Jesus.*[107]

What Max and orthodox Christian doctrine are saying is that while lists may help us, the one essential integrating, facilitating, and empowering ingredient to our living into the "will of God" is Jesus. What Max is suggesting is this: by taking on the heart of Jesus, the world would think that we were a whole lot nicer, gentler, kinder, more loving, more helpful, and so forth. What we will see is that the way we would be viewed by others would also be *just like* the way Jesus was viewed. There would be a number of constituencies that would certainly take widely varying assessments of the value of our transformation—some not so nice.

Even if we understand that the door has been opened for us to be transformed into the likeness of the Christ Jesus, and we understand something of the universal qualities that compose that likeness, we are still faced with some good news and some bad news. The nature of this dilemma arises solely from the difference in perspectives between God and the world, between the eternal and the temporal.

## From the Perspective of God and the World

What may, from God's perspective, look good and true; from the world's perspective may be considered quite foreign and worthy of derision. What may from the world's perspective be considered right and true, may be considered from God's perspective to be pure sin. Let me be clear about what I mean

---

[107] Max Lucado, *Just Like Jesus* (Nashville: Word, 2000), 1–3. Reprinted by permission, Thomas Nelson Inc. Nashville, Tennessee. All rights reserved.

by "the world." If we assume that we all are subject to sin, or a kind of self-defeating self-centeredness, and, if we can assume that the proportion of folks who are interested in the kind of transformation we have been talking about are few and far between, then we can also assume that the values of the world will be fashioned after those things that a fallen world holds to be of greatest value. This would be wealth, self-gratification, power or influence, the admiration of others, "good" looks, "nice" personality, etc. The world is very much driven by "the self." From the world's perspective, we are called to do those things that are in accord with the world's values. From God's perspective, we are called to do God's will.

What the Church would say about all this is a little tricky. Who I truly am is not what the world would say I am. Therefore, those things that the world says will make me happy and fulfilled are not the things that will truly make me deeply happy and fulfilled. We can only be truly happy when we are truly ourselves—truly who we were created to be. This is the most powerful truth the Church has to offer us. Being like Jesus does not mean being anyone other than who we are created to be. The universal characteristics of Jesus are characteristics of any of us who live fully into the will of God. It is these characteristics that allow us to live complete, fulfilled lives as we were intended to do.

## The Characteristics of Jesus
What were the characteristics of Jesus, and how would those characteristics have been viewed by the different "constituents" around him? First, let's look at some Scripture.

> Jesus stood still and called them, saying, "What do you want me to do for you?" They said to him,

How Does Jesus Open the Door for Transformation?

"Lord, let our eyes be opened." Moved with compassion, Jesus touched their eyes. Immediately they regained their sight and followed him.
*Matthew 20:32–34*

"Blessed are the poor in spirit, for theirs is the kingdom of heaven. Blessed are those who mourn for they will be comforted. Blessed are the meek, for they will inherit the earth." *Matthew 5:3–5*

"Ask, and it will be given you. Search, and you will find; knock, and the door will be opened for you."
*Matthew 7:7*

". . . and whoever gives even a cup of cold water to one of these little ones in the name of a disciple—truly I tell you, none of these will lose their reward." *Matthew 10:42*

"Let the little children come to me, and do not stop them; for it is to such as these that the kingdom of heaven belongs." *Matthew 19:14*

"You know how to interpret the appearance of the sky, but you cannot interpret the signs of the times." *Matthew 16:3*

A very large crowd spread their cloaks on the road, and others cut branches from the trees and spread them on the road. The crowds that went ahead of him and that followed were shouting, "Hosanna to the Son of David! Blessed is the one who comes in the name of the Lord! Hosanna in the highest heaven!" *Matthew 21:8–9*

And he said to them, "Do you not understand this parable? Then how will you understand all the parables?" *Mark 4:13*

"Do not think that I have come to bring peace to the earth; I have not come to bring peace, but a sword. For I have come to set a man against his father, and a daughter against her mother, and a daughter-in-law against her mother-in-law; and one's foes will be members of one's own household." *Matthew 10:34–36*

In the temple he found people selling cattle, sheep, and doves, and the money changers seated at their tables. Making a whip of cords, he drove all of them out of the temple . . . *John 2:14–15*

"Woe to you scribes and Pharisees, hypocrites! . . . You snakes, you brood of vipers! How can you escape being sentenced to hell?" *Matthew 23:13–33*

From these sources we get a whole raft of characteristics, both stated and implied, for Jesus. It should be clear, however, that different people assessed these characteristics quite differently, depending on their own vested interests.

## The View from Different Vantage Points
Let's see if we can consider them from the vantage point of a number of "constituents." What might a list of characteristics

## How Does Jesus Open the Door for Transformation?

have looked like for those whom he healed?
> Gentle
> Loving
> Kind
> The source of healing life
> Miracle worker

What about the average person who listened to him and followed him?
> Exciting
> Powerful
> Charismatic
> Innovative
> Heart warming
> Truth telling
> A prophet

What about the Apostles?
> Amazing
> Discerning
> Prodding
> Bold
> Confusing
> Frustrating
> Courageous
> Stubborn

What would the religious establishment's list have looked like?
> Vocal
> Unsatisfied
> Argumentative
> Troublesome

Viscous
Blasphemous
Evil

It is clear that Jesus looked a lot different to different people, depending on their perspective. What this says to us is that, if we are to be transformed into the likeness of Jesus, we will have to come to terms with how we will be viewed from those same diverse perspectives.

## A View from Scripture

Let's look at some Scripture where this distinction is pointed out over and over. It is particularly prevalent in the Gospel of John and in the writings of Paul.

> "The world cannot hate you, but it hates me because I testify against it that its works are evil." *John 7:7*
>
> "If you were of the world, the world would love its own; but because you are not of the world, but I chose you out of the world, therefore the world hates you."
> *John 15:19*
>
> "And now I am no more in the world, but they are in the world, and I am coming to thee." *John 17:11*
>
> God chose what is foolish in the world to shame the wise. God chose what is weak in the world to shame the strong. *1 Corinthians 1:27*
>
> If with Christ you died to the elemental spirits of the universe, why do you live as if you still belonged to the world? *Colossians 2:20*

## How Does Jesus Open the Door for Transformation?

So, what we end up with is some good news and some bad news. The good news is that being like Jesus for the world will mean that we will certainly be kinder and gentler, and some people will like us better for it. The bad news is that the world's assessment might be just exactly the opposite of what we might like. If you are looking for people to love you more, watch out.

In the end, being transformed into the perfect likeness of Jesus does not involve a checklist; it involves being changed in such a way that a new integrity takes over, and all the checklists simply fall into place—at least from God's perspective. We will be looking at the *process* of transformation eventually and should get a better appreciation for the superficial lesson of this chapter: it is not about lists and it is not about satisfying the expectations of the world. It about satisfying the expectations of God—the God who knows us better than we know ourselves, who built into us some glorious capabilities and some precious limits.

# 13
# What is the Price of Transformation?

We have alluded to the fact that "the world" interprets those things that are of God much differently than God does. What do we mean by this? If the world is characterized by what we see on TV, in the movies, in the newspaper, on the computer, on Twitter, etc., and if we assume that this world is not composed of a majority of people who are in the perfect likeness of Jesus, then we can assume that the world is still stuck in some ruts. If this were not the case, we would have no need for Jesus. Given this distinction between the way the world looks at things and the way God looks at things, it should be no surprise that trying to assume the likeness of Jesus could mean trouble. In other words, there is a price to be paid for transformation.

## Sacrifice

But let me be perfectly clear here, the price is called *sacrifice*, and it involves the worldly things we give up in order to be more and more like Jesus. What we would like to do is to understand the reasons for this sacrifice, the nature of that sacrifice, and finally in the next chapter the *net* cost to us—in other words, the benefits *minus* the price. Let's start with what Scripture tells us about the sort of expectations we should have regarding sacrifice.

> . . . for Jesus himself had testified that a prophet has no honor in the prophet's own country.   *John 4:44*

> Therefore, the Jews started persecuting Jesus, because he was doing such things on the sabbath. But

## What is the Price of Transformation?

Jesus answered them, "My Father is still working, and I also am working." For this reason, the Jews were seeking all the more to kill him, because he was not only breaking the sabbath, but was also calling God his own Father, thereby making himself equal to God. *John 5:16*

"Very truly, I tell you, whoever keeps my word will never see death." The Jews said to him, "Now we know that you have a demon." *John 8:52*

"I have given them your word; and the world has hated them because they do not belong to the world, just as I do not belong to the world." *John 17:14*

"See, I am sending you out like sheep into the midst of wolves; so be wise as serpents and innocent as doves. Beware of them, for they will hand you over to councils and flog you in their synagogues; and you will be dragged before governors and kings because of me, as a testimony to them and the Gentiles. When they hand you over, do not worry about how you are to speak or what you are to say; for what you are to say will be given to you at that time; for it is not you who speak, but the Spirit of your Father speaking through you. Brother will betray brother to death, and a father his child, and children put to death; and you will be hated by all because of my name. But the one who endures to the end will be saved. When they persecute you in one town, flee to the next; for truly I tell you, you will not have gone through all the towns of Israel before the Son of Man comes.

## Into the Perfect Likeness

"A disciple is not above the teacher nor a slave above the master; it is enough for the disciple to be like the teacher, and the slave like the master. If they have called the master of the house Beelzebul, how much more will they malign those of his household!"
*Matthew 10:16–25*

"They will hand you over to be tortured and will put you to death, and you will be hated by all nations because of my name." *Matthew 24:9*

And not only that, but we also boast in our sufferings, knowing that suffering produces endurance, and endurance produces character, and character produces hope, and hope does not disappoint us, because God's love has been poured into our hearts through the Holy Spirit that has been given to us. *Romans 5:3–5*

We are fools for the sake of Christ, but you are wise in Christ. We are weak, but you are strong. You are held in honor, but we in disrepute. To the present hour we are hungry and thirsty, we are poorly clothed and beaten and homeless, and we grow weary from the work of our own hands. When reviled, we bless; when persecuted, we endure; when slandered, we speak kindly. We have become like the rubbish of the world, the dregs of all things, to this very day.
*1 Corinthians 4:10–13*

If we are being afflicted, it is for your consolation and salvation; if we are being consoled, it is for your consolation, which you experience when you patiently endure the same sufferings that we are also suffering.

## What is the Price of Transformation?

> Our hope for you is unshaken; for we know that as you share in our sufferings, so also you share in our consolation.     *2 Corinthians 1:6–7*

> Therefore when we could bear it no longer, we decided to be left alone in Athens; and we sent Timothy, our brother and co-worker for God in proclaiming the gospel of Christ, to strengthen and encourage you for the sake of your faith, so that no one would be shaken by these persecutions. Indeed, you yourselves know that this is what we are destined for. In fact, when we were with you, we told you beforehand that we were to suffer persecution; so it turned out, as you know.
> *1 Thessalonians 3:1–4*

What this seems to say unabashedly, over and over again, is that the pathway toward Jesus is a difficult one. There is no question that the way of Jesus is the way of love. If this is so, why is it that the world despises this kind of love? Well, as long as love is defined in worldly terms, then, in fact, the world does not have any trouble with it. There are plenty of wonderful Christians who are well beloved by the majority of the world. Billy Graham might be one of them, for example. Certainly, there are pockets of people who hate anything that smacks of Christianity, but in general they didn't hate Billy. They just ignored him. No one I know was trying to string him up. So, isn't he doing what we are all called to do? He certainly has devoted his whole life to spreading the Gospel. And one might say that he has made worldly sacrifices in order to do that.

There is a whole line of devout Christians, many in our own parishes, who have acted as servants and have bountifully increased the amount of love in the world. Mother Teresa comes to mind. The message of Martin Luther King, Jr. was certainly one of love and sacrifice. But the Civil Rights Movement also shows a different side—one that challenges our understanding of the price of witnessing to the truth.

## The Challenge of Truth

The problem is not so much the "love" side of the equation. The problem comes on the flipside—the "truth" side of the equation. When we start to become truth-tellers, as certainly Jesus was, we start to ruffle feathers—and when we start to ruffle feathers, there begins to be a deeper cost and sacrifice to being like Jesus.

Within the spiritual literature there is none more compelling and insightful than the Eastern Orthodox writings of the spiritual masters found in the *Philokalia*. One of the writers was a man called Ilias the Presbyter. He probably became a monk after leaving his position as presbyter (what we would call today a lawyer) and then was ordained to the priesthood. Although the years of his life are not well documented, he probably lived around the end of the eleventh century, about the same time as Anselm. Although the manuscript, entitled *A Gnomic Anthology*, has many proposed authors, Ilias seems to be the best choice. In the common style of spiritual writers of the first 1000 years of the Church, Ilias wrote in short highly concentrated paragraphs. In other words, the paragraphs are theologically loaded. Here are a few that relate to the topic of suffering.

*Here you will find, if you truly search,*
*A flowing spring, a pure fount of moral teaching.*

1. No Christian believing rightly in God should ever be off his guard. He should always be on the look-out for temptation, so that when it comes he will not be surprised or disturbed, but

## What is the Price of Transformation?

will gladly endure the toil and affliction it causes, and so will understand what he is saying when he chants with the prophet: 'Prove me, O Lord, and try me" (Psalm 26:2). For the prophet did not say, 'Thy correction has destroyed me', but, 'it has upheld me to the end' (Psalm 18:35)

2. The first step towards perfection is spiritual knowledge put into practice and practice imbued with spiritual knowledge. For practice without such knowledge is of no value, and so is such knowledge when unaccompanied by practice.

9. Suffering deliberately embraced cannot free the soul totally from sin unless the soul is also tried in the fire of suffering that comes unchosen. For the soul is like a sword: if it does not go 'through fire and water' (Psalm 66:12)—that is, through suffering deliberately embraced and suffering that comes unchosen—it cannot but be shattered by the blows of fortune.

10. Trials and temptations subject to our volition are chiefly caused by health, wealth and reputation, and those beyond our control by sickness, material losses and slander. Some people are helped by these things, others are destroyed by them.

21. The body cannot be purified without fasting and vigil, the soul without mercy and truth, and the intellect without contemplation of God and communion with Him. These pairs constitute the

principal virtues in these three aspects of the human person.

22. When the soul moves in obedience to these virtues, her citadel—patient endurance—is not disturbed by temptations. 'You will gain possession of your souls through your patient endurance' (Luke 21:19), says the Logos. Otherwise the soul will be shaken by fits of cowardice, as an unwalled city is by a distant uproar.

34. The greater the pain that you feel, the more you should welcome the person whose reproof makes you feel it. For he is bringing about within you that total purification without which your intellect cannot attain the pure state of prayer.

49. In addition to voluntary suffering, you must also accept that which comes against your will—I mean slander, material losses and sickness. For if you do not accept these but rebel against them, you are like someone who wants to eat his bread only with honey, never with salt. Such a man does not always have pleasure as his companion, but always has nausea as his neighbor.[108]

What is it that he appears to be saying about suffering? The first thing he says is that at least some of our suffering results from temptation. Certainly, we could add the idea that sin itself

---

[108] G. E. H. Palmer, et al., ed., *The Philokalia-Vol. III* (Winchester, Massachusetts: Faber and Faber, 1986), 32–9.

# What is the Price of Transformation?

results in suffering, but unfortunately that suffering more often than not goes unnoticed, tolerated, or even interpreted as happiness. Those of us who are indulging our various appetites might not recognize our own sinfulness, let alone see how we are suffering as a consequence. Obviously, Ilias is assuming that we, his readers, have moved beyond this level of delusion. So back to temptation. What he is suggesting is that our growth depends on some amount of suffering associated with the struggle with temptation, just as Jesus experienced. This suffering is good for us, and we might even value it for the positive results it brings.

**Thought vs. Practice**

Ilias presses further, however, positing that spiritual knowledge needs to be tied to *practice*. It is the practice that gets us into trouble and results in suffering. It is not the prayer itself or the intellectual pursuit that comes into conflict with those around us. It is the practice. What we actually do. If all we did was to go to church and Sunday school and think about the Bible, we would be worse than nowhere. Not only would we be doing nothing, but we would also be practicing a high level of delusion—a delusion predicated on the assumption that what we believe does not need to be translated into action.

So, this action or practice is what sets us up, not only for real growth, but also for real trouble. Then he links courage with practice and contemplation—the practice of spiritual knowledge. Again, it is the courage tacked on to the practice that creates bigger and bigger trouble. If Jesus had had no courage, he certainly would not have riled up the Pharisees the way he did. So Ilias is implying that suffering flows directly from our practice of the characteristics of Jesus. These characteristics are intimately related to Jesus' understanding of suffering in obedience to the will of his Father.

Into the Perfect Likeness

**Suffering**
Now we get to the good stuff. Ilias then makes a really important distinction between chosen and unchosen suffering and asserts that the first must be accompanied by the second. For Ilias, chosen suffering arises directly from the choices we make that have consequences for our health, wealth, or reputation. Now isn't that interesting. Think of the things that we might choose to do in the name of goodness or truth or Jesus. Ilias corralled the greatest fears of all of us, that we might be hurt, we might lose money, or we might lose good standing in our community, social group, or, God forbid, our church. Most of us would probably say we were making a huge sacrifice if we were willing to be fired from our $100,000/year job for a moral principle. Those who sacrificed their lives at the Chernobyl nuclear accident, or the first responders who died to save others during the 9-11 attack made choices that resulted in the sacrifice of their lives. Many who took a difficult stand during the civil rights struggles sacrificed standing in their more conservative communities. Clearly this kind of suffering is very similar to the kind of suffering that Jesus endured. Ilias would agree that this suffering is an essential part of our journey—but he says it is not enough.

It must be accompanied by suffering that is "unchosen." He tells us that sickness, material losses, and slander are the three major categories of unchosen suffering. In other words, we could one day find out that we have inoperable cancer of the pancreas, or the stock market just crashed and we were penniless, or that it was just reported on the front page of the local newspaper that we had just been accused (unjustly, by the way) of being the mastermind of an international Ponzi scheme. Good grief, now what? This kind of suffering is precisely what the biblical book of Job is all about. One unchosen suffering

## What is the Price of Transformation?

heaped upon another and another. Ilias says that the willingness to endure this unchosen suffering is also an essential part of our journey. What should our response be to this kind of suffering?

**Obedience and Willingness**
Ilias then talks about the relationships between obedience and the virtues of the body that are "fasting" and "vigil." Fasting is, of course, a kind of chosen suffering, and obedience is a kind of posture that makes us supple in hands of God. We could say that the posture of obedience is the same posture that allows us to exercise 'patient endurance' for some greater good.

Now number 34 seems particularly grim, but again let me stress that this is about a posture of willingness. If the posture reflects total willingness, then the pain is in some sense irrelevant. It has no effect on my life in God.[109] If the posture does not reflect total willingness, then the pain can be used to *affect* a posture of greater willingness. Finally, he repeats what he said before about suffering that comes against our will. What he adds is the idea that we might either accept the suffering or rebel against it. What he is suggesting is that each involuntary bit of trouble is an opportunity to grow in our willingness to accept those things that befall us—to be more and more supple to the will of God.

## God's Perspective on Suffering
If we assume that the world defines suffering from its own values such as wealth and reputation, then what are God's "values" when it comes to suffering? From God's point of view, there is

---

[109] Clearly, it is hard to see pain as irrelevant. We certainly must deal with it, and it has material impact on our ability to function, but from God's point of view, it may not be seen as having a concrete influence on how I am called to live my life.

only one thing that is essential, and that is union with God. Separation from God is death, but union with God is life. What we have been saying is that union with God is through union with Jesus. We participate in the life of God more and more as we live into the likeness of Jesus more and more.

So, from God's perspective, worldly suffering looks much less like suffering than it does from the world's perspective. If my house burns down, from the world's perspective that is suffering; but from God's perspective that may be irrelevant; and from Ilias's perspective it is a tremendous opportunity to grow into the life of Jesus and thus into the life of God.

## Two Aspects of Suffering

We need at this point to understand two things about suffering. First, it is an integral part of our journey toward Jesus, both as a result of our acting like Jesus and as a result of our growth process toward Jesus' very being. Second, the closer and closer we grow toward Jesus, that very same suffering takes on less and less importance until eventually what others call suffering, we might even call a blessing.

In the end, a godly perspective turns everything on its head. From God's perspective true suffering may be the feeling of abandonment by God. Recall the words of Jesus from the cross:

> And about the ninth hour Jesus cried with a loud voice, "Eli, Eli, la'ma sabach-tha'ni?" that is, "My God, my God, why hast thou forsaken me?"
> *Matthew 27:46*

This may represent the most profound suffering the world has ever witnessed—the Son of God feeling abandoned by his

## What is the Price of Transformation?

Father. We will deal much more with these thoughts in the next chapter.

# *14*
# What is the NET Price of Transformation?

So far, we have explored what it might look like if we were to look more and more like Jesus and how the world's perception of that transformation might not be particularly endearing. We have also looked at how suffering will undoubtedly become an integral part of our transformational journey and how the world will perceive this suffering. Our own perception should be quite different, to the point that for us, true suffering would be to reject the journey. In fact, the whole of salvation history is centered on this kind of suffering.

> God so loved the world that he gave his only begotten Son that all who believe in him should not perish but have everlasting life. *John 3:16*

The whole point of the Christ event is to heal the suffering that we as a people experienced as a result of our separation from God. That is why we must assert that the journey into the likeness of Jesus Christ is the whole point of Christianity.

## Tallying Up the Debits and Credits

When we put all this together and tally up the pros and cons, the pluses and minuses, the debits and credits, what do we get? That is what this chapter is about. If suffering were guaranteed to be our plight, why would anyone choose this path? The central question we should ask is: What is the benefit? That may sound a bit course and materialistic, but in fact, if there is no benefit in some form, then the whole thing makes absolutely no sense

## What is the NET Price of Transformation?

whatsoever. The problem is determining where to look for this benefit. Is it prosperity or stature in this life, or is it bliss in the next—or even some kind of bliss in this life? Let's look at some Scripture to set the stage.

"... anyone who hears my word and believes him who sent me has eternal life ..." *John 5:24*

"... those who hear will live." *John 5:25*

"Peace I leave with you; my peace I give to you." *John 14:27*

"... that they may have my joy fulfilled in themselves ..." *John 17:13*

... in order that the promise may be guaranteed to all his descendants ... ... *Romans 4:16*

... since we are justified by faith, we have peace with God, through our Lord ... *Romans 5:1–5*

For I delight in the law of God in my inmost self ... *Romans 7:22*

To set the mind on the flesh is death, but to set the mind on the Spirit is life and peace. *Romans 8:6*

God has destined us for salvation ... that we might live with Him. *1 Thessalonians 5:9–10*

... peace ... *2 Thessalonians 3:16*

| | |
|---|---|
| ... reward ... | *1 Corinthians 3:14* |
| ... rejoice together ... | *1 Corinthians 12:26* |
| ... raised in glory ... | *1 Corinthians 15:43* |
| ... victory ... | *1 Corinthians 15:57* |

All of these portions of Scripture refer to some kind of reward: life, eternal life, peace, joy, glory, rewards, delight, and victory. The first thing that jumps out at us is the often-repeated reference to "eternal life." First of all, the word "eternal" means "not pertaining to time," in other words, not temporal. It is the life of God. It does not mean "life everlasting," or lasting forever in time, although Scripture often uses the phrases interchangeably. Unfortunately, we have come to take any reference to eternal life or life everlasting to refer to heaven, and we take heaven to refer to that place the saved will go after they die a physical death. Let me talk first about heaven.

## Going to Heaven?

One prevalent theme in our popular religion is that the reason we walk the walk is to *go to heaven*. Pastors often suggest that the most compelling question a Christian might ask a non-Christian is, "If you died tomorrow, are you sure that you would go to heaven?" (instead of the "other place") Of course, this ploy is designed to send the objects of this communication into some form of nervous reaction that will drive them into the arms of Jesus. It is neat, clean, and simple. It appeals to our most basic instincts for survival and happiness—and aversion to withering heat.

The problem is that it betrays the central theme of the Incarnation and, as such, is not by itself orthodox. The God-man

## What is the NET Price of Transformation?

brings salvation to us right here, right now. Sure, there is a dimension of the plan that involves resurrection and life after death. We even have a number of very popular books from the evangelical tradition that describe heaven in considerable detail. I don't mean obvious allegories such as *The Great Divorce* by C. S. Lewis, but novels that imply that the author really knows from Scripture what heaven will be like.[110]

Let me say unequivocally that we do not know what heaven will be like. We know some things that it will not be like from the words of Jesus to the Pharisees, and we know some characteristics of the kingdom of God from the many parables of Jesus. We even have what appear to be some opaque details in the Book of Revelation. However, orthodoxy does not spend much effort on the details of where we go after we die. These details are left to the poets. We know enough to believe that our desired goal is life with God and that this life promises a level of joy that we can only point toward in faith. We have absolutely no idea what heaven is going to be like.

One thing is for certain, however, it is not like any joy we have experienced here. It is not like the time the University of South Carolina basketball team blew out the Tennessee Volunteers. (That has only happened once in my recollection.) It is not like the time Laurel Wheeler and I briefly dated one summer. (I had spent the whole school year quivering whenever she was near.) It wasn't even like the bliss of being with my first true love, Leah Dale. It is not like receiving the acceptance letter from Penn State Graduate School (that was the only place I wanted to go, so I had put all my eggs in that one basket), and so on and so forth. We cannot know, but we can trust. We can trust that our sense of heaven is all part of our ongoing faith that

---

[110] For example, Mitch Albom, *The Five People You Meet in Heaven* (New York: Hatchette Books, 2004).

allows us to put one faithful foot in front of another along the path we have chosen. This heaven on earth is all about faith and hope. What we do believe is that the alternative is what we call *Hell*!

## The Peace of God

Now if eternal life isn't essentially about heaven, then what is it about? Well, it certainly is about the kingdom of God. Orthodox Christology states unequivocally that Jesus died that we might have life, and life eternal—but when? The answer is critical to our understanding of our transformative journey into the likeness of Jesus. And the answer is *now*. That is the deal. So the payoff, so to speak, is in the here and now. Eternal life begins now. This is what Jesus referred to as the kingdom of God. In order to understand what that means, we need to look further at some more Scripture. Look at John 14:27 above. The operative word is *peace*. Consider the following:

> And the peace of God, which surpasses all understanding, will guard your hearts and your minds in Christ Jesus. *Philippians 4:7*

This blessing by Paul captures something important about the peace that Jesus offers us. It is the peace of God, and it is so wonderful that, when we experience it, we cannot even understand how to get it, how to keep it, or even how to manipulate it. It is a gift pure and simple, and it is the payoff. In this life, the payoff of being transformed into the likeness of Jesus is the peace of God that passes all understanding. It is the life of God that is outside of time and space. It is eternal life, right here and now. But where can we find this kind of life elucidated?

# What is the NET Price of Transformation?

**The City of God**
Now let's take a moment to hear from St. Augustine of Hippo (A.D. 354–410), who wrote one of the most important treatises on Christian doctrine called *The City of God*.

> But not even the saints and the faithful worshipers of the one true and most high God are secure against the manifold temptations and deceptions of the demons. For in this abode of weakness and in these evil days such anxiety is not useless, since it makes us seek with more fervent desire for that security *where peace is fullest and most certain*. There the gifts of nature given by the Creator of all nature will be not only good but everlasting, not only in respect to the spirit, which is healed through wisdom, but also in respect to the body, which will be renewed by resurrection; there the virtues, no longer struggling against any vice or evil whatsoever, will have as the reward of victory *eternal peace* which no adversary may disquiet. For this is the final blessedness, this the ultimate perfection, the unending end. Here, surely we are called blessed when we have *peace*, however small a portion can be had in a good life; but this blessedness is discovered to be mere misery. So when we mortals possess such *peace* as this mortal life can provide, virtue, if we live rightly, makes the right use of good things; but when we have no peace, virtue makes good use even of the evils a man suffers. But true virtue is to subordinate all the good things it uses and everything it does in making good use of good and evil things and itself as well, to that end where

our *peace* will be so excellent and so great that it cannot be improved or increased.[111]

It is clear that Augustine is true to his entire doctrinal foundation, that we cannot have much peace in this life and that we get the real peace of God in the next. But if you press his logic, as thank goodness the Church has, you come to the orthodox conclusion, as the Church did, that the peace of God that surpasses all understanding has indeed been made available to us in *this life*, abundantly.

## Hebrew Scripture

The Hebrew Scripture is full of references to peace that have laid the groundwork for the writings of the New Testament above.

> For a child has been born for us, a son given to us; authority rests upon his shoulders; and he is named Wonderful Counselor, Mighty God, Everlasting Father, *Prince of Peace*.     *Isaiah 9:6*

> May the Lord give strength to his people! May the Lord bless his people with *peace*!     *Psalms 29:11*

These references could easily be dismissed as referring to a societal peace in the world—the absence of conflict. We could miss the implications concerning our own personal transformation. In fact, peace does mean the absence of conflict. How does this apply to us as individuals?

---

[111] *Augustine of Hippo: Selected Writings*, translation and introduction by Mary T. Clark (New York: Paulist Press, 1984), 451–2. Reprinted by permission, Paulist Press, Mahwah, New Jersey. All rights reserved.

What is the NET Price of Transformation?

## Integrity

We start by asserting that each of us was created for some purpose centered on the image of God that is built into us, and that God intends that our actions and thoughts operate within that purpose. This is called the *will of God*. As long as we function within the will of God, then all the pieces of our being are in accord with each other and with the image of God that is within us. As long as we operate in this way, there is no internal conflict. When we choose to go our own way, as we all seem to do, we are by definition *conflicted*. The parts are not *integrated*, and we are not operating with the ultimate level of *integrity* that is intended for us. We have no peace. Thus, we cannot experience the ultimate joy that comes from the peace of God, a peace that passes all understanding. But can this happen in this life? Have we seen anyone who somehow reflects this kind of peace?

## As It Is in Heaven

Let's look at a modern author, John Chryssavgis, who writes from the Eastern Orthodox tradition.

> In tenth-century Constantinople, Symeon the New Theologian, Abbot of the Monastery of St. Mamas, warned his community that to believe the ways of the heart are not a reality experienced in contemporary times but restricted only to the distant past is doctrinally and spiritually dangerous:
>
>> I call heretics those who say that there is no one in our times and in our midst able to keep the commandments and become like the Fathers. . . . Now those who claim that this is impossible have not fallen into one particular heresy but rather into all of them,

if I may say so, since this one surpasses all of them in abundance of blasphemy.[112]

In modern-day Greece, the same conviction is affirmed by Archimandrite Vasileios, Abbot of the Monastery of Iveron on Mount Athos or the Holy Mountain, as it is known—a peninsula in north-eastern Greece and a key center of Orthodox monasticism since the tenth century. . . . After introducing the spiritual life and liturgical prayer of monks on the Holy Mountain, Fr. Vaseleios endeavors to convey to the reader the indisputable reality of his conclusions, by sketching the portrait of a monk who remains unnamed, yet whom he claims to know. "Such monks," he writes,

> unknown and anonymous, but full of light, exist. I know one. He literally overflows. That is an expression that gives some idea of the truth about him. He has a treasure of inexpressible joy hidden in an earthen vessel, small and fragile. And this joy overflows and spreads all around him, filling his surroundings with its fragrance. Light shines from his being. . . . In his presence you feel that the saints of old continue to live amongst us, just as he himself, being dead to the world, lives among us in another way, in the Holy Spirit. . . . You understand too how the Christian doctrine of

---

[112] *Catechetical Discourse*, 39, 3-5. in Classics of Western Spirituality (New York: Paulist Press, 1980), 311–3.

## What is the NET Price of Transformation?

> the immortality of the soul is to be interpreted, how the resurrection of the body will be. Things present and things to come are made clear, not by discursive reasoning, but by appearing, by being made manifest in life.... So the presence of the saints of old becomes evident. And the grace of the saints of our own time transcends history, *leading us here and now into eternity*. ...[113]

*Leading us here and now into eternity?* The compelling idea of this chapter is that the peace of God has been made available to us all right now—and will carry on into eternity. Those things that the world would call struggle and sacrifice, God calls either irrelevant or good, and we could, if we were perfectly surrendered to the will of God, call *peace and joy*. It doesn't get any better than that—and that is the payoff.

---

[113] Originally appearing in Greek in 1974, *Hymn of Entry* was published in English by St. Vladimir's Seminary Press in 1984. The passage quoted above is taken from chapter 6 (126–31). This quotation is found in *Paths to the Heart*, James S Cutsinger, ed., (Bloomington, Indiana: World Wisdom, Inc., 2002), chapter 6, *Paths of Continuity: Contemporary Witnesses of the Hesychast Experience* by John Chryssavgis, 112–4.

# *15*
# How Much Transformation Has Been Offered to Us?

Now we finally get to the home stretch. How much transformation has been offered to us? Exactly how much like Jesus can I be? How good is it possible for me to be? How honest? How righteous? How perfect? How much like God? If there were one issue that is at the core of Christianity and at the same time points out the distinct differences between the different mainline denominations, this is it. This is where the rubber meets the road. And yet very few Christians even know that this issue is even the least bit controversial. Most of us take our position for granted and quietly assume that all others share the same position.

What has emerged from a simple study of priests, pastors, bishops, and theological professors is that this issue may be the headwaters of a set of doctrinal rivers that have become the diverse expressions of modern Christianity. If the problem with modern Christianity is a certain muddled understanding of who Jesus was and what he offered to those of us who follow him, then what we have been calling orthodox Christology had better be very clear about all of this.

## Pickin' and Choosin'
To begin, let's look at some Scripture, with one caveat. While many would like to believe that Scripture solves every doctrinal debate, the fact is that Scripture is not perfectly consistent. One can make a case for just about anything, if one picks and chooses the right scriptural passages. And let us not delude ourselves—we all pick and choose. Anyone who holds up the Bible as their

## How Much Transformation Has Been Offered to Us?

ultimate source of authority independent of the history of the Church and its doctrinal development must be careful to acknowledge the source of their interpretation. The subtle trap is that they may be merely holding themselves—or their interpretation—up as the authority, not the Scripture.

Whenever we hear anyone discussing a point based on Scripture, we all must recognize what is going on. We might state boldly that it is not important what any one of us thinks is the correct basis for our Christological doctrine, or any other doctrine for that matter, but what the Church thinks. We need to recognize the power of the Church in prayerful deliberation and discernment over a very long period of time. We need to appreciate the movement of the Holy Spirit in that communal process. We are not Christians alone. Presbyterians, Catholics, and Anglicans will look to their own history and doctrinal statements. Baptists, Lutherans, and Methodists will do the same. In any event, we need to recognize the place of the Church body and doctrinal development in any statement of authority concerning doctrine. Whatever doctrinal development has taken place in the body of Christ over the years is certainly first and foremost grounded in Scripture and the apostolic traditions reflected therein. It is also the result of the ongoing struggle of the body of believers to understand, with the activity of the Holy Spirit, the depth of meaning Scripture contains.

So, having offered a little caveat, let me do some pickin' and choosin' of my own.

> "Be perfect, therefore, as your heavenly Father is perfect." *Matthew 5:48*

> "Heal the sick, raise the dead, cleanse lepers, cast out demons." *Matthew 10:8*

## Into the Perfect Likeness

So Peter got out of the boat and walked on the water
...                    *Matthew 14:28–33*

"I am the light of the world."           *John 8:12*

"You are the light of the world."        *Matthew 5:14*

"Whoever welcomes you welcomes me, and whoever welcomes me welcomes the one who sent me."
*Matthew 10:40*

". . . the one who believes in me will also do the works that I do; and, in fact, will do greater works than these . . ."           *John 14:12*

". . . I am in my Father, and you in me, and I in you."
*John 14:20*

"I am the vine, you are the branches. Those who abide in me and I in them bear much fruit, because apart from me you can do nothing."     *John 15:3–5*

"The glory that you have given me I have given them, so that they may be one, as we are one." *John 17:22*

"I in them and you in me, that they may become completely [perfectly] one . . ."         *John 17:23*

". . . that the love with which you have loved me may be in them, and I in them . . ."         *John 17:26*

How Much Transformation Has Been Offered to Us?

But Peter put them all outside and knelt down and prayed; then turning to the body he said, "Tabitha, rise." And she opened her eyes . . .   *Acts 9:36–43*

On Peter's arrival Cornelius met him and falling at his feet, worshiped him. But Peter made him get up, saying, "Stand up; I am only a mortal."   *Acts 10:25*

And a young man named Eu'tychus was sitting in the window. He sank into a deep sleep as Paul talked still longer; and being overcome by sleep, he fell down from the third story and was taken up dead. But Paul went down and bent over him, and embracing him said, "Do not be alarmed, for his life is in him." And when Paul had gone up and had broken bread and eaten, he conversed with them a long while, until daybreak, and so departed. And they took the lad away alive, and were not a little comforted.   *Acts 20:9–12*

But we have the mind of Christ.   *Romans 2:16*

You were made free from sin through the Holy Spirit . . .   *Romans 7:18*

Just as we have born the image of the man of dust, we will also bear the image of the man of heaven.
*Romans 15:49*

and in him there is no sin. No one who abides in him sins.   *1 John 3:4–10*

Into the Perfect Likeness

> No one has ever seen God; if we love one another,
> God lives in us, and his love is perfected in us.
> *1 John 4:7–21*

When one picks and chooses these passages, and if one takes them at face value, one makes a pretty strong case that:

1. Jesus intended for us to act like he acted and thereby participate in his own perfection.
2. Jesus intended for us to have the same intimate relationship with the Father that he experienced.
3. Paul interpreted Jesus' call not only to act like Jesus, but also to have the *mind* of Jesus.
4. Paul interpreted this transformation of mind as resulting in a total rejection of sin and a reflection of the perfection that is found in Jesus.

Now you might say that these are my own interpretations and that I have left out a lot of Scripture that implies that this much perfection has not been offered to us, and you would be absolutely correct. This is why it is important to see this Scripture as signposts pointing toward what the Church has concluded about Jesus and his radical call to us. But how radical is this call. What is this business of being "perfect?"

## Be Perfect

In *Mere Christianity*, C. S. Lewis directly addresses the issue of the extent of the call.

> In the last chapter we were considering the Christian idea of "putting on Christ," or first "dressing up" as a son of God in order that you may finally become a real son. What I want to make clear is that this is

not one among many jobs a Christian has to do; and it is not a sort of special exercise for the top class. It is the whole of Christianity.[114]

The Christian way is different: harder, and easier. Christ says "Give me All. I don't want so much of your time and so much of your money and so much of your work: I want You. I have not come to torment your natural self, but to kill it. No half-measures are any good. I don't want to cut off a branch here and a branch there, I want to have the whole tree down. I don't want to drill the tooth, or crown it, or stop it, but to have it out. Hand over the whole natural self, all the desires which you think innocent as well as the ones you think wicked—the whole outfit. I will give you a new self instead. In fact, I will give you Myself: my own will shall become yours."[115]

When he said, "Be perfect," He meant it. He meant that we must go in for the full treatment. It is hard; but the sort of compromise we are all hankering after is harder—in fact, it is impossible. It may be hard for an egg to turn into a bird: it would be a jolly sight harder for it to learn to fly while remaining an egg. We are like eggs at present, And you cannot go on indefinitely being just an ordinary, decent egg. We must be hatched or go bad.[116]

---

[114] C. S. Lewis, *Mere Christianity* (Westwood, NJ: Barbour and Company, Inc. 1952), 165.
[115] Ibid., 166.
[116] Ibid., 168.

> And yet this is the other and equally important side of it—this Helper who will, in the long run, be satisfied with nothing less than absolute perfection will also be delighted with the first feeble, stumbling effort you make tomorrow to do the simplest duty. As a great Christian writer (George McDonald) pointed out, every father is pleased at the baby's first attempt to walk: no father would be satisfied with anything less than a firm, free, manly walk in a grown-up son. In the same way, he said, "God is easy to please, but hard to satisfy."[117]

What is so interesting about Lewis is that he speaks as if these are his own opinions. He never rests on the authority of the Church in sorting out the things he is concluding. He doesn't talk about the Church Fathers or the councils or a modern catechism that has resulted from these struggles within the Church. As a matter of fact, he quotes little Scripture, and yet many Christians read his writings, study them, and take them to be their guide. What is equally interesting is that he is completely orthodox in all but the subtlest points he makes. An Episcopal priest once told me that Lewis interpreted Catholic doctrine for Anglicans. I would agree, because there is no body of Anglican doctrine from which he could have drawn these conclusions of such a radical transformation.

## A Radical Transformation

And of course, this is precisely the point of this chapter. Orthodox Christian doctrine states that Jesus, the Christ, calls us into a total transformation into his perfect likeness. At this point let

---

[117] Ibid., 171.

How Much Transformation Has Been Offered to Us?

me lay out some of the most radical statements that talk about the amount of transformation that has been offered to us.

> **St. Irenaeus (130–200)**
> "The word became man in order to make us what he is himself."
>
> **St. Athanasius (296–373)**
> "He became man that we might become divine."
>
> **St. Thomas Aquinas (1225–1274)**
> "The only begotten Son of God, wishing to enable us to share in his divinity, assumed our nature, so that by becoming man, he might make men gods."

These are the most radical statements in all of Christianity—and there is no doubt that they can be unsettling, troubling, and even grossly misunderstood. I hope you will see, if they are properly interpreted, that they are simply the logical conclusion of the saving work of Jesus Christ. We might even say that they *define* that saving work. Jesus saves by his actions on our behalf on the Cross and by his very being that closes the gap between God and mankind. Anything short of a radical transformation into the perfect likeness of Jesus Christ is simply a falling short of what has been offered to us—an incomplete closure of the gap. Jesus intends to slam the gap shut.

## Maximus the Confessor

There is one Church Father who we all need to know about for a variety of reasons. We now call him Saint Maximus the Confessor, and he lived in the sixth and seventh centuries. He was born in A.D. 580 to a prominent family in Constantinople. When he was still in his thirties, he was appointed to the position of "first secretary" in the court of the emperor Heraclius. Three years later, he resigned the position and moved into a monastery in what is now Scutari, Turkey, where he soon became abbot. He eventually made his way to North Africa where he participated in one of the fundamental disputes of the early Church.

The controversy, which to us may seem a bit obscure, centered on whether Jesus had both a divine will as well as a human will, or whether he had only a divine will. Max (I use this only as a deeply affectionate diminutive) understood that once you strip Jesus of his human will, you flush the Incarnation down the toilet. (He might not have put it in exactly those terms.) He made his views known so forcefully that the Church had only two choices, either agree with him or shut him up. Eventually he was arrested by the order of Emperor Constans II and brought to Constantinople where, during one of the most poignant trials in the history of the Church (that is completely documented, by the way[118]) Max was found guilty of treason and banished in A.D. 655. He still would not shut up, so he was returned to Constantinople where he was condemned to mutilation. His tongue, by which he proclaimed the truth, was ripped out, and his right hand, by which he wrote the truth, was chopped off. Shortly thereafter he died. It was August 13, 662.[119] Oh, my dear Max—that I too should have that wisdom and courage.

The point of all this is that Max was not only a model of Christian courage, but also one of the most profound theologians of the seventh century. Again, like so many writers of that period, he wrote in short succinct paragraphs. Let's look at some writings from his *Various Texts on Theology, the Divine Economy, and Virtue and Vice*.

---

[118] George C. Berthold, translation and notes *Maximus Confessor* (New York: Paulist Press, 1985), The Trial of Maximus, 17–31.
[119] Ibid., 1–5.

## How Much Transformation Has Been Offered to Us?

62. A sure warrant for looking forward with hope to the deification of human nature is provided by the incarnation of God, which makes man god to the same degree as God Himself became man. For it is clear that He who became man without sin will *divinize human nature* without changing it into the divine nature, and will raise it up for His own sake to the same degree as He lowered Himself for man's sake. This is what St. Paul teaches mystically when he says, '. . . that in the ages to come He might display the overflowing richness of his grace'.

68. Those who are beginners and stand at the gate of the divine court of the virtues are called 'God-fearing' by Scripture. Those who with some measure of stability have acquired the principles and qualities of the virtues, it describes as 'advancing'. Those who in their pursuit of holiness have by means of spiritual knowledge already attained the summit of that truth which reveals the virtues, it entitles '*perfect*'.

73. God, who yearns for the salvation of all men and hungers after their *deification*, withers their self-conceit like the unfruitful fig tree. He does this so that they may prefer to be righteous in reality rather than in appearance, discarding the cloak of hypocritical moral display and genuinely pursuing a virtuous life in the way that the divine Logos wishes them to. They will then

live with reverence, revealing the state of their soul to God rather than displaying the external appearance of a moral life to their fellow-men.

74. The principle of active accomplishment is one thing and that of passive suffering is another. The principle of active accomplishment signifies the natural capacity for actualizing the virtues. The principle of passive suffering signifies experiencing either the grace of what is beyond nature or the occurrence of what is contrary to nature. For just as we do not have a natural capacity for what is above being, so we do not by nature have a capacity for what lacks being. Thus we passively experience *deification by grace* as something which is above nature, but we do not actively accomplish it; for by nature we do not have the capacity to attain *deification*. Again, we suffer evil as something contrary to nature which occurs in the will; for we do not have a natural capacity for generating evil. Thus while we are in our present state we can actively accomplish the virtues by nature, since we have a natural capacity for accomplishing them. But, when raised to a higher level, we experience *deification* passively, receiving this experience as a *free gift of grace*.

75. The qualities of the virtues and the inner principles of created beings are both images of divine blessings, and in them God continually becomes man. As His body He has the qualities

of the virtues, and as His soul the inner principles of spiritual knowledge. In this way He *deifies* those found worthy, giving them the true stamp of virtue and bestowing on them the essence of infallible knowledge. [120]

Now, I know this is tough stuff to digest. But for our purposes there are two words that jump out at us: *deification* and *perfection*.

## A Transformation of Being

It is clear that Max takes for granted that we are in a process of perfection, which he seems to mean the process of being drawn into the life of God.[121] In other words, to become like God, but not just like God in every way—but to become so much *one with God* that when someone sees our actions and experiences our compassion they experience the actions and compassion of God. This is the process of *deification* or *becoming god*. Notice the usual care taken here is to use a small "g" to designate that we do not become all of God, but we become part of God. It is something like being a glass of water that is thrown into the Atlantic Ocean. That water does not become the entirety of the Atlantic Ocean, but certainly does become "ocean" in a very real sense. That would be the "ocean-ification" of the glass of water. As we are perfected in Jesus, who is God, we become Jesus-ified or deified. Paragraph 62 therefore becomes one of the most powerful expressions of orthodox Christology. It is worth repeating.

---

[120] G. E. H. Palmer, et al., ed., *The Philokalia-Vol. III* (Winchester, Massachusetts: Faber and Faber, 1986), 177–82.

[121] While the concept of perfection might take on different meanings for different cultures and philosophies, it clearly points to a state that reflects no falling short. Here we would call this a state without sin. In other words, a state that is in accord with the will of God. That is our goal.

> A sure warrant for looking forward with hope to the deification of human nature is provided by the incarnation of God, which makes man god to the same degree as God Himself became man.

God reaches out in Christ to draw us to himself and into himself. If this seems a bit far-fetched and radical, it is. This is precisely why Jesus was so controversial and one of the reasons why he, like Max, had to be silenced. The difficulty of comprehending this radical call to transformation is well illustrated by the life of a wonderful spiritual seeker, Henri Nouwen.

## Becoming the Father

Nouwen was born in 1932 in Holland and ordained into the Catholic priesthood in 1957. Although his life was spent in a widely varying journey, one that took him from solitude at the Trappist monastery at Genesee Abbey in upstate New York to the academic setting of Yale University to the slums of Peru, there was always a constant drive to translate his personal journey into the written word. He wrote such spiritual treasures as the *Genesee Diary: Report from a Trappist Monastery* (1976) as well as such insightful commentaries on the Christian life, such as *The Return of the Prodigal Son* (1992). He passed away in 1996 at the age of 65. It is this latter work that is of particular interest here.

*The Return of the Prodigal Son* was written as a response to Nouwen's encounter with the Rembrandt painting depicting the biblical story in Luke 15:11–32. It is basically a meditation on the characters in the scene, the younger son, who is being welcomed back into the family after a life of profligacy, the dutiful elder son, who is exhibiting a bit of disgust at the ease with which the other is received, and finally the father, who is shown tenderly holding the prodigal son who is kneeling before him in abject humility. What is so compelling here is the realization of Nouwen concerning the importance of the father and the Father. Here are his words.

## Conclusion: Becoming the Father

*"Be compassionate as your Father is compassionate."*
*A Lonely Step*

When I first saw the detail of Rembrandt's Prodigal Son, a spiritual journey was set in motion that led me to write this book. As I now come to its conclusion, I discover how long a journey I have made.

From the beginning I was prepared to accept that not only the younger son, but also the elder son would reveal to me an important aspect of my spiritual journey. For a long time, the father remained "the other," the one who would receive me, forgive me, offer me a home, and give me peace and joy. The father was

## Into the Perfect Likeness

the place to return to, the goal of my journey, the final resting place. It was only gradually and often quite painfully that I came to realize that my spiritual journey would never be complete as long as the father remained an outsider.

I am amazed how long it has taken me to make the father the center of my attention. It was so easy to identify with the two sons. Their outer and inner waywardness is so understandable and so profoundly human that identification happens almost spontaneously as soon as the connections are pointed out.

But what of the father? Why pay so much attention to the sons when it is the father who is in the center and when it is the father with whom I am to identify? Why talk so much about being like the sons when the real question is: Are you interested in being like the father? It feels somehow good to be able to say: "These sons are like me." It gives a sense of being understood. But how does it feel to say: "The father is like me"? Do I want to be like the father? Do I want to be not just the one who is being forgiven, but also the one who forgives; not just the one who is being welcomed home, but also the one who welcomes home; not just the one who receives compassion, but the one who offers it as well?[122]

---

[122] Henri J. M. Nouwen, *Return of the Prodigal Son: A Story of Homecoming* (New York: Doubleday, 1994), 122. Reprinted by permission, Doubleday, a division of Random House, Inc. All rights reserved.

## How Much Transformation Has Been Offered to Us?

Perhaps the most radical statement Jesus ever made is: "Be compassionate as your father is compassionate."[123] God's compassion is described by Jesus not simply to show me how willing God is to feel for me, or to forgive me my sins and offer me new life and happiness, but to invite me to become like God and to show the same compassion to others as he is showing to me.

What I am called to make true is that whether I am the younger or the elder son, I am the son of my compassionate Father. I am an heir. No one says it more clearly than Paul when he writes: "The Spirit himself joins with our spirit to bear witness that we are children of God. And if we are children, then we are heirs, heirs of God and joint heirs with Christ, provided that we share his sufferings, so as to share his glory." Indeed, as son and heir I am to become successor. I am destined to step into my Father's place and offer to others the same compassion that he has offered me. The return to the Father is ultimately the challenge to become the Father.[124]

Notice the shift in the use of "father" to "Father." Make no mistake about it; four years before his death, after many books on the Christian life, Henri Nouwen finally *got it*. And he knew he had gotten it. He knew that he had to spread the word because he also knew that there were many, many others just like himself

---

[123] Luke 6:36. The RSV translation of this line is, "Be merciful, even as your Father is merciful." A similar but more compelling line in Matthew (5:48) is, "You, therefore, must be perfect, as your heavenly Father is perfect."
[124] Ibid., 123.

who did not get it—especially those who did not have the theological training or the years of serious searching that he had. And as Lewis would say, the transformation into a new Christ-being is not just one of the central points of Christianity, *it is the only point*. Our transformation into the perfect likeness of Jesus, whom we call God incarnate, *is the only point*.

## The Only Point

There is one crucial issue that we have touched on before that tends to block dialogue concerning this radical transformation. Has this transformation into perfection been offered to us in this life? Here is Lewis again.

> Here is another way of putting the two sides of the truth. On the one hand we must never imagine that our own unaided efforts can be relied on to carry us even through the next twenty-four hours as "decent" people. If He does not support us, not one of us is safe from some gross sin. On the other hand, no possible degree of holiness or heroism which has ever been recorded of the greatest saints is beyond what He is determined to produce in every one of us in the end. The job *will* not be completed in this life: but He means to get us as far as possible before death.[125]

Now herein lies the rub. Lewis uses the word "will" and the correct word is "may"—unequivocally. There is nothing in orthodox teaching, unless one takes St. Augustine as the definition of orthodoxy, which the Church has not, that blocks us from the perfection of Christ. Now this is where Catholic teaching about

---

[125] Lewis, *Mere Christianity*, 172–3.

How Much Transformation Has Been Offered to Us?

Mary, the mother of Jesus, becomes particularly interesting and compelling.

## Something about Mary

Mary has always been of supreme importance to both the Roman Catholic and Eastern Orthodox churches. One could almost echo the words of Paul by saying that for Protestantism, Mary is a stumbling block, but for Roman and Orthodox Catholics Mary has reflected the wisdom and power of God.[126] What is it about Mary that, on the one hand, taps into our deepest fears or on the other captures our highest expression of veneration? There is no doubt that there has been error on both sides. For the Catholics, I am told, part of Vatican II was focused on correcting some of the excesses regarding Mary. While Protestants would say that Catholics worship Mary, Catholics would say that they "venerate" her, and they would say that this is a huge distinction. On the other hand, while Catholics would say that the Protestants ignore her, Protestants might say that they simply have her in proper perspective, a perspective that is consistent with Jesus' own words.

While Luther tended to maintain an essentially Catholic understanding of Mary, it is clear that, as Protestantism took hold, later leaders saw Mary's position as a threat to the centrality of Christ in the salvation story. What we end up with is the appearance that some Protestants ignore her to their own detriment, and some Catholics venerate her to the point of becoming dangerously close to worship. Neither position is really in line with the

---

[126] The actual quotation is: "For Jews demand signs and Greeks desire wisdom, but we proclaim Christ crucified, a stumbling block to Jews and foolishness to Gentiles, but to those who are the called, both Jews and Greeks, Christ the power of God and the wisdom of God" (1 Corinthians 1:23).

best of either tradition.[127] The orthodox truth about Mary, on the other hand, can only be appreciated in light of orthodox truth about Jesus. Only after we understand Jesus and the radical call to transformation that he offers us, can we understand the important role of Mary in the full expression of the Incarnation.

Here is how it works. If indeed perfection is offered to us on this earth through the saving work of Jesus' Incarnation and atonement, then we must ask if there has been anyone whom the Church has said has lived fully into that possibility. And the answer is an unequivocal yes. The first to do so other than Jesus himself was Mary. Now you may ask, how is it that Mary can live into the perfection that is offered to us by her son when her expression of that perfection takes place before Jesus' work of salvation has been completed and, in fact, before he is even born.

While this is all part of the mystery of the Christ event, we can say that the event, although in time, is in some way eternal in its effect. Thus, Mary can participate in the salvation offered to us through Jesus before it takes place in time. So, ignoring time factors, Jesus reestablishes the bridge between God and mankind, and Mary walks over it. But she is so important that we need to spend a bit more time with her.

To understand Mary is also to understand Jesus and *vise versa*. We have already established that Jesus had free will, and thus was subject just as much as we are to the possibility of sin. We must also assert that he was born without the taint of "original sin." In other words, he was not a slave to sin *by nature*. We participate in Jesus' nature through *grace* as expressed in the sacrament of Holy Baptism. We have also asserted that Jesus had to struggle just as we do to "appropriate" or live into his *nature* just as we must struggle to appropriate or live into the *grace* that

---

[127] It is also interesting to note that the editor of Luther's Works in English converted to Catholicism. One wonders if Luther convinced him.

## How Much Transformation Has Been Offered to Us?

has been offered to us. In other words, Jesus was without the necessity of sin *by nature* but was without the actual sin *by choice*. We are without the necessity of sin through *baptism* but are without actual sin *by choice*. Unfortunately, we always seem to make the wrong choice. But as we said before, after baptism we must take responsibility for all our sin. We no longer sin because we are human. We sin because we choose to. Now this is where Mary really gets interesting.

The Catholic Church has articulated a formula that offers Mary the same benefits that we get through baptism.[128] Since baptism is a temporal sacrament that happens at a point in time and space, she is a bit stuck, because she obviously cannot partake of the sacrament of Holy Baptism before it is instituted. How does the Church overcome this dilemma? Well, it is called the Immaculate Conception. The Church asserts that Mary was conceived without "original sin." Mary is simply offered through the Immaculate Conception the same benefits of the salvational work of Jesus as we are through baptism. She is not given any extra help. She is simply brought up to par with us. Does this make Mary sinless? Not by a long shot! Mary is without actual sin *by choice* just as Jesus was and just as you and I could be if we so chose.

What the doctrine of the Blessed Virgin Mary accomplishes is to give us another model of one who lived into perfection through grace. As Catholics assert that she is "full of grace,"[129]

---

[128] There is no question that the Catholic formula related to Mary are problematic for many. The point here is the ultimate consequence of this formula and not the details.

[129] This is actually Jerome's translation of "most highly favored one" and is a bit of a stretch until one sees the role of the Catholic Church in developing doctrine consistent with the "big picture. The Latin *gratia plena* would have been used if the strict translation would work. The Church

they proclaim the possibility that you and I could also be full of grace, if we surrendered to the will of the Father as she did. Her words could become our words. "Here am I, the servant of the Lord; let it be with me according to your word" (Luke 1:38). And someone could say to us, "Blessed are you among humanity, and blessed is the fruit of your spirit" (Luke 1:42). And we start to imagine the kind of surrender to the will of God that would result in her words becoming our own words.

> "My soul magnifies the Lord, and my spirit rejoices in God my Savior, for he has looked with favor on the lowliness of his servant. Surely, from now on all generations will call me blessed;" *Luke 1:46–55*

What we can say, in summary, is that *Mary has never been about Mary*, per se. The title Mother of God (Theotokos) was not intended to elevate Mary to some exalted status—it was intended to assert unequivocally that the one born of woman was, indeed, God. To say that Mary was without sin, was not intended to elevate her status so that we would revere her above all other human beings, but to assert that we too have been given access to the same state as she reflected. In other words, Mary was first about Jesus and second about us.

There is nothing in this that is inconsistent with the gift of eternal life here and now that has been offered to us. The challenge for us is to see how these very same statements could apply to us. Under what conditions could we make these statements. In other words, to test these waters, we might want to

---

has kept his translation in its Hail Mary because it more accurately reflects the status of Mary as the Mother of God and a perfect example of one living fully into the likeness of Jesus.

How Much Transformation Has Been Offered to Us?

follow the advice of C. S. Lewis and "try on" radical statements such as these.

## Miracles

One of the most challenging aspects of Christian Transformation is the problem of miracles. Before we engage in the process of "trying on," we need to revisit something of our general posture toward the will of the Father. Clearly, we are all called to believe that Jesus "performed" miracles. Above we talked about how our understanding of those miracles is closely related to his intimate relationship to the Father, the authority of the Father and the obedience of the Son. If this is, indeed, true, then what does this model say about us? Jesus makes statements that imply that we are to do the same sorts of things that he did and "greater things." How are we to understand this call? Are we supposed to be able to snap our fingers and raise Grandma from the dead? Are we supposed to lay hands on anyone who is sick and heal them? Are we supposed to walk on water whenever we want?

Actually, the answer to these legitimate questions is quite simple and looks exactly like our understanding of the miracles that Jesus performed. If the Father wants Grandma raised from the dead through me and I am the faithful obedient instrument of that will, then Grandma is "comin' up." Otherwise Grandma will rest in peace just like most of the rest of the folks who experienced normal human death.

If the Father wants me to walk on water and I am the faithful obedient instrument of that will, then I can walk right out there. Otherwise I will sink like a rock just like the rest of normal people who have normal buoyancy. OK, well not exactly like a rock, but you get the idea.

In other words we are called to function just exactly as Jesus functioned: live a life of ceaseless prayer in communication with the will of the Father and respond to that will just as Jesus did, recognizing that most of the time the will of the Father is to "play the game." Play the human limited cards that are dealt us with the same universal characteristics of his Son, Jesus Christ. With this radical openness to the will of the Father in mind, let us "try on" Jesus.

## Trying on the Words of Jesus

One question that should arise is whether we see in Scripture any of the followers of Jesus using words that look very much like the words he spoke. Let's look at a few passages.

> Stephen, full of grace and power, did great wonders and signs among the people. . . . Then they dragged him out of the city and began to stone him. . . . While they were stoning Stephen, he prayed, "Lord Jesus, receive my spirit." Then he knelt down and cried out in a loud voice, "Lord, do not hold this sin against them." When he had said this, he died.
> *Acts 6:8, 7:58, 7:59–60*

> "I am now rejoicing in my sufferings for your sake, and in my flesh I am completing what is lacking in Christ's afflictions for the sake of his body, that is, the church."
> *Paul in his letter to the Colossians, 1:24*

> "Therefore I intend always to remind you of these things, though you know them and are established in the truth that you have. I think it right, as long as I am in this body, to arouse you by way of reminder, since

How Much Transformation Has Been Offered to Us?

I know that the putting off of my body will be soon, as our Lord Jesus Christ showed me."
*Peter in his second letter, 1:12–14*

In each of these cases, Stephen, Paul and Peter saw themselves as responsible not only for acting but also speaking in radical tones the truths that had been conferred upon them. They saw as their responsibility not only to speak *about* Jesus, but to some extent to speak *like* Jesus, recalling at every turn that, just as Jesus "did nothing on his own authority," so neither Stephen nor Paul nor Peter nor any of the other Apostles, nor any of the saints of the Church who followed, nor any of us modern Christians, do or say anything on our own authority. In this light there is only one last thing to do in this regard. We simply must "try on" Jesus.

In fact, we should consider a central spiritual exercise that of "trying on" the words of Mary, Peter, Paul, and all the Apostles that point toward a radical transformation. In other words, the challenge here is to see how we might say these very same words about ourselves—to try them on. These statements are simply a logical consequence of these people's belief in the possibility of total transformation into the perfect likeness of Jesus. This final exercise directly links us to this radical transformation into the full stature of Jesus. This exercise is to look at Jesus himself, at his actions and his words, and "try them on." As I pointed out in Chapter 12, there are an infinite number of "actions" that we might consider copying in order to get a clearer idea of just what is meant by this transformation into the likeness of Jesus. But we also said then that the transformation is more about "posture" than it is about specific kinds of actions.

Let me carry that a bit further while developing the idea of "trying on" Jesus. Let me start by offering a meditation—some might call it a daydream. Some years ago, I was thinking about this whole process of transformation and the picture came to my mind of Jesus standing next to me with another of his garments neatly folded. He holds it out to me and says, "Here, Jonathan, put this on." And I reply, "But Lord this is your garment, I couldn't possibly put it on." At which point he looks at me both sternly and yet with a reflection of profound compassion for my confusion and says, "Jonathan, unless you put it on, you have no part in me." As I reflected on this little meditation, I began to realize that even in our imperfection, we are called to dress up like Jesus, exactly as C. S. Lewis said.

A wonderful and powerful preacher, Cynthia DeBerry Freeman once said, "God has to shape us up and use us all at the same time."[130] To take on the mind of Christ is first to be willing to try. So, I went to a fabric store and got some course cotton material called osnaburg and had a Jesus robe made up from a costume pattern. Then in one of the classes on *Scratching the Surface of Christian Transformation*, we tried it on.

It is funny how many different emotions the exercise brought forth, but no one was totally indifferent. Some, like myself, were reluctant even to try it on. This is a long way of saying, as Lewis did, that we are called first of all to try on the spiritual and intellectual, if not the material, garment of Jesus. As I mentioned in the Introduction, my Roman Catholic priest friend who taught theology in Rome said, "Don't go out and *follow* Jesus—go out and *be* Jesus." One further way to get an idea of what this means is to return to the idea of the spoken word. As we considered trying on some of the words of the followers of Jesus, we now must consider the significance of trying on the words of Jesus himself.

---

[130] She said this often as part of her sermons at Abundant Life Outreach Ministries, Columbia, SC.

## How Much Transformation Has Been Offered to Us?

One way to try on his words is to see what the minimum number of changes we must make for us to be able to make those same statements about ourselves. If we are indeed called in some sense to "be Jesus" for the world, we must find our radical voice as he did and be willing to articulate with bold words the way in which this transformation has effected not only what we do but also what we say. One thing is for certain: Jesus was crucified not so much for his radical actions but more especially for his radical words.[131] When he said, "I and the Father are one," the Pharisees were enraged. How much less would our friends and pastors be put off, if we started to make such statements about ourselves.

Let's be very careful here. Neither I nor the orthodox doctrine that I am trying to communicate, would suggest that we start lifting his statements about himself and start touting them as our own. But let me give you an example of what I mean. It would certainly be true for me to say, "Inasmuch as I show you the truth and love of Jesus, I show you Jesus, and therefore I show you the way, the truth and the life." Now I know this is tricky. I am not trying to puff us all up. I am merely trying to suggest that, as we are transformed more and more into the likeness of Jesus Christ, our language should be more and more transformed and look more and more like the language of Jesus.

Here is another one. "Inasmuch as Jesus lives in me and I do the will of God, I and the Father are one." In other words, if I were to choose to do the perfect will of the Father as Jesus did, I would be "at one" with God at least in one sense as he was. This is, in fact, the call that Jesus makes to us. This is, in fact, what is supposed to happen. Notice, however, that I am very careful to

---

[131] It might seem a bit contradictory to the admonition of Ilias to put into "practice" what we believe. Here Jesus' words are precisely the putting into practice of what he believed to be true about himself and about the problems he was addressing.

qualify each statement. It is certainly not true that I can make any such statements independently of Jesus' working in my life. I must always tie myself to him and in so doing to God. But the qualifications are relatively simple for those who are "in the way" of the perfect love and truth of Jesus.

Finally, we might assert that "Inasmuch as I reflect perfectly the image of Jesus, I am perfected." Now this is absolutely true. The reason it is true is that it has to be true, by definition. It is a tautology. It is circular, because we as Christians *define* perfection in terms of this perfect transformation into the image of Jesus.

If this process of "trying on" makes you feel a bit uncomfortable, here is another one that should give you pause. You know that "Christ" was not Jesus' last name. It meant anointed one of God. So, if we are called to be one with the Father as he was one with the Father, and if we are called to show the world the face of Christ, then we too might gingerly consider the possibility of being an anointed one of God. Not the first, but certainly a legitimate heir.

Now don't try this in public or people will think you are—well, they will think the same thing about you that the Pharisees thought about Jesus. But in the quiet of the morning right after you have waked up, try placing the word "Christ" after your own first name. For me that would be Jonathan Christ. For you it might be Deborah Christ or Serge Christ or Penny Christ or Gregory Christ or Ned Christ or Michael Christ or Susan Christ. And just let the whole set of overwhelming implications start to sink in. You might only try it for a few seconds and then jump up and brush your teeth, but on another day in which you feel more bold and secure in your call to be transformed into the perfect likeness, you can give it more time.

How Much Transformation Has Been Offered to Us?

Don't, for goodness sake, put it on your business cards but know that the exercise is perfectly consistent with the call to radical transformation. This exercise might just be the most powerful expression of our belief that Jesus, in fact, did offer all of himself to us. His humanity is the full and complete model for our humanity.

Finally, here is another good one.

> "Truly, truly, I say to you, he who receives any one whom I send receives me; and he who receives me receives him who sent me." *John 13:20*

Certainly if Jesus sends us out into the world to be for the world the one who sent us, just as the Father sent Jesus out into the world to be for the world the one who sent him, then this bold statement should be just as much true for us as it was for Jesus. I know it feels uncomfortable, but don't give up. Keep trying him on. Be reminded that it is only through this transformation that we receive the gift of eternal life, the life of God, the peace of God that passes all understanding.

## A Journey into God

Once we become clear about the wonder and power and beauty of this gift, then we are compelled, no *propelled*, into the journey toward God—and not just toward God but *into* God. We never look back. We no longer ask the question, "Why do we believe in this radical transformation?" but "How do I begin?" While the history of the Church is full of critical twists and turns that have led us to our present understanding of Jesus and the overwhelming nature of the gift of the Incarnation, we cannot stop there. We must ask the question, "How do I proceed on this journey toward perfection, toward complete transformation into the perfect likeness of Jesus Christ?"

# 16
# What is the Process of Transformation?

This part of our journey is called *life*. It is not, as C. S. Lewis so clearly stated in the last chapter, some part of the Christian experience, it is the whole of the Christian experience in this life. So, once we are convinced that this transformation into the likeness of Jesus is the whole point of our earthly lives as Christians, then the real interesting and compelling part of our journey begins. What do we do? We are seeking the gift of an answer. But to ask this question is to desire an answer and even this desire is a gift.

## The Divine Desire
The mystics would have called the desire for God the *divine desire*, because the desire for God is itself a gift of God. We are promised that if we have this divine desire, God will respond. Recall Jesus words.

> Ask and it will be given you; search, and you will find; knock, and the door will be opened for you. For everyone who asks receives, and everyone who searches finds, and for everyone who knocks, the door will be opened. *Matthew 7:7–8*

Sometimes it is hard to grasp the meaning of this passage, if we are thinking about material things. There are certainly plenty of things we wish we had that we don't get. There are plenty of very poor folks who would like to make use of this passage to achieve only the bare minimum necessary for survival. In this

What is the Process of Transformation?

regard, I do not know how to explain the meaning of this passage to them. But what I do know is that in matters of the heart and spirit, the divine desire is the beginning of our journey toward Jesus, who withholds nothing of himself from us. He offers all of himself to us, and all we have to do to begin receiving is to have the desire to ask and search and knock. While the gift of Jesus' own being is certainly a "pearl of great price," the appropriation of that gift must start with the desire to receive it.

## The Posture of Jesus

Secondly, before we start to talk about this process, it is critically important to understand what we mean by becoming indistinguishable from Jesus. There are so many ways to become distracted from the central idea that we must be extremely clear that we are talking about a psychological, intellectual, and spiritual *posture*. This is the *posture of Jesus*. To attempt some meager explanation of this posture is to delve into the depths of the spiritual treasures of the Church. We could say that it cannot be comprehended with the mind but can be apprehended with the heart—it is *heart wisdom*.

However, while we cannot analyze the posture of Jesus and write an exposition of it, we can point toward it and more particularly toward the path that can lead us to it. We can say some things about it. This posture is life and light and joy and peace, while its absence is death and darkness and sadness and conflict. What I think we can start with is the fact that it is the posture of surrender. A beginning might be to stand up, hold your arms straight out to your side, and turn your palms up. There is something about this physical posture that begins, and I mean just begins, to capture a bit of the posture of Jesus. It is the posture of the cross, so powerful in its depiction of sacrifice and the love that that sacrifice denotes.[132] It is also the posture of the journey.

While we can talk around it, we can't exactly put our finger on it. It is something that must be experienced. Having said all this, and probably left you in a state of considerable confusion, let me invite you on this journey toward Jesus. Ultimately, if we were willing to enter this journey we would walk around this central idea of posture and look at it from a host of different directions and methods. I hope in the end you will have a clear picture, not necessarily an explicit sure-fire road map, but a first step you might take on your own personal journey.

## The Ladder of Divine Graces

To begin, let me offer a poem by one who was known as Theophanis the Monk (as opposed to Thelonious Monk, the jazz piano player). Unfortunately, we have no biographical information on him, although his writing is part of the traditional spiritual literature.

### The Ladder of Divine Graces
*which experience has made known to those inspired by God*

The first step is that of purest prayer.
From this there comes a warmth of heart,
And then a strange, a holy energy,
Then tears wrung from the heart, God-given.
Then Peace from thoughts of every kind.

---

[132] This ancient posture (or something close to it) is actually called the orans position, is well known among charismatic Christians, and is used in Catholic, Anglican, Lutheran and Orthodox liturgies. Another alternative that is even more stunning is the posture of prostration—to lie on the floor face down before the cross with your arms outstretched. This is a common posture of religious and those being ordained to the Catholic, Anglican, and Orthodox priesthood.

## What is the Process of Transformation?

From this arises purging of the intellect,
And next the vision of heavenly mysteries.
Unheard-of light is born from this ineffably,
And thence, beyond all telling, the heart's illumination.
Last comes—a step that has no limit
though compassed in a single line—
Perfection that is endless.

The ladder's lowest step
Prescribes pure prayer alone.
But prayer has many forms:
My discourse would be long
Were I now to speak of them:
And, friend, know that always
Experience teaches one, not words.
A ladder rising wondrously to heaven's vault:
Ten steps that strangely vivify the soul.
Ten steps that herald the soul's life.

A saint inspired by God has said:
Do not deceive yourself with idle hopes
That in the world to come you will find life
If you have not tried to find it in this present world.
Ten steps: a wisdom born of God.
Ten steps: fruit of all the books.
Ten steps that point towards perfection.
Ten steps that lead one up to heaven.
Ten steps through which a man knows God.

The ladder may seem short indeed,
But if your heart can inwardly experience it
You will find a wealth the world cannot contain,

## Into the Perfect Likeness

A god-like fountain flowing with unheard-of life.
This ten-graced ladder is the best of masters,
Clearly teaching each to know its stages.

If when you behold it
You think you stand securely on it,
Ask yourself on which step you stand,
So that we, the indolent, may also profit.
My friend, if you want to learn about all this,
Detach yourself from everything,
From what is senseless, from what seems intelligent.
Without detachment nothing can be learnt.
Experience alone can teach these things, not talk.

Even if these words once said
By one of God's elect strike harshly,
I repeat them to remind you:
He who has no foothold on this ladder,
who does not ponder always on these things,
When he comes to die will know
Terrible fear, terrible dread,
Will be full of boundless panic.
My lines end on a note of terror.
Yet it is good that this is so:
Those who are hard of heart—myself the first—
Are led to repentance, led to a holy life,
Less by the lure of blessings promised
Than by fearful warnings that inspire dread.
'He who has ears to hear, let him hear.'

You who have written this, hear, then, and take note:
Void of all these graces,

What is the Process of Transformation?

> How have you dared to write such things?
> How do you not shudder to expound them?
> Have you not heard what Uzzah[133] suffered
> When he tried to stop God's ark from falling?
> Do not think that I speak as one who teaches:
> I speak as one whose words condemn himself,
> Knowing the rewards awaiting those who strive,
> Knowing my utter fruitlessness.[134]

This is just a beginning, but it is a pretty good one. It is a small dose of the kind of wealth that exists in the writings of the spiritual masters. What does this tell us about our spiritual journey toward Jesus? We might begin by saying a few things about this ladder.

**It's a Ladder**
First of all, it is a *ladder*. While the mountain top experience may be crucial in the beginning of one's journey, it is only a beginning. To say that I was saved on January 10, 1976, is a bit misleading. Orthodox doctrine would say that I was saved the moment I was baptized. This is the point at which the Church says that God makes salvation available to me through grace and the saving work of Jesus—who opens the door for me to complete transformation into his likeness. In other words, I am no longer enslaved to sin. My mountaintop experience might represent the

---

[133] "And when they came to the threshing floor of Nacon, Uzzah put out his hand to the ark of God and took hold of it, for the oxen stumbled. And the anger of the Lord was kindled against Uzzah; and God smote him there because he put forth his hand to the ark; and he died there beside the ark of God." (2 Samuel 6:6–7)
[134] Palmer, et al., *The Philokalia-Vol. II*, (London, Faber and Faber), 67–9.

point in time that I changed direction and made a conscious decision to follow Jesus—and that would be of life-changing importance. What it certainly does not mean, however, is that I will fully appropriate the grace that has been offered to me. That I must do by my choices through time. This is a bit tricky, because we don't want to say that we earn our own salvation by our own efforts. Neither do we want to say that our salvation is in no way related to the choices we make. Sin still separates us from God, and to be separated from God is to turn our backs on the salvation that has been offered to us. So there is some kind of collaboration between God and mankind required to accomplish our individual restoration into the people God intends us to be.

**Perfection as a Process**
Thus, the ladder points to a process that we participate in by choosing to climb the ladder, but at each rung what is gained is gained only by the grace of God. We don't earn it. We simply make ourselves available to it. So, what does Theophanis say to us? First, we make a choice to develop a deep and transformative prayer life. Out of that prayer life follows one gift after another. He is clear that the goal is some form of perfection. But it is interesting that even perfection is not an endpoint, but itself an endless process. This idea of goal as process is just the kind of paradox the mystics love. They are unwilling to allow themselves or us to clutch at something that may deceive us into believing that we can grasp it like a brass ring on a merry-go-round or "achieve" it like we achieve merit badges in Boy or Girl Scouts. This posture that is not grasping but open to God is an essential part of our journey. This kind of elucidation is why reading the mystics is so important if we desire to enter this journey. We need help from those who have gone before us.

# What is the Process of Transformation?

## A Collaborative Effort

Theophanis then makes a bold statement concerning our efforts in this life. He said, "Do not deceive yourself with idle hopes that in the world to come you will find life if you have not tried to find it in this present world." He is being pretty clear that our own personal salvation is somehow a collaborative effort. God wants us back, but we must help—in this life. He follows by noting that the point of our journey is to *experience* the transforming nature of God. This is not an intellectual exercise—but an experiential one. We can make ourselves available to the grace of God through some level of intellectual activity, but ultimately, we must wait on the grace of God as a free gift, one that we cannot make happen. It might be like putting the coin in the vending machine and then sitting down on the floor and waiting for the candy to drop—having no idea when or if it will happen. It all happens in *kairos* or God's time. This posture of openness to the timing of God is all part of the posture of Jesus.

## Humility and Openness

One of the greatest traps that lies before us is the possibility that we will be deluded about how we are doing on our journey. Many like to bask in the idea that they have a "simple faith," which asks nothing of them. Others take great comfort in daily worship or regular prayer exercises—that leave them unchanged—comfortable, but unchanged. Others, like myself, may understand intellectually the call to radical transformation, but have not yet come to terms with the demands that it places on our lives. In other words, it is really impossible to know on what rung of the ladder we stand, and the degree to which we take solace from our personal delusions is probably the degree to which we probably are on a rung that is much lower than we would like to think. This humility and openness to the truth is another part of that posture of Jesus.

## More on Detachment

He then talks about the importance of detachment from everything. But what does this mean? Let's spend some time on this one because it forms the basis of most teachings on the spiritual journey and is a core aspect of a posture of Jesus. To understand *detachment* we must first understand the concept of *attachment*. As we discussed in Chapter 6, the best way to do this is to review our two simple examples. Recall, if you throw a tennis ball for your dog to fetch, how do you know, after he has retrieved it, whether he is *attached* to it? Try to take it away. Some dogs will let you take it easily and wait excitedly for you to throw it again, and others will hold on tightly. The one who holds on is *attached*. How can you tell if baby is *attached* to "blankie?" Just try to take it away. We know that for the baby's health, we must wash blankie, so we must think of some deceitful way of getting blankie away from baby—at least for a while. We are like this with most of the things of our lives, our house, cars, clothes, friends, jobs, children, parents, our lives and even our understanding of God—maybe even especially our understanding of God.

Anything we hold dear, in general, we are attached to. The mystics would say that any attachment whatsoever separates us from God. God wants us to be so supple in his "hands" that he can mold our will to his without resistance. Now this doesn't mean, for example, that we are not supposed to love, but we are called to love without attachment. When our child grows up and must leave home, we must be willing to let go. If we suffer some kind of financial setback, we must be willing to reorder our lives and give up those things that are a financial burden. This is easy to do if we are not attached or if we don't have much to begin

## What is the Process of Transformation?

with. The folks who jumped off a building as a result of tremendous financial loss during the stock market crash of 1929 clearly were *attached* to their lifestyle and status that depended on their wealth. Poor folks didn't jump—they just sucked it up and continued to try to survive. Those who had wealth could not imagine their lives in the context of financial poverty. They were attached to their wealth. Although we are all attached to some things, the challenge is to get unattached or detached.

Let me offer a simple example of the way attachment is related to expectations. The more I develop concrete expectations regarding my own life and the way people should act around me, the more attached I become to those expectations. It is as if I am standing in a wind, and I expect the wind to continue. Consequently, I begin to lean into the wind. Ah, now I no longer struggle against the wind but simply let it counteract my inclination in its direction. That is so much easier—until the wind stops or shifts direction, at which point, I fall flat on my face. The stronger the wind (expectation) the greater the leaning (attachment) and the harder the fall. The spiritual call for detachment keeps us light on our spiritual feet and more willing to sense and respond to the will of God as we are able to ascertain it.

One more aspect of attachment has to do with our anger. When we see something that somehow is an attack on who we think we are or what we want, often our anger bubbles to the surface. Sometimes that anger is initiated by something that is truly unethical or unhealthy. In other words, we might say that there are things in the world that should make us angry. But all anger is not the same. The anger that flows from our own self interest finds its roots in attachment. When we get that kind of anger, we might say that we are *hooked*. It is this kind of anger that Jesus is referring to when he says:

## Into the Perfect Likeness

> But I say to you that every one who is angry with his brother shall be liable to judgment; whoever insults his brother shall be liable to the council, and whoever says, 'You fool!' shall be liable to the hell of fire.
>
> *Matthew 5:22*

But all anger is not of this kind. There is something called righteous indignation that arises out of a process of discerning truth from lie, right from wrong, good from evil. This is the anger of Jesus when offering the "Woe to you" speech to the Pharisees. It is anger that is not self-centered but God-centered. How can we tell the difference? Well, I can tell you how I determine the difference. It is by looking within myself to see whether I am leaning—yes, that leaning—leaning into the wind. It really is pretty easy to see if I am hooked because I have lost my balance. I have lost my ability to see others as Christ sees them. It has become all about me. I am massively attached.

But here is an equally important distinction. Detachment is not indifference. To be on a journey into the life of Christ is to be intrinsically involved in the world. Not of the world but deeply in the world. To be on a journey into the life of Christ is to care deeply without being attached—without seeing your own wellbeing as dependent on any specific outcome. As Paul might say: we are called to plant the seed, maybe even water, but God gives the growth. (see 1 Corinthians 3:6–8). In other words, we are called to do the will of God without seeing the outcome as an influence on our happiness or state of mind. This kind of paradox—detachment without indifference—is one of the most challenging aspects of any spiritual journey into Christ. How do we care without caring? The answer is found deep in the treasures of the spiritual mysteries of the faith. Good luck with that one.

## What is the Process of Transformation?

Finally, let me talk about the attachment we have to the important people in our lives. While we love our parents, when it is time for them to depart this life, we should let them go with grace. If our child is tragically killed in an accident, it is only viewed as tragic by those who are attached (which would be most of us). But the challenge is to see their lives with us as a gift and not an expectation. If they are drawn home early, then we should be supple in our faith enough to see God's hand in all things.

Now let me see if I can clarify something here. How should we think of the sadness we feel at the parting of a loved one from this world? On the one hand we can be devastated and even incapacitated because our lives had become defined in terms of the other—we are sad because of our personal attachment. The mystics would say, however, that there is a higher plane on which to operate that has been made available to us the closer we get to God, but to understand this plane is a bit tricky. Certainly, the Apostles were very sad at the loss of their Lord and friend Jesus. Jesus himself wept at the death of Lazarus. Every time I think of my friend Earl Yerrick, who died of stomach cancer at a relatively young age, I am sad to the point of tears. The same thing is true when I think of my friend Ned Badgett, who died from complications related to leukemia. This kind of sadness may have something to do with attachment, but it may also have to do with a recognition of the precious value of the other without the loss incapacitating us. One has to do with me and the other has to do with, well, the other. One is focused on my loss and the other is focused on the other's value. While most of us tend to practice the former, the latter is the one that is part of the pathway toward God. The former is grounded and stuck in our worldly life, while the latter is grounded in our eternal life. As we make our journey towards God, we will be trying to make the transformation from one to the other—or from me to *the other*.

**Compassion**
This concern for the other takes us squarely into one of the most compelling and yet demanding of the spiritual qualities of Jesus. We alluded above to Jesus' emotional response to the death of Lazarus. One way to understand his reaction is in terms of compassion—a deep understanding of and connection to the people around him. This emotional link can be seen as the most powerful driver of his entire ministry. All of his directives and responses to others were profoundly connected to his ability to look deeply into the hearts of others and see their motivations and brokenness. The challenge for us is somehow to plumb the depths of this compassion, articulate its characteristics, and learn how to reflect it within our own hearts and minds.

I am reminded of a delightful little movie entitled "The Holiday"[135] in which two women, played by Cameron Diaz and Kate Winslet, exchange homes for the holiday, one in rural Surry, England and the other in Beverly Hills, California. In one scene, Cameron Diaz talks with Kate's brother played by Jude Law. In it, Jude says that he is a great "cry baby" when watching movies, to which she responds that she has never cried since her parents divorced when she was 15. It is clear that these two characters respond to encounters with others in very different ways. One is emotionally available and the other is emotionally bound up—tighter than a drum. This difference takes on important significance as their relationship develops. The whole issue of crying is a powerful stimulus for our contemplation of the nature of compassion.

---

[135] Sony Pictures, 2006.

What is the Process of Transformation?

Let me state something as a basic premise: crying is the way we humans demonstrate connection, empathy, compassion. While we may cry out of total self-centeredness, we also my cry out of true compassion for others. When we see something that "touches us deeply" we cry. Not bawl uncontrollably but experience a movement of the heart that often results in a tear. In fact, in movies, the picture of that tear slowly running down the cheek of the actor is one of the most powerful elicitors of emotional response available to actors, directors, and screen writers.

In other words, the tears referred to in the Ladder, point to this very same deep connection. When we are touched by deep truth, our bodies react with a visceral response that is not something that we control or guide. It is a connection of the heart, and it is this kind of connection that we are talking about when we allude to the compassion of Christ. What it is and how to avail ourselves of it may be one of the great spiritual mysteries, but to experience it is in some small way to be touched by God—to be engaged in the process of being transformed into the perfect likeness of the one who's compassion was the very core of his ministry, his teachings, and his model for our lives.

## A Relationship with Jesus

We have been laying a lot of emphasis on the idea that if we are to understand the nature of the transformation that has been offered to us, we must understand who Jesus *was*. The historical Jesus, the man of flesh and bones, the incarnate Lord, is the one who shows us who we are intended to be. It is now time to make a shift. It is time to start talking about who Jesus *is*. It is the living Christ who energizes our transformation, here and now. Without him we can do nothing. As Paul would say:

> I have been crucified with Christ; it is no longer I who live, but Christ who lives in me; and the life I now

live in the flesh I live by faith in the Son of God, who loved me and gave himself for me.   *Galatians 2:20*

Through him God can accomplish anything. As a matter of fact, most of our spiritual literature stresses this ongoing relationship with Jesus Christ. As the evangelicals would say, we need a "personal relationship" with Jesus. Our understanding of the goal of that relationship might now be different, but the ongoing nature of the relationship is the same. The Jesus who *is* transforms us into the Jesus who *was*.[136] Now our "personal relationship" is much more than having him beside me—it is more like having him inside me. As Max Lucado said, it is as if Jesus takes over my being. That is much different than a personal relationship with someone else like a friend or colleague. It has everything to do with an indwelling of the spirit of Christ. What may seem a bit overlapping and confusing is the difference between the spirit of Christ and the Holy Spirit. Recall his promise to the Apostles at the last supper:

> "If you love me, you will keep my commandments. And I will ask the Father, and he will give you another Counselor, to be with you for ever, even the Spirit of truth, whom the world cannot receive, because it neither sees him nor knows him; you know him, for he dwells with you, and will be in you.
>
> "These things I have spoken to you, while I am still with you. But the Counselor, the Holy Spirit, whom the Father will send in my name, he will teach you all things, and bring to your remembrance all that I have

---

[136] Now in fact, it is much deeper than that, but it is a good starting point.

## What is the Process of Transformation?

said to you. Peace I leave with you; my peace I give to you; not as the world gives do I give to you.
*John 14:15–17, 25–27*

What we must assume is that the role of spirit after Jesus' ascension is played by the Holy Spirit. In other words, the very idea of a Trinity, the three persons of which have the same nature, is that the language we might use to describe their work is somewhat inclusive: the spirit of God, the spirit of Christ, the spirit of Jesus are subsumed in the third person of the Holy Trinity, the Holy Spirit. We are thus confronted by the role that the Holy Spirit is to play in the whole transformation process.

Linking the divine desire with the posture of Jesus has intimately to do with our openness to the activity of the Holy Spirit in our lives. In other words, to ask for God is to open oneself to the activity of the Holy Spirit. To take on the posture of Jesus is to open oneself to the activity of the Holy Spirit. The question we might ask is sort of a chicken and egg problem. Does the Holy Spirit open us up to God, or does our openness to God allow the Holy Spirit to work in our lives—and the answer is yes—both/and.

This small discussion of the critical role of the Holy Spirit is just a pointer. As you might have guessed, a real discussion of the process of transformation is far beyond the scope of this effort, as well as my own abilities. With this little introduction to that process, however, I hope all of us can see the immense possibilities that can be revealed through further investigation and practice. I would like to comment, however, on one critical component—the community of faith.

# 17
# The Community of Faith

From the very beginning of Jesus' ministry, there has been a community. The Apostles formed a group that could act out the possibility of transformation through their relationship not only with Jesus, but also with each other. The Church has also from the very beginning been about how we relate to each other. It has been about the community of believers—the community of faith. What is so important about this dynamic when "two or three are gathered together in my name?" (Matthew 18:20) What is essential about the role of the community of faith in the process of transformation? There are six aspects of this issue that I would like to address here:

1. Knowledge
2. Opportunity
3. Compatibility
4. Dialogue
5. Safety
6. Responsibility and Accountability

Notice that much of what we are going to be talking about is the church with a small "c." By this I mean our own particular parish where we worship, attend Sunday school, and participate in a host of programs and functions. If you are engaging this discussion in the context of a Sunday school setting, then I hope it might expand your understanding of some additional possibilities. If not, then this may form an impetus for you to experience a community of faith in addition to worship. In any case, it is good to understand the rationale for an authentic community of faith. This rationale includes a number of dimensions but ultimately each is intended to encourage our transformation into the perfect likeness of Jesus Christ.

## Knowledge

No one can enter the process of radical transformation without some fundamental understanding of what it is all about. No one! The history of the Church has stressed the idea of learning as the basis for our spiritual journey. Jesus was understood first as a teacher. Paul's missionary work was centered on teaching not only through the preaching of the good news, but also through what may be considered the first attempt at systematic theology. As we have seen, some of Paul's formulations are crucial to our understanding of the Incarnation. In fact, we may consider ourselves not only Christians, but also Paulines. We have been greatly influenced by the teachings of Paul. The early Church through its creeds tried to clarify its basic teachings. Finally, the history of doctrinal development is one of continuing the process begun by Jesus, continued by the Apostles, and furthered by the Church to this day. The way we get access to this teaching is to place ourselves deliberately in a learning situation. Our life journey is always one of continual learning.

Not only do we need to stay in school, but we also need to demand that our learning experiences are rich in transformative potential. That means that we not only should learn cognitively, but also experientially. Our learning experiences must not only stimulate our minds to think in a new way, in other words to take on the mind of Christ, as Paul would say, but also to offer us opportunities for testing out these new ways of thinking and behaving. Thus, the entire church experience is a school. When we participate in a mission and outreach committee, one of our express purposes is to put into action what we understand about the transformative journey we are on. We should be stretching ourselves, not only by thinking, but also by doing.

Now here is a trap. During the Reformation there was an important distinction made between being saved by works and being saved by faith.[137] We understand the current orthodox position to be one of works being driven by faith. The Reformation backlash against the perception that the Catholic faith placed too much emphasis on works may have been, however, well founded. The Catholic Church underwent an important correction as a result of this criticism. Nonetheless, there was a tendency to move away from works as the overarching measure of one's salvational "status."

In the mid-nineteenth century, the "social gospel" movement arrived on the scene to proclaim the central importance of ministry to the poor. The hallmark of this position was the understanding that unless the Church was active in this ministry, the whole enterprise was hollow. In fact, this idea found its culmination in what is known as "liberation theology," a blend of social gospel and Marxism that became popular in South America after 1950 and spread to other sectors of the Church throughout the world. Only recently has this expression of Christian theology and action been repudiated by the guardians of orthodoxy as too narrow an interpretation of the radical transformative potential of the Gospel.

The trap is this. To be in the perfect will of God, one must find the perfect balance between thinking and doing—between faith and works. One without the other is empty and distracting. Consider the following:

---

[137] By the way, no one would disagree that salvation is by *grace*, the free gift of God. The challenge has always been to determine a correct understanding of the relationship between faith and works.

## The Community of Faith

> What does it profit, my brethren, if a man says he has faith but has not works? Can his faith save him? If a brother or sister is ill-clad and in lack of daily food, and one of you says to them, "Go in peace, be warmed and filled," without giving them the things needed for the body, what does it profit? So faith by itself, if it has no works, is dead.
> *James 2:14–17*

For example, we are concerned about the environment not only because we believe that it is the most respectful position to take toward God's creation, or because we care about future generations, but also because such caring is in itself transformative. To be *willing* to spend our time on a worthwhile cause is part of our spiritual journey. To be *willing* to adjust our consumption for some larger purpose that we might assuredly call "the will of God" is part of our journey toward God. We must first understand something of that journey before we can use our environmental concern as a mechanism for that journey. Otherwise we are distracted by actions that are not essentially transformative. In fact, much of what we see as equivalent to our journey is merely a distraction. Participating in church-league basketball is a distraction unless grounded in some understanding of transformation. Working on the property and grounds committee or the church governing body is a distraction unless similarly grounded.

We may also reverse the trap. If we think that an intellectual understanding of a problem is sufficient to influence our transformation, then our intellect has become a distraction. Studying the Bible for its own sake is a distraction unless that study is grounded in a desire to be transformed. Without the willingness to do, the thinking or faith or belief is without fruit. You will recall that Jesus shriveled up the unfruitful fig tree (Mark 11:12–

14). We will be known by our fruit; but fruit is by definition the fruit of something. That something is faith. In other words, balance, balance, balance. Get a good solid base in transformative Christology as a foundation for your wondrous array of fruitful actions. Go to Sunday school and demand that your learning experiences are rich and transformative.

## Opportunity

As we have just said, learning without action is of no value in our journey. Church allows us an array of opportunities to turn our learning into action. Particularly, we are thrown together with people of different character and temperament that may or may not match our own. Just like Jesus was certainly of a different temperament than those he encountered, we too are faced with the challenge of loving and working with those of different temperaments from ours. The idea here is to see these challenges as opportunities for growth. As is said in Scripture, you get no "credit" for loving your friends (Matthew 5:43–48). Try loving those you dislike or those who dislike you. Church is a wonderful place to surrender to this challenge.

G. K. Chesterton, in his book entitled *Heretics*, put forth a fascinating discussion of the family in his chapter, "On Certain Modern Writers and the Institution of the Family." What he says about the value of the family is precisely what we are talking about in terms of the community of faith. Here are some of his words:

> The common defence of the family is that, amid the stress and fickleness of life, it is peaceful, pleasant, and at one [all in agreement]. But there is another de-

fence of the family which is possible, and to me evident; this defence is that the family is not peaceful and not pleasant and not at one.[138]

The modern writers who have suggested, in a more or less open manner, that the family is a bad institution, have generally confined themselves to suggesting, with much sharpness, bitterness, or pathos, that perhaps the family is not always very congenial. Of course the family is a good institution because it is uncongenial. It is wholesome precisely because it contains so many divergencies and varieties. It is, as the sentimentalists say, like a little kingdom, and, like most other little kingdoms, is generally in a state of something resembling anarchy. It is exactly because our brother George is not interested in our religious difficulties, but is interested in the Trocadero Restaurant, that the family has some of the bracing qualities of the commonwealth. It is precisely because our uncle Henry does not approve of the theatrical ambitions of our sister Sarah that the family is like humanity. The men and women who, for good reasons and bad, revolt against the family, are, for good reasons and bad, simply revolting against mankind. Aunt Elizabeth is unreasonable, like mankind. Papa is excitable, like mankind. Our youngest brother is mischievous, like mankind. Grandpapa is stupid, like the world; he is old, like the world.[139]

---

[138] G. K. Chesterton, *Heretics* (Sam Torode Books, Amazon.com, Kindle Edition, 2017, originally published 1905), Chapter XIV, 77.
[139] Ibid., 81.

## Into the Perfect Likeness

What we see in Chesterton's discussion of the value of the family is exactly the value of a legitimate community of faith: first, you can't choose the members and, second, the diversity offers essential opportunities for growth. Those who suggest that the way to spiritual growth is to find a congenial small group the members of which are all comfortable with each other are missing the fundamental truths of spiritual growth. We don't grow without challenge, struggle, and often painful change that comes from our necessary encounters with those who are different from ourselves.

Not only do we have opportunities for personal interaction, but we also have opportunities to get exposed to areas outside our comfort zones. Church is a place in which we will be challenged to take responsibilities for things with which we are not necessarily comfortable. Accepting those responsibilities, at least for a period of time (e.g. for a year), will offer us a tremendous opportunity to grow in our surrender to the larger will of God. There is one thing we know about God, unequivocally, God wants us to grow. So, try it, you may like it. In fact, our faith should be predicated on the idea that we *will* like it if it is transformative.

Finally, our churches will provide us with special opportunities for spiritual growth. I recall helping to organize a day of quiet to which no one except the organizers came. The criticism was that no one was comfortable with the concept. We might assert that the folks who should have come were those who might have used that discomfort as an impetus for spiritual growth. Just possibly the ones who should not have come were those who had been to many quiet days, loved them, found great solace in them—and needed to work on other areas of their spiritual growth. Let me assert in summary that church is a place to find a host of opportunities for transformative growth.

## Compatibility

One of the great truths about our journey of transformation is this: it is impossible to be on a meaningful faith journey by yourself. As bumpy as your journey may be, you need fellow travelers to lean on, confide in, and engage in meaningful dialogue. There needs to be some important level of compatibility among the members of any given community of faith. For example, if you were going to choose a baseball team from a group of people, you would like to know that the people all liked baseball, knew the rules and had some baseball skills. All team sports depend on this kind of compatibility. Well, we might stick our necks out and say that Christianity is fundamentally a team sport.

What are some important areas of compatibility? What we find in our vast variety of Christian denominations are different styles of worship, different levels of formality, different emphases on doctrine and even different doctrines. It is important when choosing a church community to find one with which we feel *compatible*. It does not necessarily mean the same thing as one where we feel *comfortable* but one in which we are somewhat "on the same sheet of music." We may not be playing with the same level of expertise, we may have different abilities to follow the conductor, but at least we agree on the piece of music we are playing—the transformational fugue in E-minor by Jesus Christ. In other words, we need a place where we fit in but also where we can grow spiritually. You should be able to see that this is another balance issue that may be very difficult to discern, let alone achieve. At least if we understand this natural tension between compatibility, comfort, and growth, we can start to make better decisions about where and why we worship.

## Into the Perfect Likeness

From the church's point of view, one of the challenges is to address the need that is characteristic of a committed Christian and at the same time to be inclusive of those who have not yet begun their journeys. The trap that many churches fall into is that they water down the radical nature of the gospel in order not to "turn people off," which sadly results in the rest of the congregation, who want and need something richer, being starved. I have been in a situation in which the comment was made that we should not put the word "God" in the title of a Sunday school class lest we "turn off" those not interested in God. While this certainly is way out on the end of the spectrum, variations of this problem often arise in many churches, especially those that are striving to appeal to a broader segment of the population. Interestingly, some churches have made a move in the other direction, reflecting the idea that they were not going to water down the historical message and were going to find their strength in those who are grounded in that message. This inclination may be seen as the other end of the spectrum. We might say that no matter what our position, our challenge is to find the balance that reflects the will of God.

A church which is totally exclusive will not only exclude people who may dilute the possible movement of the Spirit but may exclude people who will begin their journeys as well as give others valuable opportunities for growth. A church that is totally inclusive will draw many people in and offer many opportunities for limited growth but may block any possibility of radical transformation for those who are ready for it. Somehow, through deliberate planning and decisions, our churches must try to find the balance, while appreciating both traps. Recall Ken Wilber's discussion of translational and transformational religion. Some exclusivity is good, but too much is not good. Some inclusivity is good, but too much is not good. The challenge is to find a deliberate balance that draws people into a journey and allows those who are on their journey to pursue it to the highest level.

## Dialogue

Learning, opportunity, and compatibility are not enough to form a fertile field for transformative growth. We must be in meaningful dialogue with others on the same journey. We must be sharing our lives, our problems, our challenges, our successes, our breakthroughs, our deepest fears, and our greatest joys with each other. It is one thing to share these things with a friend or relative because we believe they care about us. It is an entirely different thing to share these aspects of our lives as a "sacramental" aspect of our faith journey. I say sacramental because these shared thoughts are indeed an outward and visible sign of the inward and spiritual grace associated with our journey. We simply must share them if we are to grow and if we are to be an instrument for others' growth. We as Christians grow together, and to do this we must be in continual meaningful dialogue with each other.

We do that in the community of faith. The more we understand the role this dialogue plays in our respective journeys, the more open and transparent we will learn to be.

Let me take this opportunity to talk about the issue of relativism in the Church and the implications for the dialogue in the community of faith. One of the fundamental tenets of the Christian faith is that there is one God and therefore one "will of God." To say that one truth is just as good as another is tantamount to saying that there is no God. Now, that is quite different from saying that my *perception* of truth is just as good as another's. In fact, the issue of perception is at the crux of the matter. If we "see through a glass darkly," (1 Corinthians 13:12, King James

Version) then we must all recognize that our individual perceptions of the truth are all flawed until we "see face to face." Even in a state of human perfection, we still would not "see" with the mind of God. To believe that there is an absolute truth that emanates from God is not the same thing as saying that I have it.

A belief in an absolute truth, however, sets the tone for the dialogue. For two or three to come together in dialogue to try to discern the truth of God is precisely what should be taking place. The process of discernment in community is the same process that has taken place in the councils of the Church from the very beginning. Thus, the interplay between our individual journeys in the community of faith and the Church's journey as the body of Christ is one of the fundamental dynamics of transformation. Inasmuch as individuals drive the Church's discernment process, these two journeys are inextricably intertwined. Orthodoxy is simply the result of the Church's discernment process through dialogue in community.

## Safety

One thing is for certain: there is often nothing sillier than people wandering around trying to look like Jesus. We will make really dumb mistakes. We will assert ourselves at times when we should be reserved, and we will be reserved when we should assert ourselves. We will sing out boldly when we should be quiet, and we will be quiet when we should sing out boldly. We will lay on hands for healing when we should wait for God's direction, and we will dumbly wait for God's direction when he is "yelling" for us to go for it. We desperately need a place where we are safe to "try on" Jesus. If every time we try on Jesus, we are laughed at or scorned, we will stop.

The main thing that keeps us from being like Jesus for each other is that most of us *will have none of it*. Often, I am not interested in *your* being Jesus for me. I remember recently at a high school reunion a classmate was telling me of the power of prayer. My first inclination was to inform him of my advanced status (high on the ladder) on my spiritual journey. God let me know in no uncertain terms that first of all I was not that all-fired advanced and second that *my job* was to receive the Christ in this faithful servant, since receiving the Christ of others is just as important as offering it. We need to be willing not only to try on Jesus ourselves, but also to allow and encourage others to do the same. To do this we need a safe place, and that is our church.

The source of this safety comes from *hesed* (pronounced with a little gurgle for the "h")—the Hebrew word for steadfast love or even better, covenant loyalty. The idea is that even though we make mistakes, others will not stop loving us. No one will abandon us. This is the same kind of safety net that exists in marriage that allows for much deeper levels of intimacy. It is the same kind of committed steadfast love we are taught to expect from God. This kind of committed relationship should also be the model for relationships in the community of faith and thus form the basis for much deeper transformative experiences.

## Responsibility and Accountability

We need to take responsibility for our journey, and we need to be given responsibility for our journey. The free gift of the characteristics of Jesus through grace[140] and our own free choice allow us to take responsibility for our journey. This is orthodox Christology. This responsibility is part of the growing up that Christ offers us. We no longer can say, "I sin because I am human." I now must say, "I sin because I choose to." The community of faith is the place where we are given responsibility for our journey.

---

[140] The early Church Fathers would have said, "What Jesus was by nature, we are called to be by grace."

## Into the Perfect Likeness

In other words, the Church has expectations. In the history of the Church we have seen where these expectations have been both a blessing and a curse. From the earliest time, one was not allowed to participate in the life of the community of faith until one had demonstrated an understanding of what the community was about. This transition from being a learner to being a practitioner was the sacrament of Holy Baptism. In later years the Church split the process into two pieces, infant baptism based on a pure act of grace and "mature" confirmation based on an act of intellect and will. While some denominations have rejected this split, the sum total is the same. At some point in our lives we needed to learn something and then decide if we believed it.

In the early church, if an "inductee" fell away from those basic tenets, they would be sent back to a position that was outside the community, or "excommunicated." All that meant was that one needed to do more work before being readmitted to the most sacred symbol of the community, Holy Communion, lest he or she dilute the powerful transformative work taking place. This makes some sense. In other words, there was a responsibility of each member of the community to uphold the values of the community, and they were held accountable to the community for failure to do so. If this accountability and responsibility broke down, the community ran the risk of devolving into a social group.

During the Middle Ages up to the Reformation, the Church embarked on much more strident forms of discipline, exemplified by the Spanish and Roman Inquisitions. Those whose thinking was contrary to the thinking of the Church were called heretics and were often burned at the stake, the idea being (I guess) that you could do little damage if you were separated into millions of little tiny smoke particles and blown off on some errant wind. During the Reformation, excommunication was common, and intolerance was practiced at a fever pitch both by Catholics and Protestants alike. Here responsibility was held to a high doctrinal standard. Today some churches adhere to much higher levels of church discipline than others. While the Catholic Church is the most centralized in its doctrinal control, some Protestant parishes exercise much more control over their local parishioners than do many local Catholic parishes. What was originally known as the Supreme Sacred Congregation of the Roman and Universal Inquisition (1542, or the Holy Office, 1908) changed its name in 1965 to the Congregation for the Doctrine of the Faith, but the task is still to vet doctrinal issues throughout the Catholic Church. Its existence is one reason why we are looking at Catholic orthodoxy—because it is easy to find.

Discipline is an ongoing balancing act that most churches do not address explicitly; but certainly, one of the important values of being part of any community of faith is that there is a shared understanding and expectation of a shared responsibility and accountability. In other words, we should be talking about how we fall short of the goodness of Christ and we should be encouraging each other. The trap is when we move from encouragement to meddling. It certainly is a big ego boost to pick the speck out of my neighbor's eye and miss the log in my own (Matthew 7:5), but as we practice higher and higher levels of transparency and willingness to submit to the journey, we become more and more supple in the face of the "encouragement" of others.

I used to expect my mother, when she was alive, to correct me if I looked like a bum. I probably would be put off, however, by such criticism by anyone else. But we should understand that the more intimate our relationship with each other, the easier it is to assume a level of abiding love as an essential component of that correction. We are reminded of a question from the Hebrew Bible, "Am I my brother's keeper?" If we recall Ezekiel 33 and the responsibility we have to "blow the trumpet" in warning, the answer is an unequivocal "yes." How we act out that responsibility is not in the least straightforward, but it is clear that the safest place to acknowledge and act it out is in the community of faith. Often our negative response to the possibility of some form of accountability in our churches is simply a product of our lack of intimacy in our church community.

While some may think that they can commune with God on the golf course, all evidence points to the fact that our journey into the perfect likeness of Jesus Christ requires a shop with a lot of sophisticated spiritual tools and a number of workers who know how to use them. We all are a work in progress, and the workshop where that takes place is the community of faith.

# 18
# Transformation in Action

One of the most challenging problems we all face as members of a modern technologically advanced society when we try to compare ourselves to Jesus Christ is that he was able to walk wherever he needed to go because first-century Palestine was quite small compared to our sprawling metropolitan and suburban and even rural areas. He didn't need a phone, because there weren't any. He didn't need a charge card or a bank account, because the technology of exchange was very simple. We are tempted to say that he had it much easier than we do in trying to live a simple life. Our lives are quite complex compared to his. For this reason, it seems like it might be very useful for all of us to try to look at a few specific areas of our complex lives and see if we can imagine what that aspect of our lives might look like if we were transformed into the perfect likeness of Jesus. In other words, we might play Max Lucado's game and try to imagine how we, functioning as Jesus, would operate in our modern technologically sophisticated world.

One thing to keep in mind: the examples we have seen of those who have experienced the most transformation often are those who are cloistered in monasteries or convents.[141] That is a whole different kettle of fish than trying to live like the rest of us with a worldly job, with worldly needs such as housing and

---

[141] I'm not saying being cloistered is easy. Living a cloistered life has its own massive challenges, but they are quite different than trying to negotiate rush-hour traffic most of the week. One does not enter a convent to escape problems. One enters a convent to replace one set of unchosen problems with a whole other set of chosen problems—to recall Ilias the Presbyter.

material necessities and with worldly communication and transportation requirements. I am stuck in the same world as you are without any particular credentials that allow me to get paid for working on this transformation stuff. I need all the things in life that you do and have experienced periods of confusion, frustration, and poverty, just like many of you have. Let me assure you, many of you are much farther along this path than I am. Consequently, the following observations are the most profound example of "scratching the surface of Christian transformation." I will simply be sharing some of the modest insights that form my own starting point. So, let's take a little journey out into the streets of our lives and kick the transformational tires together.

## Prayer and the Life of the Spirit

If we are fortunate enough to find ourselves blessed in a rich and transformative community of faith, we have the external environment to grow in the Spirit of Christ—the Spirit of God. But this growth requires not only an external nourishing fertile soil but also an internal posture that will turn that nourishment into true transformation toward and into the life of God. This is the life of prayer and the activity of the Holy Spirit.

If there is one area in all of this that I am least qualified to speak on, it is this. I go to church regularly, teach Sunday school classes when needed, come to most special services like Thanksgiving and Easter. At least in this regard I am not an $H_2O$ Christian (in the Jewish tradition, high-holy-only). I read a lot about Christianity, because I think it is the most challenging and possibly the least generally understood religion. I like trying to figure things out, especially where to draw the line between things that are figure-out-able and those that are mysteries. I do pray in the morning, before I bounce out of bed (well, not exactly bounce) and at night as I am waiting for the shade of sleep to draw down. I bought a prayer bench some years ago with the

## Transformation in Action

intention of committing myself to regular formal prayer but didn't use it too much. That was probably my best effort. In fact, as I write this, I am thinking that I should do that again. What I do know is that a transformational life is a life in the Sprit based on a vital life of prayer.

The one thing I feel very comfortable with and comforted by is extemporaneous prayer, so let me talk about that a little. Here is the way I think of it. What we are doing when we offer to say grace at the dinner table or offer to say a prayer at the end of a Sunday school class, is to prime the pump, so to speak, and then let the Holy Spirit pray through us. The idea that it is the Holy Spirit who is actually praying is a well-known spiritual principle. In the Catholic tradition, we pray *to* the Father, *through* the Son, *in* the Spirit, so we simply start by opening up a line of communication by saying, "Heavenly Father" and then trust the Holy Spirit to fill in the rest. We finish with "through Jesus Christ our Lord, Amen," or some such ending. We all know where to look for prayer in the five standard forms: thanksgiving (the things we are thankful for), contrition (things we are sorry for), praise (acknowledging the wonder of God), intercession (praying for someone else), and supplication (asking for something).

I would add the prayer of discernment, because one of the most important things we do in our journey toward transformation is to discern the will of God. As we have mentioned a number of times, this must have been one of the most important modes of prayer for Jesus. I also find myself praying for the desire to change. As we said above, all transformation starts with the desire to be transformed. It is known as the "divine desire" because it is a desire that is a free gift of God, if the one receiving it is open to that gift, but we certainly can ask for it.

Finally, I do try to get to church early, not to chat, but to pray. One can and should avail themselves (me especially) of deliberate opportunities to commune with God. This is one of the essential aspects of any transformational process.

While my own prayer life may be feeble, there are a couple of things that I have found in the treasures of the Christian spiritual life that might be useful for us to understand and maybe appreciate: the rosary and speaking in tongues.

## The Rosary

Some years ago I read one of the classics of Christian spirituality, The Way of a Pilgrim, written by an anonymous 19$^{th}$ century Russian monk. At some point in his life he is driven by Paul's admonition to "pray ceaselessly" to find a spiritual director (called a starets in Russian) who can lead him in this direction. When he finds one, the starets directs the monk to pray the Jesus prayer, "Lord Jesus Christ have mercy on my," three thousand times, and then six thousand times and then twelve thousand times. After each exercise, the monk reports back to his starets his feelings. Eventually the monk realizes that the repetition of this simple prayer over and over again has a wondrous effect: the intellect gets totally bored and goes away, leaving the one praying in direct spiritual contact with God.

Upon reading this, I thought of ways that I myself might do this—but I needed a counter. I thought I might use and abacus, or I might use a mechanical counter that I had from my childhood that I traded for a bunch of marbles, or I might use...at this point I became literally flushed with one of those precious gifts of physical response to some deeper connection...at this point I might use a *rosary*. As an Episcopalian, I had never before thought of that prayer tool as something of interest, let alone of power. All of a sudden, I saw it as a simple counter that offered the possibility of entry into another spiritual dimension. It's just a counter. In other words, whether one says the Marian Rosary (Hale Mary, full of grace, the Lord is with thee. Blessed art thou among women and blessed is the fruit of thy womb Jesus. Holy Mary, Mother of God, pray for us sinners now and at the hour of our death.") or whether you say the Jesus prayer, the rosary becomes a way to count without thinking and may have wonderful spiritual benefits. That is about the best I can do on that one.

**Speaking in Tongues**

When attending one of Cynthia DeBerry Feeman's services at Abundant Life Outreach Ministries, she asked anyone who would like to be saved to "rest on your feet." Since I felt (probably unduly) secure in my own salvation, I ignored the prompting—until I got a prompting of a different sort. It was as if God were tapping me on my shoulder and saying, "Jonny, would you do this for me?" I was perfectly willing, but my only problem was that I had no idea what "rest on your feet" meant—at which point someone stood up. Ahh! So, I got up. Kathryn Larisey, not to be left behind, stood up with me.

We, along with several others, were taken to another room where were read Scripture from Paul's letter to the Romans (10:9): "If you confess with your lips that Jesus is Lord and believe in your heart that God raised him from the dead, you will be saved." We all agreed and were thus, according to the ministers, saved. Then they read us something from 1 Corinthians concerning the activity of the holy spirit and were asked to pray in tongues as the spirit moved us. Oops! That was a new one. I had heard Cynthia pray in this way but certainly had never tried it myself. Ok, hear goes! I rocked back on my heals, squinted my eyes closed, took a deep breath and...wait a minute. The lady who was holding my hands gave me a little shake. She said you don't have to do that. Just relax.

Well the upshot of this experience made one thing abundantly clear to me. The main thing that prevented me from praying "in the spirit" was my own self-consciousness. I thought if I could practice enough to get rid of that, I might actually get my intellect out of the way and pray at a much deeper level. Hmm, maybe Paul was right when he said:

> For one who speaks in a tongue speaks not to men but to God; for no one understands him, but he utters mysteries in the Spirit.
>
> Now I want you all to speak in tongues, but even more to prophesy.
>
> I thank God that I speak in tongues more than you all.
> *1 Corinthians 14:2,5,18*

While these two little stories certainly don't fling open the spiritual doors for you, they may open up a crack to see some wondrous possibilities. Prayer seems to be like a pool that we can dip our toes in, or we can jump in and get totally immersed. We might go so far as to say prayer is not just a communication with God but an essential part of our transformational process. We don't pay just to get something or to get something done for us. We pray in order to be changed into something new. Unless prayer is transformational, it may be at some level a distraction. When Fredo Corleone says a Hail Mary in order to catch a fish in the movie *The Godfather Part II*,[142] this is a massive distraction. He has totally missed the point (Evidently, all the Corleones missed the point). A deeper understanding of the transformational efficacy of prayer may be a call for all of us to *dive in*.

---

[142] Paramount Pictures, 1974.

Transformation in Action

*Father, give me the desire
to discern your will through a deeper
connection to you through prayer.*

## Spiritual Exercises

Spiritual exercises are those things we do explicitly to elicit a response, to expose a weakness, or to practice a virtue. Here is a little example. Once after Sunday school class, I asked who would be willing to pray for us. No one raised his hand. Ah, not surprising. I then asked everyone to raise their hand as an exercise—just to loosen up the muscles. It was a hoot. Hands went up gingerly and tentatively. You could see the trepidation in their eyes. Then I would launch into some very simple prayer: "Dear Heavenly Father, thank you for this day and the opportunity to follow your Son, through Jesus Christ, Amen." We did that exercise after a number of classes until I would ask someone to step out in faith to take a shot. The raising of the hands was a spiritual (as well as physical) exercise.

Another spiritual exercise was the trying on of the "garment of Jesus" found in Chapter 14. The very idea of trying on a crude robe that might have looked like the one that he wore, with the express purpose of trying to put ourselves in his place, is a bold move designed to expose our inner feelings about the whole project of transformation. It is only when we uncover those fears, that we can begin to address them. It is also important to do these kinds of spiritual exercises in the context of a community of faith. It is truly amazing how the shared experience and the acknowledgement of shared fears can tend to heal those fears.

We often find folks not participating in one activity or another because they are not "comfortable" doing that. The quiet day we held that no one came to is a good example. What we are not so good at recognizing, however, is that those kinds of things are perfect examples of spiritual exercises precisely because they take us into new territory that requires of us a certain amount of faith and courage. They are not supposed to feed our comfort; they are supposed to change us. In other words, church activities may not only be an integral part of our spiritual life but may also offer the opportunity, as spiritual exercises, for us personally to stretch (or for God to stretch) our own personal spiritual envelopes.

In other words, spiritual exercises are all those things we deliberately choose to do to loosen up our spiritual muscles, take us out of our comfort zones, allow opportunities for us to grow out of our fears, and give us the courage and confidence to "press on toward the goal to win the prize for which God has called me heavenward in Christ Jesus" (Philippians 3:14).

*Father, give me the courage*
*to choose exercises that challenge myself*
*to be like your Son.*

With the importance of prayer and spiritual exercises in mind, let's forge ahead.

## How is Driving Transformed?

Oh, this is a tough one for me. I get so impatient with drivers who are lollygagging. "Keep up!" I say. The challenge before all of us is to reorient our focus away from our own needs and desires to those of others—to be other-oriented. What are the deep needs and challenges of those around me? How do I develop the same kind of empathy that Jesus had for everyone? How do I operate with integrity in such a way that I don't allow bad behavior to go unchecked and still not become "hooked" by some implicit feeling that my own wellbeing depends on the behavior of others? Ah, *hooked*. Recall our discussion in Chapter 15. Driving is a perfect opportunity to address this issue.

# Transformation in Action

Whenever we get upset with the driving behavior of others, we are acknowledging some connection between our own peace of mind and that behavior. I know that I am "hooked" by the way my stomach muscles engage and my frustration level rises. The transformative spiritual challenge is to try to look more deeply into why other drivers act in what appears to me to be a self-centered fashion.

Here is an example that has something to do with traffic. When I am walking on the indoor track during a gym workout, I notice that some folks refuse to walk in the "Walking Lane." I have a couple of choices: how to feel and how to respond. I think that there are only two reasons someone would do that: ignorance and self-centeredness. The challenge for me is to be in some sense indifferent to where they walk. I just need to be concerned about where I walk.

But there is a counter part of the puzzle. I do need to be concerned about other people. As we mentioned, I am my brother's keeper. I do have a responsibility to care about others. So, it is not an option for me simply to say that their behavior is none of my business. How can I care and not get hooked? There is the rub. Secondly, I need to decide how to respond. If they simply don't know which is the walking lane (they have not seen the somewhat obscure sign), then my informing them of that fact could be appreciated. That has actually happened. If they don't give a darn what the sign says, then their response will be, "Mind your own business." That leaves the next challenge as to how to feel when met with this retort. Hooked again? Ugh! The simple act of walking on an indoor track with other fallible human beings like myself offers a great opportunity for spiritual growth, if I don't simply plug up my ears with headphones and ignore the world around me. (more on this in the next section).

Certainly, the same thing is true when driving. I love to notice what others are doing as I drive along. Sometimes someone is missing a taillight. If I have a chance, I will point that out to them. Most often people are appreciative, but every once in a while, you get someone who knows the light is out, is tired of people reminding him or her, and tells you to "mind your own business." It is hard not to get hooked on such a response.

*Father, help me to see my wellbeing only in you and to treat others with your compassion.*

## How is our use of Technology Transformed?

One of the major changes that has taken place over the last forty years has been the proliferation of computers, the internet, smart phones and now smart watches (Thank you, Dick Tracey), just to name a few. The "Internet of Things" is growing rapidly, drones are invading our privacy, and our access to information is boundless. Some would rather text than talk, with the concomitant loss of subtle "information." Our ears are plugged in to the music on our phones, so that we must remove the earphones in order to engage in simple greetings and conversation. What we need is some sort of guideline that helps us regulate this behavior so that we not only do not slide further into a feeling of self-sufficiency and isolation but use the technology to enhance our ability to relate to one another at progressively deeper levels. Hmmm, the answer is far from obvious.

First, we might differentiate between data and information. Access to data is really neutral in terms of its negative effect on our relationships, unless we become addicted to data analysis to the detriment of our relationships. But what we may be missing is the subtle information that comes from true dialogue. As Pope Benedict once said, "There is no true dialogue as long as we are only talking about *something*."[143] What he was saying is that for true dialogue to take place we must be sharing something of ourselves and receiving something of the self of the other person. To the extent that modern technology stresses data at the expense of more subtle information, it is a detriment to the development of the kinds of social interaction that build community and offer transformational opportunities.

Of course, some of the major traps associated with technology are associated with computer games and simulations. With the advent of virtual reality, we are taken further and further away from real human interactions into the world that the game designers have created for us. The more lifelike the games, the more we are seduced into that alternative reality. It is hard to imagine the world of Jesus in the context of these kinds of life simulations. What we want is life with more reality, not less. It is not at all clear what adjustments we might make to these amazing technologies and how we use them to be more transformational, but we need to try.

In other words, technology can be wonderful if we know how to use it and how to limit its use. Most of all we need to have a yardstick to measure the pros and cons of different technologies and different ways of using them. In our case, the yardstick is Jesus. The question we must ask is how would he have used these tools. Reverting to a primitive lifestyle as the Amish do, for example, is probably not an option for most of us, although we must at least consider the possibility that such deliberate simplification might be the only way to deal with some of the modern trends in our culture.

---

[143] Joseph Cardinal Ratzinger, *Introduction to Christianity* (2d ed.; San Francisco: Ignatius Press, 2004), 95.

Into the Perfect Likeness

*Father, help us to imagine how your Son would utilize modern technologies for his purpose of offering true life and love to others.*

## How is Dieting Transformed?

Now, if I were nice and slim with a very high metabolism, I might not know how to address this issue, but this is certainly not the case. It is very clear to me that the "will of God" for me is to lose weight. It is like *really clear*. We have a plethora of dieting plans. We have your Atkins low carb diet and your paleo nut diet and your psychologically transforming Noom diet, or Jenny Craig, or Weight Watchers, and so forth and so on. The options are endless. For us on this transformational journey, what is the central question? The spiritual question is really simple: what is the will of God for me regarding my eating habits? Does God want me to eat that Reese's cup—or two? Does he want me to have that extra serving of lasagna? Once I have a very clear picture of "the will of God," which in this case is not at all hard, then the challenge is how to respond. How do I develop the spiritual discipline to live into that will? Clearly, this is not easy, because we see many people "of the cloth" who are greatly overweight. So, being close to God in one sense does not necessarily mean we are close to God in every respect. In fact, we might think that we are closer to God than we really are, if our weight is out of control. In other words, losing weight can be a great spiritual as well as physical exercise.

Well, I just had my second Reese's cup, so this is clearly a case of the pot calling the kettle black. But it is an important challenge to our spirituality that we need to address, if we are to move further along on our journey.

*Father, help me to surrender to your crystal-clear will for me and act accordingly.*

## How is Fear Transformed?

Right after I saw the movie *Silence of the Lambs*,[144] I remember being nervous in the dark of my apartment. It was a great opportunity to adjust my thinking about what I was afraid of. I was standing at the top of the stairs, thinking of descending into the pitch dark, and thinking about whether I actually trusted God. Hmmm, good question. I then changed my attitude on the spot and said out loud, "Bring it on!" That was the end of the fear—at least on that evening.

What this episode points toward is that there are two obvious dimensions of fear: whether something bad could happen to you and what your attitude towards it should be. Consider Rabbi Kushner's book, *When Bad Things Happen to Good People*.[145] The issue he is addressing has something to do with the definitions of *bad* and *good*. Here let's concentrate on the word bad, because that is what we are afraid of. In general, our assessment of bad centers on the consequences of something happening to us. In other words, what is the worst thing that could happen? Now, here is where the cross comes in. If we think that we are offering our whole lives to God, then the perspective of what is bad comes from the cross of Jesus Christ. It is hard to think of a more painful way to feel, having a guaranteed ending in death. We might say that if he could do that for me, certainly I can do that for him. At that point we become like the martyrs of the early Church. This is precisely the way they could go to the lions in peace, trusting in God. What this posture allows us to do is to operate with truth in love irrespective of the consequences because of our boundless trust in God. In other words, how we view what is bad is changed because of Jesus Christ, as is our

---

[144] Orion Pictures, 1991.
[145] Random House, 1981.

response to it. Now, this is easy to say and hard to do, but we have ample opportunities to step out in faith, take a chance, and trust that, if we are operating in truth and love, we have nothing to fear.

> *Father, give us trusting hearts that we might live a life of truth and love without fear, in emulation of our savior Jesus Christ.*

## How is Pride Transformed?

The very idea that "pride goeth before the fall" (Proverbs 16:18) has always presented a problem for those who think that we "take pride" in those we love and feel some sort of natural pride in our own accomplishments. So, what is the big deal? Is there a good pride and a bad pride? Of course, we should be used to the fact that once we start to travel down the road of Christian values, we are called to examine our values through a different lens. All pride is based on the assumption that individuals, either ourselves or others, have accomplished something on their own. In the Christian journey, we are called to believe that all we accomplish is done through the grace of God. The realization of our total dependence on God is fundamental to the transformative process.

So, how should we look at pride and its opposite, humility? The quotation from Screwtape in Chapter 5 does a great job of offering us a vision of how we should view our own accomplishments. We are called to value the accomplishment while being indifferent to whomever accomplished it.

The real question is whether pride is an indication of self-centeredness and related autonomy—the idea that I am the only one who matters and that what I accomplish, I do on my own. I don't need to recognize the contributions of others to my success.

Transformation in Action

One interesting phenomenon in this regard is related to the individual celebrations on the football field when a player receives a touchdown pass in the endzone. The way it often looks is that somehow that player did it all by himself and that others played no significant part. The quarterback didn't throw the ball, the offensive line didn't protect the passer, the other tight ends and wide receivers didn't run their respective diversionary routes. I caught the pass and I am going to keep the ball for my mantle. It would be nice to see some genuine humility in recognizing that everything—not just some things but *everything*—depended on others: being born, being raised, being taught, being coached and finally participating on a team whose hard work together and tight coordination made the play possible.

I am not just talking about manners. I am talking about a deep awe for all the things that others had to do in order to make it possible—especially the God given talent that allowed the player even to play the game. That deep appreciation for his complete dependence on God was the most obvious characteristic of Jesus and should grow into our own similar appreciation. When he says, "I do nothing on my own authority," he implicitly is also saying I do nothing on my own account or under my own capability.

*Father, help me to see my utter dependence on you and on all those around me whom you have placed there to nurture me, guide me, and enable me.*

## How is Sex Transformed?
This is really tricky for me, because one's sexual experiences involve other people whose privacy must be respected. It is clear, however, that my understanding of this topic comes from experience and an abiding faith in an evolving understanding of the love of Christ. Let me start by stating the obvious. Sex in not

about self-gratification—it is about *mutual* gratification. It is about the remarkable possibilities that human intimacy holds for not only touching the very soul of another but also touching the transcendent—that which is beyond myself. Maybe it is too bold to state unequivocally that it is about touching the face of God, but it is close. Even mystics think of their highest point of contact with God as a kind of erotic experience.

The most interesting and inviting aspect of the relationship between a man and a woman is that it is a relationship between unlike entities and requires a recognition and submission to that disparity. That, in and of itself, takes love to a higher plane than the love between like entities. Even the love between like entities just as the love of David for Jonathan in the Hebrew Scripture and the love of Jesus for the beloved apostle, John, are quite different than the love of a man for a woman and vice versa. Consequently, I will focus on the latter in this discussion. If we are concerned with the challenges that lead to transformation, the challenges associated with the struggles of men and women to understand and love one another are possibly the most profound opportunities for growth.

How can we set this up? Let me start by referring to the story in the Hebrew Scripture about the creation of Adam and Eve. Even if we take the story as allegorical, clearly, it is intended to point out the intimate connection between man and woman and, at the same time, the innate differences that are built in. The book *Men are from Mars, Women are from Venus* by John Gray[146] is an attempt to develop and clarify the implications of those differences.

The challenge is to see the differences as complementary and not antagonistic. In our modern world of women's liberation, we

---

[146] New York: Harper Collins, 1992.

## Transformation in Action

often rebel against any such characterization as a kind of profiling intended to constrain rather than liberate. Many of us may have a long way to go before we can once again recognize and rejoice in those differences without fear of type casting. Let's be clear: there are many women who are better at some traditionally male tasks than many men, and there are many men who are better at some traditionally female tasks than many women. We must get to the place that we recognize ability irrespective of gender.

That does not mean, however, that there are not in general innate characteristics that are "baked in" that make women more nurturing, more social, better multitaskers and men more individualistic, transparent, and focused. Ok, I know this is very dangerous territory, but at some point, we must start to identify and delight in some set of differences, whether those that I have identified are correct or not. The admonition "Vive la différence" did not arise out of pure fiction. There clearly is something there.

The major shift in our modern culture may be captured in one simple metaphor: "power steering." If men are supposed to be better at everything than women, what are women supposed to do with all that estrogen. If women are supposed to be better at everything than men, what are the men supposed to do with all that testosterone? It used to be that strength was a natural source of the division of labor in any household—and then power steering came along. Strength was no longer an issue. Now what? Well, we are still trying to figure that out, but there should be a few guidelines that we can articulate that might just help us put all this in some sort of perspective.

Before I take my best shot at this, let me tell you a story about a weekend workshop I attended that was sponsored by St. John's Episcopal Cathedral in Denver. An Episcopal Priest psychologist and his family and marriage therapist wife gave the workshop on the Myers Briggs personality profiling system. In the workshop, we first answered a questionnaire that was designed to determine whether we were Extroverts or Introverts, Sensors or Intuitors, Thinkers or Feelers, Judgers or Perceivers. Once that was done, we were separated into groups of like type and asked to build a cathedral out of tinker toys. As an Intuitor, I was part of the group that thought deeply about the abstract "meaning" of a cathedral and determined that a cathedral was a group of people who were intimately related—so we had a circle of stick people all holding hands. Then someone found a propeller in the pile of pieces— "Look," they said, "here is the *wind of the Spirit*." So, we rigged up a cross bar and put the propeller in the center so that the wind would blow through the circle of people all holding hands. It wasn't pretty, but it had great "intuitive" meaning. The Sensors, on the other hand, built a beautiful soring spired building.

Having built our prototypes, we were then asked to stand up and present our offerings. The Extroverts all wanted to jump up and offer something, while the Introverts had to vote on who would be burdened with the presentation. Here is the point of all this: as it became abundantly clear that we were all operating in perfect accord with our respective profiles, we all started to laugh. No, we were all in convulsions. It was without a doubt the most hilarious time I have ever spent being perfectly transparent and perfectly loving and accepting of those wondrous differences.

Then, after we were all done, the leaders told us about themselves. The wife was an extrovert, and the husband was an introvert. They had to struggle to understand the natural differences between the way each one responded to different situations. The grand finale bottom line was this: if you want to grow, marry someone unlike yourself, if you want the be comfortable, marry someone like yourself. Since we are in the business of transformation, the more unlike the better. In summary, marriage between a man and a woman has the potential to be the most profoundly transformative experience available to human beings, especially if understood and approached in this light.

So, now let's try to distill some guidelines:

1. Learn to appreciate and delight in other people's differences, including their weakness and strengths, as did Jesus.
2. Learn to be perfectly transparent, as was Jesus, so that others might see these differences, including your own weaknesses and strengths.
3. Learn to express that appreciation and delight in appropriate ways, including sexual intimacy with a spouse.
4. Learn that sexual intimacy is more about mutual giving than mutual taking. To offer yourself to the other and to receive that offer from another may be the most sublime form of sacramental love that mankind has been offered.

This is probably wholly inadequate, but at least it is a start in realizing that our sexuality is a gift from God and must be treated as a profound opportunity for transformation.

*Father, help me to see my own sexuality*
*as a gift to be shared in committed relationships*
*in which only mutual giving is honored.*

## How is Ambition Transformed?

Ambition has to do with desire. It may be justified, as in the case of a highly gifted scientist, athlete, or musician, or it may be delusional, as in the case of a cult leader. The first task is to assess accurately the gifts that have been given us. The second task is to ask how those gifts are to be used. In other words, we must learn the two dimensions of the will of God for us. Of course, the assumption is that there is a single will of God for us—the idea that God has built us for some purpose. This is one of the many articles of faith by which Christians live their lives. Our task then it to discern that will through prayer and examination, trial and error.

The problem with ambition is that it can be blinding. Yes, that "blind ambition." What does it mean for us to be blinded by our ambition? The first problem is that we see certain payoffs associated with a particular pathway and we become attached to the prospect of those payoffs. The same kind of attachment the baby has for the blankie.

One great example of this kind of blinding ambition is found in the movie *Amadeus*.[147] In it, Antonio Salieri is a court composer to Emperor Joseph II. When he is first exposed to the undeniable genius of the strange young man, Wolfgang Amadeus Mozart, his jealousy kicks in and his ambition is immediately threatened. The movie is all about how this blind ambition drives Salieri crazy. What he failed miserably to recognize was that he was a magnificent music critic. He was the first to recognize the vast talents of the rambunctious youngster. Had he understood he real talent, his whole life could have been one of peace and support to a kindred spirit. In the end, his ambition destroyed him.

What we learn from this sketch is that ambition must be tempered by truth and love. We should be very interested in developing our gifts to their highest degree by diligence, study, and performance. We should also be very attuned to our weaknesses as exhibited in our failures and our strengths as exhibited in our

---

[147] Orion Pictures, 1984.

successes. What we need to do at all times is to recognize the dependence we all have on the original gift and handle that gift with care, especially as we discern the nature and limitations of the gift.

> *Father, help me to see only one ambition worth following:*
> *my life in your Son.*

## How is Competition Transformed?

As we said above, clearly some people are better at some things than others. These are God-given abilities that should be utilized in our families, towns, friendships, and communities of faith. Consider the following:

> And his gifts were that some should be apostles, some prophets, some evangelists, some pastors and teachers, to equip the saints for the work of ministry, for building up the body of Christ, until we all attain to the unity of the faith and of the knowledge of the Son of God, to mature manhood, to the measure of the stature of the fulness of Christ.   *Ephesians 4:11–13*

The abilities we have are gifts from God. We get no personal credit for them. And yet we still have competition for jobs, for recognition, for promotion, and for outright winning. Don't just get a piece of the pie. Take it all. In economics this is called *the law of increasing returns*. Microsoft Word is an example of this phenomenon: as more and more people used the word processing program, it behooved more and more people to use the same program until it became the last program standing. That is the ultimate in competitive strategy. In a world in which competition is built so intimately into the fabric of our society, how should we Christians view it? This is not an easy question to answer.

Consider the problem of investors. If you are trying to get a new innovation to the marketplace, and it requires funding for manufacturing, marketing, and administration, you will need investors, and these investors will require a return on their investment. You, as an individual, might be willing to share the benefits of your invention as Christ might, but suddenly you have people who have a stake in your venture and have other expectations. This complicates your journey into Christ considerably. Oh, if you only could go to the monastery and not worry about such vulgar administrative details.

How can we parse this problem in order to see a pathway that somehow balances our personal journey with the agreements that must be forged in the marketplace? The opening we seek seems to be in the difference between the nature of contracts and the way we operate personally—those things we agree to do and the way we choose to do them. Let's see how this might work.

Suppose we return to our manufacturing example. We have invented a new widget and have one angel investor who has bought 30% of the company Widgtech, Inc. for $3 million. That values the whole company post financing at $10 million. You agree to a marketing plan with increasing returns that promises to capture the entire widget market in five years—the whole enchilada—at which point you can raise prices indiscriminately. It is called monopoly pricing.[148]

How do you balance the push from your investor to do just that against your own moral position that "fair" pricing should

---

[148] Recall the recent pricing strategies of some pharmaceutical companies.

## Transformation in Action

allow the company to recover its investment and give a fair return to the investors? How do you approach this considerable dilemma? Wow! This is a tough one. It may very well be that you sell your share of the company and get out, because the "game" is essentially rigged in such a way that questionable behavior is necessary to survival. This is a very important aspect of marketplaces that many don't understand.

Let's dwell on this a bit more. Remember Michael Milken, the "junk bond" guy from Drexel Burnham Lambert investment bank. What happened was a dramatic shift in the market for corporate bonds toward what were known as "high-yield" or "junk" bonds. Other banks had a decision to make: jump on the bandwagon or suffer considerable loss of business, potentially resulting in bankruptcy. This is a terrible dilemma for businesspeople who would like to operate with integrity but are staring down the barrel of failure or complicity. It may just be that your own personal integrity forces you to jump ship and apply your business skills in an area less fraught with problems.

Let me make a confession of sorts. I spent a few weeks in the penny stock market in Denver. Yes, *that* notorious penny stock market. I am glad to say that I never sold one share of stock to anyone, but it was clear that the ethics were questionable. One weekend, while my firm of Chesley and Dunn[149] has suspended operations as they tried to recover from a capital shortage, I listened to a tape of a financial advisor who noted an admonition of Andrew Carnegie to his daughter: "Never invest in anything you don't control." The next Monday I resigned. Resigning is sometimes the best option. What you cannot do, if you are on the journey, is to sell your soul.

---

[149] You guessed it. There were no actual people named Chesley and Dunn. It just sounded very financial.

How are we to view competition on the playing field? Well, we sort of addressed this with the little meditation in Chapter 9 regarding Peter's imaginary recollection. How could Jesus play a game with enthusiasm and yet not be captured by a self-centered competitive spirit? The answer is the "contract." When we play a game, we have an implicit contract with all the participants that we all will try our best. The trick is to play the game while enjoying the success of your opponents just as much as you enjoy your own success. In other words, the score is totally irrelevant—*totally*. Now, that is particularly hard in the case of school, college, and professional sports. One way to approach it is to play the game as Christ would and somehow appreciate the difficulty that others have in doing that too. In other words, with a heap of compassion. Again, imagine how Jesus would play football. If you can't do that or if you think that Jesus would not play football because he was too busy teaching or healing, then your football is not saved. Remember, "Quod non est assumptum, non est sanatum."

*Father, help me always to operate*
*with integrity and compassion,*
*no matter what the stakes are.*

## How are Politics Transformed"

One of the things most of us are familiar with is that we seldom hear blatant political electioneering from the pulpit, lest the church lose its tax-exempt status. While we might agree with this approach, especially when we are dealing with a politically diverse congregation, we would like to think that the Church (with a capital "C") has something to say about our choice of political leaders. We live in a country that still has as its motto, "In God we trust." If this is indeed true, at least for those reading this

## Transformation in Action

book, how are our political proclivities and decisions influenced by a transformative spirituality?

Well, there probably are a few things we could state unequivocally. First of all, Jesus was not a conservative or a liberal. He was the man of truth and love. Often his positions look conservative to conservatives and liberal to liberals, but this is just wishful thinking—one might call it delusion. If this is the case, then what was he doing? Well, as we said, he was the man of truth and love. Whatever diverged from truth and love he would have considered the work of the "other guy." Hate is simply not an option. Lie is simply not an option. Recall Screwtape's goal was simply to get his "patients" to participate in untruth. Whenever you see those two values threatened, *run*.

Unfortunately, we see truth and lie popping up wherever we look, particularly when we are dealing with the all-important "issues" of the day, e.g. abortion, homosexuality, immigration, etc. As a result of our religious beliefs, most of us have clear opinions on each of these issues and would probably assert that Jesus would have agreed with us. Don't be so sure. He was continually turning common thinking on its head.

What we do know is that there are three focal points: issues, leaders, and our democratic system of government. We can either focus on the issues, on the character of our leaders, or on the way in which our constitutional and representative form of government works—or on some combination of the three. One thing should be clear, however: if we are in a legitimate transformative process, we should be looking carefully at all three to see where truth and love are operative and whether your conclusions serve your own agenda or God's agenda. Remember this: the devil will always give you something you want—*in exchange for your soul*.

## How are Violence and Anger Transformed

One of the most stunning results of our technological age has been the proliferation of representations of extreme violence on TV, in the movies and particularly in video games. Is this something really new. It seems that the spectacles in the Roman Coliseum were the same kind of extreme violence—only real. At least we don't do that anymore, although mixed martial arts is starting to move in that direction. What are we to do with all this violence? The first thing that we should realize is that, whether we like it or not, this exposure results in some level of desensitization. We probably don't understand all the ramifications of this effect, but we should be concerned. The message it seems to send is that violence and the anger that seems to be its root are to be regarded as staples of our modern life. Two examples will serve to show how seductive this problem is and how challenging it may be to solve. Law and Order is a great television series that has spawned several sub-categories. One of the most attractive features for me is that I really like the cast members, the intricacy of the stories and the challenges portrayed in the legal problems that have to be solved, not always successfully. It is a great series—but it is violent. Another is NCIS. Again, I really like the characters and the actors who play them. Their interactions are anything but trivial and the complexity of the stories are intriguing—but it is violent. Both series are about murder, rape, and pillage. Ugh!

The challenge for me is to regulate my exposure to these kinds of shows, if not eliminate them completely from my palate. The question is whether any of us are able to get to the point that we can watch these expertly developed stories as spiritual exercises that move us forward rather than experiences that move us backward. If there is any clear message from Jesus' admonition to "turn the other cheek" is that such violence and an-

# Transformation in Action

ger are totally antithetical to his teaching. We might try to consider exposing ourselves to activities and stories that build up rather than tear down the kind of transformative behavior we are seeking.

As we alluded to in Chapter 16, anger can be manifest in two general ways: first, there is self-centered anger that is predicated on the idea that some external factor or person directly impacts my own wellbeing and second, what we call righteous indignation that is simply a response to some external factor or person that is predicated on the will of the Father to challenge some untruth. The question is how do we tell the difference and how do we begin to abandon the first?

The answer to this question seems to be through the development of our sense of compassion. Here we need to consider palpable consequences of unhealthy anger and concrete indications that we are making the transition. Of course, this is a difficult challenge, but let me take a shot. If we recognize this kind of anger as a persistent knot in our stomach accompanied by a kind of distraction that yields frustration and even hatred, we, at least, have the information we need to begin the process of transformation. What we do then involves the whole set of spiritual tools that are begun with the divine desire to rid ourselves of these kinds of debilitating feelings. That process was alluded to in Chapter 16 but really is beyond the scope of this brief treatment. One question, however, is worth noting. How do I know if I am making any progress?

As we said, the key is compassion, but how do I know if I am really experiencing the compassion of God. Let me assert that one concrete way is the feeling of empathy. Now this is really important, because it is a God-given physical and psychological response that we talked about when we discussed the topic of compassion. It is that mysterious response that comes right before we feel a tear forming. It really is quite indescribable and yet very clear. It may or may not result in a tear, but clearly it is associated with what I can best describe as a flush.

These precious moments of connection occur whenever we are touched deeply or moved by, for example, a painting reflecting some profound truth, a scene in a movie expressing a relationship that resonates with us, or a photograph of someone risking life and limb for others. We feel it. We may not know why. We certainly can't make it happen. It is purely spontaneous. We could say that it is a pure gift from God. We are touched by God in some very special way. This visceral response is one indication that we are starting to make deep connections that arise out of compassion and empathy. Our hearts are warmed. But that very statement points beyond itself, because we know that our physical hearts do not experience an increase in temperature. It is the best we can do to describe something that we would assert is a pure gift of God. Pay attention to these moments. They may be a direct result of our being made in the image of God.

> *Father, help me to pay attention to*
> *and nurture those precious moments*
> *when you break into my world*
> *with wondrous tenderness.*

## How is Humor Transformed?

One of the most interesting aspects of Jesus Christ is the nature of his sense of humor. I am reminded of an episode of *Seinfeld* in which Jerry and George are discussing whether Superman had any sense of humor. George is looking at the data (comic books and movies) and insisting that he did not, and Jerry is saying, "He's Superman. He must have a super sense of humor." Of course, the whole exchange was designed to be absolutely ridiculous and was intended to place the TV viewers in a state of hysterics. Actually, the question as to whether Jesus had a sense of humor has the same form but a much different significance. We really don't have much data on his laughter. We don't see him cracking a joke, although there are places where one might infer a twinkle in his eye. When he is addressing the Syrophoenician woman at the well, we can almost see that twinkle.

But there is much more at stake with Jesus than with Superman. How can he be the model for our lives and not show us how and when to laugh? How can our humor be saved, if he knew no humor? Recall the first time any of us saw the picture of a laughing Jesus. It was radical. The artist was asserting unequivocally that Jesus not only had a sense of humor, but that he had a wonderful sense of humor that resulted not in a serene smile or a controlled chuckle but in a raucous laughter that was absolutely contagious. If we accept this as a fundamental part of his character, even though we have little concrete evidence for it, we should try to unpack the kinds of things that would have been humorous to him.

If we look back at the Myers Briggs workshop, we can assert that transparency and trust breed a humorous response. We all need to be able to laugh at ourselves and laugh with others about themselves. My dad, Robert Fletcher, use to say, "We are not laughing *at* you; we are laughing *with* you." The problem I always had as a kid with that concept was that I was never laughing at myself when he said it. What I learned was that I determined whether people were laughing at me or with me. The more I was able to laugh at myself the more delightful the laughter became. When we take ourselves too seriously, we leave ourselves open to… well, you get it. That doesn't mean that there are times that we are called to take ourselves and others very seriously, and laughter is truly inappropriate, but we should get better at telling the difference.

So, we might say that Jesus was very good at seeing our foibles and very eager to laugh with us about them. He must have

## Into the Perfect Likeness

been just as good at discerning our sensitivities and knowing when that laughter would have been hurtful. It is precisely this kind of deep sensitivity that we are striving to achieve in our transformational process.

What are some of the traps associated with humor? What are some things that we laugh at that are destructive to others and to ourselves? Many of us, in our studies of philosophy and literature have run across "Lucretian Pleasure." The simplest meaning is that it is the kind of pleasure one might take from seeing the misery of another and realizing that you are not experiencing that misery, as when someone else falls in a mud puddle. In that sense, we get a kind of pleasure in seeing cartoons in which the subjects engage in mind numbing fury and corporeal devastation. The only problem with this kind of humor is the sorts of insensibilities it breeds. The more we probe into what is going on, the less it seems like humor and the more it seems like unhealthy masochism. We might say that we should get better at being sensitive to the kind of conditioning that some humor is promoting.

Finally, we might recognize a kind of humor in which two parties observe something untoward and laugh at the fact that each is having precisely the same thought. The humor is not in the act being observed but in the commonality of the response. One would think that, as we get better at paying close attention to what is going on around us, especially to the feelings and responses of others, we will find delight in that connectedness.

As we discussed above regarding anger, we might consider the same kind of question here: how do we know if we are making progress in transforming our humor from that which is self-centered and unhealthy to that with is of God?

Just as we pointed out the kind of feeling we get when we make a deep connection through compassion and empathy, we make the same precious connection through humor. When we see or hear something that resonates with us, we often feel the thrill of humor. Actually, the word "humor" refers precisely to the fact that it arises from some indeterminate region of our being that we cannot find or control. At its best, it is so much like the feeling of empathy that we could say that it is one more way in which we are touched by God. We feel a smile spontaneously develop and a delight emerge. It is clearly a gift that we do not control. It is one more piece of evidence that God is acting on us.

> *Father, help me to pay attention to*
> *and nurture those precious moments*
> *when you break into my world*
> *with wondrous delight.*

## How are Church Ministries Transformed?

One of the things we tend to take for granted is that anything associated with our church activities must be an important part of our responsibility to God. As Ken Wilbur pointed out, most of those activities are translational. There are, in fact, two different dimensions of this kind of translation: those activities that minister to us and those activities that minister to others. Our tendency is to believe that the latter are the most important aspect of our religious experience. What we should recognize is that the feelings we get from doing good works can simply be another form of translation—the activities that make us feel comforted, secure, and in "the way."

What we might like to do is to look a little more closely at the dynamics of these kinds of activities to see whether there is real transformation going on. Consider a field trip to participate in Habitat for Humanity. Clearly the feeling of ministering to others and the sense of intense community can be very uplifting and point the way toward radical transformation, but it is also true that these feelings can simply be seen as an end in themselves, rather than a launch pad for authentic transformation. Without understanding the nature of the transformational goal, the chance that participation in church ministries will launch us into deeper transformation probably is slim to none.

Let's look at another dimension of church ministries. Consider participating in the church choir. We might gather once a week and work on the music for the next Sunday's worship service. Before the service we gather to review the music, polish any rough spots and make any final preparations to execute the music to the best of our ability. What is usually missing is any effort to understand this ministry in terms of transformation. In the case where the church schedule precludes the choir from participating in Sunday School, the problem is compounded. One might make the bold statement that, unless transformational content is intentionally woven into the ministry, it becomes more of a distraction than an aid. The same thing might be true for those involved in Sunday school teaching, worship ministry, church administration, and so forth. The challenge is to evaluate all the programs that parishioners are involved in to determine the degree to which the activity includes some dimension of transformational instruction and guidance.

One very interesting ministry is that of foreign mission work. This may represent one of the most profound commitments to a particular lifestyle that the church offers. The call to mission work is certainly powerful and life changing. Few are called to such work without a deep abiding faith in the importance of sharing the Gospel with those who may not have heard it or giving solace to those who are trying to act out their Christian faith in hostile environments. One might suggest that this kind of work is the most inherently transformative. We might just suggest that it may be important to include this aspect of the work in the initial training and in the ongoing guidance.

## Transformation in Action

When difficult situations arise, as they must, one needs an orientation that sees those difficulties as profound opportunities to be seized rather than problems to be avoided. Having never made that commitment, I must speak very tentatively here and acknowledge my profound respect for those who have.

Finally, we should mention Sunday school itself. It is so very easy to use the time to study the Bible, if you are Protestant, or examining a host of other topics if you are in other traditions. Let me offer one possible guiding principle. Back in 1970, Marshal McLuhan and Quentin Fiore wrote a book entitled *The Medium is the Message*.[150] The concept was that, in the use of any medium to communicate some idea or message, the very medium you use has a kind of message inherent in itself.

One of the most important aspects of any Sunday school effort is that the content may be important, but the way in which the class is executed is much more important than the content. If the way the class is organized and executed is the message, then the medium is the most important part of the message. In other words, discussion and dialogue are much more valuable than lecture. Developing a trusting environment in which participants can be transparent is critical. Seeing this kind of trust result in self-deprecating shared humor is probably the most important indicator that participants are being changed by the experience. This takes considerable work by class leaders but should be a central motivation for holding the class in the first place. Remember, transformation is the ultimate goal, not memorization of Bible verses, knowing the details of church history, or learning about the Holy Land. All of these are interesting and potentially valuable within the context of authentic transformation.

---

[150] London: Penguin Books, 1967.

Into the Perfect Likeness

> *Father, help us to see all that we do*
> *in our church communities of faith*
> *as a tool in our journey toward*
> *authentic transformation.*

## How is Happiness Transformed?
Finally, we should talk about happiness. We might call it joy. As we mentioned above, pleasure can take on many forms: the pleasure of eating, of swimming, of competing, of drinking, of watching, of smoking, etc. Each of these and many more have an upside and a downside.

The upside is related to how we have been made by God:

> For you created my inmost being; you knit me together in my mother's womb. I praise you because I am fearfully and wonderfully made; your works are wonderful; I know that full well.
> *Psalm 139:13–14*[151]

The point here is that we have been made for happiness, but some happiness is pleasurable in the short term and destructive in the long term, other happiness is a blessing both in the short term and the long term, and still other happiness is difficult in the short term and a massive blessing in the long term. Our challenge is to tell the difference.

Gerald May wrote an important book in 1987 entitled *Addiction and Grace*.[152] In it he talks about the possibility that anything can be addictive, if we interpret the pleasure that is received as something that can be repeated at will and tends to anesthetize us to some form of pain. The idea that some things

---
[151] NIV.
[152] New York: Harper & Row, 1987.

are there simply for our pleasure without any ancillary benefits can be a huge trap into which we can be drawn and from which it may be hard to extract ourselves. It could be ice cream, chocolate, dieting, marijuana, the adulation of others, and on and on. We see this over and over again with people who seem to "have everything" and yet commit suicide or overdose on narcotics.

What is the problem? It would seem that the problem is that many of us really don't know what true happiness is. All we have to do is return to our understanding of the Net Price of Transformation in Chapter 14 to understand that God wants peace and happiness for us but does not want us to fall into the traps of short-term pleasure and long-term destruction. The challenge for all of us is to be able to tell the difference between those things that are of God and those things that are of the "other guy." Let me restate an important truth: *The Devil will always give you something you want—in exchange for your soul.* What this statement admonishes us is to be careful of those things that we think give us happiness and yet result in our loss of orientation. It should be clear to all of us as Christians that only God gives us our true orientation and only in him is there true happiness.

*Father, help us to discern true happiness*
*and peace that only abides in you*
*and give me the courage to follow that pathway*
**into the perfect likeness of Jesus Christ.**

# 19
## Some Final Thoughts

The journey toward communion with God that was made possible through the saving work of Jesus Christ must begin with a clear understanding of who Jesus was and how much of himself has he offered to us. Who are we called to be as Christians? I hope a case has been made for the Church's teaching regarding a radical transformation *into the perfect likeness* of Jesus Christ. It is not necessary that we see this perfection in our lifetime. It may be completed in our next life in the presence of the glory of God, but there is no question regarding the orthodox understanding that the whole enchilada has been offered to us *in this life*. The Gospel message asks us to trust in some understanding of heaven, but even more so, it asks us to trust in the possibilities of heaven in this life. Just maybe, heaven has never been solely about what happens after we die but is also about how that understanding and hope conditions our activity in this life.

This effort has not treated in any systematic way the process of transformation, let alone the many barriers to that process. A conviction that we are called to *be* the face of Christ in the world says little about the process of *becoming*. The great spiritual teachers of the Church serve as the resources for this journey. Once we become convinced of the goal, we are compelled to ask how we get there. Where is the map? Which roads do we take? What are the best hotels to stay at that will give us the most refreshment on our journey? Where are the gas stations at which we might refuel? What if we have a breakdown—where are the mechanics who can help us get up and running again? We could carry this metaphor to an absurd limit, but at least it points out that the journey needs some deliberate planning and execution,

## Some Final Thoughts

as well as the certain realization that we cannot do it alone. So far we have just scratched the surface.

Let me take this moment to offer a caveat. As our metaphor indicates, our journey is not without its potential peril. The real risk is centered on the problem of trying to undertake this journey alone. While we don't have a map to follow at this point, we can assert that there are lines on the road that one does not want to cross. We might say that one should have some sort of spiritual director who can help us avoid running off the road into a ditch—or worse. If the journey will assuredly have its challenges as we run up against the brick wall of the world's values, we desperately need an intimate relationship with the Holy Spirit in order to be guided through the brambles. We want to be prepared before we expose ourselves to challenges that could potentially result in extreme bitterness, frustration, anger, and even disillusionment. The journey, while it may be the only one really worth taking, is not for sissies. Spiritual warfare is the one thing we can be absolutely sure of. Recall Paul's description of the armor of God:

> Finally, be strong in the Lord and in the strength of his might. Put on the whole armor of God, that you may be able to stand against the wiles of the devil. For we are not contending against flesh and blood, but against the principalities, against the powers, against the world rulers of this present darkness, against the spiritual hosts of wickedness in the heavenly places. Therefore take the whole armor of God, that you may be able to withstand in the evil day, and having done all, to stand. Stand therefore, having girded your loins with truth, and having put on the breastplate of righteousness, and having shod your

feet with the equipment of the gospel of peace; besides all these, taking the shield of faith, with which you can quench all the flaming darts of the evil one. And take the helmet of salvation, and the sword of the Spirit, which is the word of God. Pray at all times in the Spirit, with all prayer and supplication. To that end keep alert with all perseverance, making supplication for all the saints... *Ephesians 6:10–18*

Remember it is who Jesus *is* who makes it possible for us to become who he *was*. The Good News is that God has chosen each one of us to be transformed ***into the perfect likeness*** of the Son, our savior, Jesus Christ.

May your journey be rich with blessings and the bumps not be too discouraging. It is the only journey worth taking.

www.ingramcontent.com/pod-product-compliance
Lightning Source LLC
Chambersburg PA
CBHW030850170426
43193CB00009BA/560